Palgrave Studies in the History of Economic Thought

Palgrave Studies in the History of Economic Thought publishes contributions by leading scholars, illuminating key events, theories and individuals that have had a lasting impact on the development of modern-day economics. The topics covered include the development of economies, institutions and theories.

More information about this series at
http://www.palgrave.com/gp/series/14585

Julius Horvath

An Introduction to the History of Economic Thought in Central Europe

palgrave
macmillan

Julius Horvath
Dept. Economics
Central European University
Budapest, Hungary

ISSN 2662-6578 ISSN 2662-6586 (electronic)
Palgrave Studies in the History of Economic Thought
ISBN 978-3-030-58925-7 ISBN 978-3-030-58926-4 (eBook)
https://doi.org/10.1007/978-3-030-58926-4

This Palgrave Macmillan imprint is published by the registered company Springer Nature Switzerland AG.
The registered company address is: Gewerbestrasse 11, 6330 Cham, Switzerland

To Petra, Robert, and Roman

Acknowledgments

I have benefited from an engagement with many scholars, who were also remarkably inspirational. This has been a long process. I would like to thank for fruitful debates in particular to Nikolay Nenovsky, Gilles Campagnolo, Antonio Magliulo, Pencho Penchev, Vladimir Avtonomov, and others.

I have always found inspiration at the Conferences of the European Society for the History of Economic Thought. Actually, the stimulus for this book happened, in June 2018, at a conference at Universidad Complutense de Madrid, where I met the representatives of the publishing house. But similarly inspirational were all other Conferences I had participated: May 2019 at the Science Po Lille, May 2017 at the University of Antwerp, May 2016 at University Paris 1 Panthéon-Sorbonne, and May 2015 at Roma Tre University.

After empty years of studying in Bratislava, I moved to Prague and I owe a great deal to those whom I had a high regard for, especially Tomáš Ježek, Václav Klaus, Lubomír Mlčoch, Karel Kouba, Jozef Zielenecz, Karel Kříž, and others. I have since learnt from many people: in Muncie from Mir Masoon Ali, Gary Santoni, Dale Umbach, in Carbondale from Subhash Sharma, Selahattin Dibooglu, Richard Grabowski, Rolf Fare, Daniel Primont, Prakash Mahat, Leonid Tolmatz, in Bonn from Jürgen von Hagen, Marco Bifulco and Bob Hetzel, in Budapest, from Jacek Rostowski, Gerardo della Paolera, Béla Greskovits, László Csaba, Tamás Réti, László Ferenczi-Fisher, József Galántai, Anja Szilágyi, Alexander Astrov, Michal Merlingen, Ákos Péter Bod, Rastislav Káčer, Marco Zoppas, in Bratislava from Mikuláš Luptáčik, Pavol Brunovský, Martin Kahanec, René Matlovič, Stanislav Biskupič, Milan Čorba, Tibor Žilka, Vladimír Krčméry, Jozef Jarab, Attila Komzsík, János Tóth, György Juhász, Marián Karvaj, Martin Šuster, Ronald Blaško, Vladimír Gazda, and in all of these places from many others. To these personalities, my deep gratitude.

Almost finally, I record my gratitude to an entity that is not a person: Central European University. Great personalities who have led the school Yehuda Elkana, John Shattuck, Michael Ignatieff, and Liviu Matei, always created exceptional work conditions, and I had the privilege to work at this institution. I would also like to thank the Department of Economics and Business for providing a friendly and competitive atmosphere.

Finally, I would like to thank Petra, who rendered the most excellent inspiration.

Contents

CHAPTER 1

Introduction

This book provides preliminary information about the development of Central European economic thought for approximately four hundred years. It is an introduction to a history of economic thought in Central Europe.

We perceive Central Europe as a compact territory of the four present-day countries: the Czech Republic, Hungary, Poland, and the Slovak Republic. This region represents a geographical concept and a concept that has acquired a political and a cultural undertone and is based on claims of shared identity, culture, and history. Central Europe varies culturally, historically, politically, and economically from Europe's other parts and regions.[1]

[1] In a similar spirit, see Mout (2006), Lindahl (2003), Kamusella (2012), Le Rider (2008), Wallace (2003). In different writings, Central Europe was also known as Mitteleuropa, l'Europe centrale, but also East-Central Europe, or Ostmitteleuropa. Before World War I, the concept of Mitteleuropa was perceived as a place where German ethnic, culture, and influence spread (Le Rider 2008). The German nation-state of 1871 was Kleindeutschland as it did not include the German-speaking areas of Austria-Hungary with which it would form Grossdeutschland, the dream of German nationalists before World War I. Kamusella (2012, p. 248). In contrast to the German concept of Central Europe as a space for German cultural, economic, and political expansion, Russians viewed Central Europe in terms of the Slavic world. Since the 1840s, different Pan-Slavism versions had become more widespread, Miller (1996, p. 7). However, after World War II in the Soviet discourse, there was no concept of Central Europe. Miller (1996, p. 15). Kobrinskaia (1997, p. 14) writes that Eastern

J. Horvath, *An Introduction to the History of Economic Thought in Central Europe*, Palgrave Studies in the History of Economic Thought, https://doi.org/10.1007/978-3-030-58926-4_1

Jordan (2006)—in an expert paper for the Permanent Committee on Geographical Names of the European Union on sub-division of Europe into regions—argues that a subdivision of Europe naturally begins with Central Europe. Once Central Europe is defined, Europe's further division to regions comes somehow naturally, even if boundaries between areas are not clear-cut. Jordan (2006) points to differences between Central Europe and other European regions. For example, industrialization in Central Europe happened more slowly than in Western Europe but faster than in Eastern and Southeastern Europe. Similarly, independent urban society counter-balanced nobility and church more slowly than in the West but quicker than in Eastern and Southeastern Europe. In contrast to Western Europe, Central Europe was typically oriented toward the continent and not overseas.

In Central Europe, traditionally prevailed ethnic and linguistic variety ended in the middle of the twentieth century.[2] Afterward, the countries became ethnically relatively homogenous, which the example of Bratislava[3]

Europe was used as a synonym for the world socialist system during the Cold War. Belonging to "former Eastern Europe" predetermined the mode of post-socialist transition bearing important psychological meaning—elites in East European countries perceived their future development in close cooperation with Western Europe. The primary goal of political elites was to get rid of this perception as "East European" and be instead considered "Central European."

[2] "In fact, the cardinal rules of the monarchy's history were that ethnic and political frontiers did not coincide, and that its diverse nationalities were scattered pell-mell throughout its territories. After 1918, the so-called successor states valiantly strove to end this unhappy state of affairs, and they succeeded to a large degree, thanks to the use of such modern techniques as forced assimilation, persecution, and expulsion." Deák (1990, p. 12).

[3] In 1890 in Prešpurk (Posonium in Latin, Pressburg in German, Pozsony in Hungarian; from 1919 Bratislava), the population was around 52 000, about 60% were the Germans, approximately 20% the Hungarians, and around 17% the Slovaks. After 1919 Bratislava began to be Slovakized, and the proportion of the Slovaks and the Czechs increased. Before World War II, about 60% of the population were the Slovaks and the Czechs, 22% the Germans, and 13% the Hungarians. The foundation of Slovak State meant the expulsion of the Czechs and the deportation of Jews. After World War II German population was deported, too, and later partially Hungarian population. Besides, some upper-class families were expelled from Bratislava in the early years of communism and replaced by the proletariat families. As a result of these movements, currently, Slovaks represent around 90% of Bratislava's population. Otto's encyclopedia (1903, vol. 20), current Slovak official data, and Salner (2001).

and Budapest[4] as well as of other large cities nicely documents.[5] There is higher homogenization in smaller cities and villages.

The affairs shared by the Central European nations define them more than their unique features separate them. Their shared past is the basis of the comparable economic and educational systems, foreign relations, cultural norms, and similar. For an extended period, they were part of the Austrian Monarchy and also of the Soviet Empire. Even in periods when these countries were independent, their development was also reasonably similar. There were disparities in individual responses to both domestic and foreign events, but shared similarities prevailed.[6]

It is challenging to write a book without some pre-conceived inclinations.[7] Nevertheless, one can somehow assess progress by bearing in mind civilizational advancements, developing non-oppressive inclusive societal structures, and favoring economic development to ideological aspirations. We take a stance that is skeptical and critical of social, economic, and political activities in Central Europe, which slowed down the regional economic development. In the period before World War II, we negatively assessed the role of land-owning classes as they were prolonging feudal

[4] In 1880, Budapest's population accounted for around 506 000, about 57% were the Hungarians, 35% the Germans, 8-9% the Slavs, and 0.5% the Romanians. According to the religion, approximately 68% were Roman Catholic, 19% Jewish, and around 11% protestants. In 2011 population size was about 1.7 million by ethnicity, 81% were the Hungarians, 1.1% the Romani, 1% the Germans, 0.4% the Romanians, 0.3 the Chinese, 0.1% the Slovaks, and the remaining did not declare their ethnicity. Otto's encyclopedia (1891, vol. 4), and current Hungarian official data. Interestingly, there are tendencies also in the opposite direction. Urban (1991, p. 777) documents that in 1988, only 8000 people in Poland claimed German ethnicity. However, in 1991, "according to official estimates in postcommunist Poland, there were 350-400 000 Polish citizens who claimed German roots for their families."

[5] Judt (1996, p. 54) argues that the Central European culture used to be cosmopolitan with most accomplished representatives were Ashkenazi Jews. Nevertheless, this culture was destroyed gradually in the twentieth century and made Central European cities just provincial cities, which lost their cosmopolitan character. Judt (1996) argues that these countries may be located in the middle of Europe, but their claim to a distinctive 'Central Europeanness' is 'at best nostalgic, at worst bogus.'

[6] For example, after the break-up of socialism initially, these countries opted for a democratic path and only gradually began to differ in nation-building's political character. However, still today, all these lands are members of the European Union and NATO.

[7] Robbins (1998, p. xvii) mentions that the author should reveal one's bias whenever conscious of it. Schumpeter (1954/2006, p. 938) points out that political preferences make the basis of some biases. However, even economic theorists have a bias as they prefer manageable patterns.

structures when the Western world has already begun to move away from them. The old feudal property relations persisted for too long, especially in Hungary.

In the twentieth century, we evaluate negatively representants of totalitarian views, whose actions caused agony and pain to a large number of people, and did not achieve most of their economic aims.[8] Finally, we also discern the negative role performed by those who place at the top of their values belief in their nation's uniqueness and spread animosity, aversion, and distrust toward other communities.[9] They are not aware of the advantages that accumulate to their nation if their neighbors prosper.[10] However, we also value those who somehow began their career standing on the totalitarian or nationalistic positions, and were able to shift and become critical to their original views. We prefer respect to an individual, which none of these universal, either totalitarian or nationalist views accept. Instead, they prefer collective to individual, nation vis-à-vis other nations, labor class vis-à-vis other classes, believers vis-à-vis infidels, and similar. A neutral approach does not differentiate between these concepts as it believes it should 'objectively' study any of them.

As we cover a relatively long period, we divide the Central European history of economic thought into shorter time fragments. The first period

[8] Fischer, Sahay, and Vegh (1998, p. 7) compare the per capita income level in Western and Central European countries. From 1937 to 1992, their data document that Czechoslovakia reached a per capita income of 70% compared to the Western European average in 1937, but only 45% after the fascist and communist control ended. Note that in this period only for two to three years, Czechoslovakia was not under the totalitarian regimes.

[9] Maybe such considerations led Friedrich August von Hayek in the Road to Serfdom to advise the West not to get involved in this region "peopled by small nations, each of which believes equally fervently in its own superiority over the others, is to undertake a task which can be performed only by the use of force." Hayek (1944, pp. 232-233). It seems Keynes held similar opinions. "Keynes lamented that the breakup of the old multinational empires of Europe created new frontiers 'between greedy, jealous, immature, and economically incomplete, nationalist states'." Markwell (2006, p. 20). See also Wolff (1994). The emphasis on the unity of one people entailed a lack of unity with any other people, and from such a concept, it was a very short step to intolerance. Webb (2008, p. 15).

[10] Some authors blame this nationalistic spirit on the over-blown importance of Central European intellectuals. The importance of Central European intellectuals reveals the limitations of political and economic elites as "Hungarians and Poles had no national bourgeoisie, the Slovaks did not even have a nobility, while the Czechs lacked both an upper bourgeoisie and an aristocracy." Szakolczai (2005: 417-418). This had led the intellectuals to formulate "overblown and aggressive, mutually exclusive claims about the 'missions' of their own people." Szakolczai (2005: pp. 417-418).

starts from the early beginnings and ends with the emergence of World War I. Afterward, we discuss the interwar period and the socialist episode. Finally, we provide some observations about the period after the break-up of socialism. We present a political and economic context that characterized the specific period, and afterward, we present a discussion of economic thought. In each chapter, we offer brief presentations of the work and life of some representatives of the economic thought in Central Europe. We describe the work and the life of those economists who impressed by their knowledge, originality, life attitude, and intellectual stories. These are not necessarily the most excellent economists as considered by these days' mainstream. Neither are they the most notable economists as seen by national histories of economic thought. However, this does not mean that there is no overlap between these approaches.

We do not follow any specific methodology in the presentation of different epochs. Our work is eclectic. We "sometimes talk about doctrine sometimes talk about persons, sometimes talk about periods."[11] We provide information to the reader, which, for the most part, was scattered in different sources and typically not provided in the English language. Our interest is then quite general, and less specifically economic, which also reflects Central European economists' spirit, as they were in various epochs more interested in issues as the organization of the society, problems of hierarchy and equality than problems of pure exchange.

There is little permanency in Central European history, and this also extends to the history of economic thought. This discontinuity in national histories creates the foundation for shared regional history. It is difficult to find the continuing existence of specific themes or particular sets of problems, which would be researched by successive generations of scientists in the same nation or across the region. To no small extent, this type of discontinuity prevented the formation of a national tradition of specific economic thinking, even if movements happened in this direction at specific periods. These discontinuities also meant that individual scholars could not continue functioning in their country of origin and needed to move to another country, which guaranteed them possibilities of continuing their work. An Appendix lists a little less than a hundred notable economists, some world-famous, born in Central Europe, and settled outside

[11] We have taken this expression from the introduction to Robbins (1998, p. xvi).

this region, mostly in Western countries.[12] One sees the flow of talent from these countries to the West, especially the United States, the United Kingdom, Germany, Austria, and other countries. This list documents the vitality and talent of economists originating from Central Europe. When working in the Western environment, these economists became more known, and their contribution was recognized as part of the Western world.

In a certain sense, we would like to save some of the authors from oblivion. These are typically authors whose importance is granted mostly in the historical context of their time. Some contributions were significant in one period and considered banal in the next period. There is another group of scholars who somehow never ceased to attract attention as their contribution remained valid through different epochs. We discuss the contributions of both categories of economists: those who were notable only in their historical context, and those whose work survived the examination of time. In this way, we present incompatible judgments about economic thought, conflicting conceptions of a social inquiry's appropriate direction. In a certain way, we judge not the correctness or incorrectness of particular opinions but the fruitfulness of the subsequent knowledge advancement.

As the political character of the Central European lands often changed, so the names and spellings changed. Names used in this book are in the Czech, Polish, Hungarian, Slovak, Latin, German, Russian, and English. Some authors mentioned in this book had consequently differently spelled names. We will signal if different versions of the name occur, and typically also point to older versions. We do not present different names of Central European regions, towns, or places that are generally familiar to English-speakers. Also, the names of universities changed quite often. We present the university's proper name as known at the actual historical time under consideration, but it might happen that, at times, we use just the stylized name.

[12] Political discontinuity also meant intolerance against some of the old academia's representatives. For example, some professors lost jobs in universities that were shut down or relocated after World War I. Among them was Karl von Balás, who lectured at the short-lived Royal Hungarian Elizabeth University in Bratislava (1912-1918). After World War I, at German-speaking universities, one observed delay in replacing professors at vacated chairs by the Czechoslovak authorities. Šišma (2004, p. 64). Toward the end of the 1930s, Czech professors lost jobs in Slovak universities. In a similar spirit, non-Marxist professors lost jobs in the socialist regimes, and later Marxist professors were constrained after the break-up of the socialist regimes.

In Central Europe, political events played determining role in economic development. All significant decisions concerning assets ownership and assets redistribution—especially in the twentieth century—were politically determined. These include partial nationalization of assets after the break-up of the former Austro-Hungarian Monarchy, nationalization and redistribution of assets in the period 1938-45, nationalization by the socialist governments, and re-privatization of assets after the break-up of socialism.[13] These critical economic events followed the results of internal and international political processes. Efficiency considerations played a small role in such important decisions. Instead, the aim was to redistribute from the representatives of old ruling classes to the new ones in the context of political changes.

Economics is not only a social science but also an ideology. At different times some intellectuals and economists appeared as civilizational missionaries (an expression borrowed from Szakolczai 2005): in the early 1950s, young communists were persuading people about the new policies to reorient the society from the West to the East, and in the early 1990s young liberals were persuading people about the need of returning to the West. These views were often presented by people persecuted in the previous political systems, which helped strengthen economic teachings' ideological aspects. Myths and stories play an essential role, as they shape the perception of the non-experts and provide them with simplified meanings of more complex economic arguments. One of the essential myths in Central Europe is that the new economic policy will benefit the country to converge to the level of development of the Western world. Communist were presenting such myths—calling them results of analysis of scientific socialism—about the positive economic effects of a planned socialist economy with just distribution, which will surpass the Western development. Even today, some governments in Central Europe present myths about the future development of their economies to the public as the right path of modern development. Such myths play an important ideological role in activating the less skeptical and more docile part of the population, even if they have no support in empirical reality and the region's historical development.

This book depends mostly on secondary sources, even if we studied some individual economists' work in detail. We concentrate on events and

[13] On the dark side of nationalization and the stealing of assets in modern Europe, see Ther (2014). See also Teich and Porter edited volume from 1993.

ideas which spread in Hungary and the Czech (Czechoslovak) lands. By far, Poland is the largest country in the region, and a more comprehensive view concerning Polish history of economic thought would require an independent endeavor. The intricacies of the political and economic reality of Poland were beyond the scope of this author. Still, we mention at least some aspects of the development of Polish economic thought.

We acknowledge authors who contributed invaluably to developing an understanding of the history of economic thought in Central Europe. Among these researchers and economists, we mention just a few. We acknowledge our intellectual debt to them as valuable exponents of the history of thought. Location of some of the contributions, particularly before World War I and to an extent also World War II, could not be achieved without dependence on the published research of these scholars. In Hungary, we mention, among others, Zsuzsa Bekker (1941–2015), János Mátyás Kovács (1950–), Éva H. Balázs (1915–2006), János Barta (1940–), István Futaky (1926–2013), Jenő Gaál (1846–1934), Márta Hild, Róbert Horváth (1916–1993), Béla Sipos (1945–), Aladár Madarász, and Antal Mátyás (1923–2016). In lands of the former Czechoslovakia, we mention, among others, Ilona Bažantová, Antonie Doležalová, Ladislav Unčovský, František Vencovský (1923–2006), Marek Hudík, Milan Sojka (1951–2009), Miroslav Jeřábek, Jaroslav Krameš, Tomáš Krištofóry, Alžbeta Kvasničková, Miloslav Rechcigl, Josef Šíma, and Tomáš Nikodym. Finally, in Poland, Jerzy Chodorowski (1920–2011), Bogusław Czarny, Jan Toporowski (1950–), Tomasz Kamusella (1967–), Jerzy Jedlicki (1930–2018), Tadeusz Kowalik (1926–2012), Robert Szymczak, and Waclaw Stankiewicz (1925–). In the international arena, we mention Hans Jürgen Wagener (1941–), Ruman Avramov (1953–), Paul Dragos Aligica (1966–), Nikolay Nenovsky (1963–), Pencho Penchev (1971–), and others. One also needs to mention great work which deals with the political economy thought in Central Europe as Trencsényi and Kopeček (2006) and Trencsényi et al. (2016).

One observes that in each specific period, ideas from the more advanced countries flow to Central Europe. This flow is natural as the research frontier in economic science seems to be related to the most developed countries' civilizational success. Research in these countries shifts the frontier of economic knowledge more often than others. In Central Europe, the development of domestic economic views was, to a large extent, influenced by the Western and during socialism by the Soviet economic thought. In Chap. 2, we present two short studies of the transfer of economic thought to Central Europe. First, we consider the transmission of ideas of Adam Smith in the early decades after the appearance of the Wealth of Nation. Second, we discuss the early transfer of ideas of the Austrian school into Central Europe.

This book deals with Central European economists who worked most of their lives in Central Europe and typically impacted economic thought and economic policy only in Central Europe. One can call such personalities as 'in-between figures.' These are people with vision, economic thinkers close to political movements, and those Friedrich von Hayek referred to as 'second-hand dealers in ideas.' They are typically more influential, in the context of their countries, than those who produce original ideas. Muller (2009, p. 215). These are the people with societal impact who understood the call of public duty and served their age.[14]

In the remaining part of the book, we proceed as follows. Chapter 2 discusses the emergence of economic thought, its evolution until World War I. Here, we also present two short studies on transferring ideas from Western lands into Central Europe. Chapter 3 includes the period between the two World Wars. Chapter 4 concentrates on the socialist period and Chap. 5 on the period after the socialist system break-up. Finally, the Appendix presents an incomplete list of economists born in Central Europe who made careers in Western countries, mostly in the twentieth century. Finally, we conclude.

References

Arestis, Philip, and Malcolm Sawyer. 1992. *A Biographical Dictionary of Dissenting Economists*. Cheltenham, Northampton: Edward Elgar.

[14] Only rarely such economists are listed in international reviews of the history of economic thought. International reviews typically list those with theoretically oriented contributions. For example, Blaug (1986), when considering one hundred great economists before Keynes, mentions only three economists from the region: Ladislaus von Bortkiewicz, Michal Kalecki, and Oskar Lange Furthermore, Blaug (1985), when considering one hundred major economists after Keynes, mentions only János Kornai from the region. However, Blaug's list includes economists who originated from Central Europe and achieved fame in the West as Nicholas Kaldor, Tibor Scitovsky, and Jaroslav Vaněk. A Dictionary of Dissenting Economists edited by Arestis and Sawyer (1992) includes Nicholas Kaldor, Michal Kalecki, and Thomas Balogh originating from these lands. We recognize both groups of people. Those who left Central Europe and contributed to the general knowledge of economic theory. Moreover, those who stayed in Central Europe and worked their way in typically more complex and challenging conditions.

Blaug, Mark. 1985. *Great Economists since Keynes: an Introduction to the Lives & Works of One Hundred Modern Economists*. Brighton / Totowa: Harvester Press / Barnes & Noble.

———. 1986. *Great Economists before Keynes: An Introduction to the Lives & Works of One Hundred Great Economists of the Past*. Brighton / Atlantic Highlands, NJ: Harvester Press / Humanities Press International.

Deák, István. 1990. *Beyond Nationalism: A Social and Political History of the Habsburg Officer Corps, 1848-1918*. New York: Oxford University Press.

Fischer, Stanley, Ratna Sahay, and Carlos Vegh. 1998. How Far Is Eastern Europe from Brussels? *International Monetary Fund Working Paper* 98 (53): 1.

von Hayek, Friedrich August. 1944. *Road to Serfdom*. London: George Routledge & Sons.

Jordan, Peter. 2006. A Subdivision of Europe into Larger Regions by Cultural Criteria. *United Nations, Working Paper No. 48*.

Judt, Tony. 1996. *A Grand Illusion? An Essay on Europe*. New York: Hill and Wang.

Kamusella, Tomasz. 2012. Central Europe in the Distorting Mirror of Maps, Languages and Ideas. *The Polish Review* 57 (1): 33–94.

Kobrinskaia, Irina. 1997. *Rossiia i TSentralnaia Vostochnaia Evropa posle "kholodnoivoiny voiny"*. Moskva: Moskovskii TSentr Karnegi.

Le Rider, Jacques. 2008. Mitteleuropa, Zentraleuropa, Mittelosteuropa A Mental Map of Central Europe. *European Journal of Social Theory* 11 (2): 155–169.

Lindahl, Rutger. 2003. *Whither Europe? Borders, Boundaries, Frontiers in a Changing World*. Göteborg: CERGU.

Markwell, Donald. 2006. *John Maynard Keynes and International Relations. Economic Paths to War and Peace*. Oxford, New York: Oxford University Press.

Miller, A.I., ed. 1996. *Tsentralnaia evropa kak istoricheskii region (Central Europe as a Historical Region)*. Moskva: Institut slavianovedeniia i balkanistiki RAN.

Mout, Nicolette. 2006. Does Europe Have a Centre? Reflections on the History of Western and Central Europe. *European Review* 14 (2): 257–268.

Muller, Jan-Werner. 2009. The Triumph of What (If Anything)? Rethinking Political Ideologies and Political Institutions in Twentieth-century Europe. *Journal of Political Ideologies* 14 (2): 211–226.

Ottův náučný slovník (Otto's encyclopedia). 1891. Prague: J. Otto, volume 4.

Ottův náučný slovník (Otto's encyclopedia). 1903. Prague: J. Otto, volume 20.

Robbins, Lionel. 1998. In *A History of Economic Thought, the LSE Lectures*, ed. Steven G. Medema and Warren J. Samuels. Princeton and Oxford: Princeton University Press.

Salner, Peter. 2001. Ethnic Polarisation in an Ethnically Homogenous Town. *Czech Sociological Review* 9 (2): 235–246.

Schumpeter, Joseph. 1954. *History of Economic Analysis*. An edition published in the Taylor & Francis e-Library, 2006.

Šišma, Pavel. 2004. *Učitelé na německé technice v Brně 1849-1945. (Teachers at German Technical University in Brno 1849-1945)*. Prague: Společnost pro Dějiny věd a Techniky.

Szakolczai, Arpad. 2005. Moving beyond the Sophists Intellectuals in East Central Europe and the Return of Transcendence. *European Journal of Social Theory* 8 (4): 417–433.

Teich, Mikulas, and Roy Porter, eds. 1993. *The National Question in Europe in Historical Context.* Cambridge: Cambridge University Press.

Ther, Philipp. 2014. *The Dark Side of Nation-States, Ethnic Cleansing in Modern Europe.* New York and Oxford: Berghahn Books.

Trencsényi, Balázs, and Michal Kopeček, eds. 2006. *Discourse of Collective Identity in Central and Southeast Europe (1770-1945).* Budapest: Central European University Press.

Trencsényi, Balázs, Maciej Janowski, Monika Baar, Maria Falina, and Michal Kopeček. 2016. *A History of Modern Political Thought in East Central Europe.* Oxford: Oxford University Press.

Urban, Jan. 1991. Nationalism as a Totalitarian Ideology. *Social Research* 58 (4) Nationalism in Central and Eastern Europe: 775–779.

Wallace, William. 2003. Where Should EU Enlargement Stop? In *Whither Europe? Borders, Boundaries, Frontiers in a Changing World*, ed. Rutger Lindahl, 7–17. Göteborg: CERGU.

Webb, Adrian. 2008. *The Routledge Companion to Central and Eastern Europe since 1919.* Abingdon and New York: Routledge.

Wolff, Larry. 1994. *Inventing Eastern Europe: The Map of Civilization on the Mind of the Enlightenment.* Stanford: Stanford University Press.

CHAPTER 2

From Beginning Until the World War I

From around the fourteenth to the sixteenth centuries, in most parts, the peoples of Central Europe inhabited the kingdoms of Poland-Lithuania, Hungary, and Bohemia. Centuries ago, they converted to Christianity, and their primary contact to the West was mainly through their relations with German lands, and through the inflow of German ethnic as traders, clergy, settlers, artisans, mining specialists, and similar. University was founded in Prague in 1348, and Krakow in 1400. In Bohemia, Poland, and Hungary, the first printing presses were established during the middle of the fifteenth century on a par with Italy and both England and France. Translations of the Bible into the vernacular appeared first in Germany and Italy, then in Bohemia and Hungary, and only after that in England and France (Bideleux and Jeffries 2007).

Also, one of the first places where Reformation occurred was the Czech lands. Initiated by Jan Hus, burned as a heretic in 1416, an event that helped spread radical movements as the Hussites and Taborites. Hus' idea of cleaning the church and increasing the importance of laymen went later together with an increasing role for the Czech culture and aristocracy. Czech Reformation, nationally oriented, made Prague, and the University, internationally and intellectually isolated in times of emergence of a more

J. Horvath, *An Introduction to the History of Economic Thought in Central Europe*, Palgrave Studies in the History of Economic Thought, https://doi.org/10.1007/978-3-030-58926-4_2

cosmopolitan Renaissance.[1] "Bohemia became notorious as the most disordered polity and ungovernable people of the day: the sick heart of the continent, beating to an unsteady rhythm" (Evans 2006, p. 78). The radicals destroyed churches, paintings, and statues, but led to more widespread literacy—the key to spreading activist ideas to a mass audience. Only later, under Rudolf II (1552–1612), who patronaged art and science, Prague has risen, once again, to political and cultural prominence.

The Habsburgs began to enter these lands once the Jagiellonian King of Bohemia and Hungary died, when defeated by the Ottoman Turks in 1526. The Bohemian Diet conferred the vacant Bohemian throne on the Catholic Habsburg dynasty. The Hungarian and Bohemian crowns thereupon passed to Habsburgs.[2]

From the early seventeenth century, increasingly Catholic royalists began to control Bohemia's key administrative positions; Czech and German non-Catholic nobles and burghers felt that their liberties being threatened. The Bohemian Diet formally terminated Habsburg rule in Bohemia in August 1619 and attempted to bring German Protestant prince to rule. The Habsburgs crushed the Bohemian insurgents in November 1620. Wealth redistribution followed with a large part of landed property became owned by Catholic loyalists, who also took the administrative and judicial power.[3]

A protracted struggle between the Ottomans and the Austrian Habsburgs for control of Hungary ended after the second unsuccessful Ottoman siege of Vienna in 1683 and the subsequent Habsburg expulsion

[1] In the second half of the fifteenth century, a moderate Hussite, Jiří of Poděbrad, faced Catholics backed by the Hungarian King Matyas Hunyadi, who ruled for most of the second half of the fifteenth century, was a Renaissance personality who founded a library of ancient and current literary and humanist writings, destroyed later in the Ottoman invasions.

[2] The Habsburg Monarchs, who ruled in the sixteenth century have considered Protestant as heretics and fought against both the Ottomans as well as Protestants. They wasted revenues from Spanish America's silver mines in fights over the Spanish throne and drove several Protestant merchants, artisans, and financiers into exile.

[3] Evans (2006, p. 85) describes the situation after 1620: "All Protestant lords and burghers in Bohemia and Moravia, however loyal their record, had to tread the path of exile, while all peasants faced forced conversion. Meanwhile the Catholic prelates regained their rank as the first estate of the realm, 200 years after the Hussites had humbled them. Ecclesiastical lands were reclaimed, or in lieu of that a financial settlement was stipulated. New churches and monasteries began to spring up and the Jesuits laid claim to a dominant role in the purified educational system."

of the Ottomans from most of Hungary. Afterward, *heretics* were persecuted in large numbers.[4] This atmosphere of constant social and military tensions and persecutions by any side helped to increase the gap in the technological and financial predominance of the West from Central Europe. West became more secular, scientific, and rationalist, while for Central Europe, intolerance, intensification of serfdom, and a concentration of landholdings in fewer hands became characteristic (Bideleux and Jeffries 2007).

In Poland situation was somewhat different but principally similar. At the end of the fourteenth century, a union between Poland and Lithuania under the Jagiellonian followed by their victories over the Teutonic Order in the fifteenth century made Poland and Lithuania a major European power. Till the notorious 1526, following Jagiellonian kings' establishment on the thrones of Hungary and Bohemia, the Jagiellonian governed about one-third of mainland Europe. The latter half of the sixteenth century became a period of decline by reducing Poland's cultural pluralism and its tolerance of diversity and humanist learning and its receptiveness to the West (Bideleux and Jeffries 2007).

During the seventeenth century, these developments moved Central Europeans downward spiral with merchant classes in decline, partly due to religious persecution, emigration, and warfare. For a while, these countries became "a granary and livestock breeder for the urban centers of the west" (Landes 1998, p. 240).

The Early Works of the Sixteenth and the Seventeenth Centuries

In the Central European region, political economy–related writings emerged from around the sixteenth century. Especially in the early phases, these writings were not close to what we call today an economic science. Nevertheless, they were writings on agriculture, farming, ethics, geography, which contained some aspects of economics as wealth, conditions of sales, labor, agriculture, trade conditions, and similar issues. The birth of economic thought in these lands is related to the work of scientists, theologians, and observers of societal and economic life. Their work appears in a scattered way in different literature, including the emerging descriptive

[4] By the 1560s, Hungary's Calvinist 'Reformed Church' had become Hungary's largest religious denomination.

statistical works and pieces dealing with agricultural development. In premodern times, economic thought locates inside the social and political ideas regulated by norms stemming from religion. The early authors' work did not stand on firm analytic foundations. Only later, from approximately the early nineteenth-century economic thought emerged in a specialized, more formal framework of the theory. That was the progress, and the price paid for it was that economic thinking gradually became disentangled from a broader societal and moral context.

Some authors connect the beginning of economic publications in the Hungarian Kingdom with Georgius Wernherus (Georgius Wernher, Wernher György)[5] (1497–1567) publication *De admirandis Hungariae aquis* (The Exquisite Hungarian Waters). Wernher was born in Silesia, studied at the University in Cracow. He worked as a teacher in Kassa (Košice) and Eperjes (Prešov), as a protégé of Zsigmond Herberstein (1486–1557), to whom he dedicated his book.

Wernher's work describes rivers and spas in the Hungarian Kingdom, especially in Upper Hungary, with scores of comments on their economic usefulness. The book is written in Latin language and was published and republished for more than a century.[6] Today, it is still of interest to those who write about the history of medical science and medical treatments. We consider this work here as it provides a classification of an endowment of resources in the country. The book describes different spas and hot springs, and customs—especially those introduced by Ottoman Turks—prevailing at the Hungarian Kingdom. Wernher also discusses the territory's different nationalities, origins of the names of various towns in the Kingdom. The book speaks about the economic usefulness of spas, mentions different rivers and fish in these rivers. This book also provides a general geographical description of the Kingdom and classifies and catalogs different spas and water resources, which still today play a valuable part in the Hungarian and also Slovak economy. The author's style also points to his erudition as often comments and quotes from antic authors

[5] Barta (2004), Dobos (2011), and Erdősi (1963). Erdősi (1963) provides a translation of Wernher's book based on the edition issued in Köln in 1595.

[6] Dóczy et al. (1934, p. 15) put the publication of Wernher book to 1505. However, multiple other sources confirm that it was published in Basel in 1549. Dóczy et al. (1934) mention that this work was republished numerous times in different languages, for example, in Vienna in 1551, in Köln in 1563, 1591, 1595, and in Frankfurt in 1600. Scriptores rerum hungaricarum veteres (Hungarian Ancient Writers), Vienna (Vindobonae) 1746, edited by Johann Georg Schwandtner, a student of Matej Bel, also reprinted Wernher's work.

as Ptolemaios, Plinius, Ovidius, and various Greco-Roman mythology episodes. Notably, the author wrote the book for a high representative of the nobility, Herberstein Zsigmond sending the signal that it was respectable for high nobility and land-owning class to acquire this knowledge and use it.

In these early centuries, we find more works that provide information and collect data about the economy's characteristics and place it into the public realm. The authors understood that there are useful objects which create value and hence wealth. Peter Melius Horhi (Melius Juhász Péter) has published a book, similar in spirit to Wernher.[7] This book title was Herbarium *Az fáknac, füveknec nevekről, termeszetekről és hasznairól* (Herbarium. On Names, Nature and Usage of Trees and Grass), printed in Kolozsvár in 1578 by Heltai Casparne. This book contains descriptions of more than six hundred herbs (virtuous plants), describing their substrate, and giving advice on how to use them or what disease they cure. Importantly he provides herbs' names in Latin and German and then typically presents more than one name in Hungarian. Similar works appeared in the Czech Lands and Poland. For example, Christoph Fischer's *Opus oeconomicuma* was published in 1679 in the Czech lands, and Jakub Kazimierz Haur's *Ekonomika ziemianska* was published in 1675 in Poland (Barta 2004, p. 10).

At the beginning of the seventeenth century, Kristof Lackner published a drama entitled *Actus oeconomicus* (Economic Actions) (Francofurti 1619) written for students and people of Sopron where Lackner was a mayor. Quoting Roman and Greek authors, Lackner provides advice for the production of grapes, improving wheat and corn quality. János Zsámboki published *Mulomedicina* in 1574 in Basel. Apácai Csere János (Apátzai Tsere János) (1625–1659) published *Magyar Encyclopaedia* in 1653 in the Hungarian language. Jesuit János Lippay (Lippai) (1606–1666), also Rector of Trnava University, published Calendarium Oeconomicum Perpetuum in 1661 in three volumes, republished at different editions in the eighteenth century. In this work, he writes about the agricultural activities such as plowing, sowing, gardening, and administrative and organizational issues. Similarly to others of that time, this work was instructional and typically did not provide a more systematic analysis. János Lyczei (around the mid-seventeenth century—after 1712) has published *Iter Oeconomicum*, *Duodena Stationum* in Tyrnaviae in 1707; his

[7] Barta (2004), Bán (1962), Csohány (2013).

book dealt with administrative improvement issues in agriculture, agricultural accounting, and the way to increase productivity and income in settlements of the aristocracy. These works provided numerous examples of the inputs required in the production of various commodities. As mentioned earlier, these works, especially those published earlier, extensively quoted Roman and Greek authors. The modern scientific approach was of less concern. Only later, more exact works appear, especially under the influence of Matej Bel (Barta 2004).

These early works represent an effort to improve agricultural development, especially as traditional feudal methods were still not challenged at a number of places. They aimed to increase animal husbandry and agriculture productivity, recommending not only more diligence but also better organization of fallow—land that needed to recover its fertility—and advised on what type of fodder to provide to domesticated livestock, and similar. However, practical productivity-increasing advice combined with thousands of years old superstitions. For instance, it was common to discuss the influence of heavenly bodies on agricultural yields or to combine practical knowledge about the properties of materials with Vergilius' warning on how not to sow during the cold north wind. In other words, these authors considered particular economic phenomena by drawing analogies to primarily Roman and Greek historical sources, as well as to natural phenomena. In social relations, they advised against landlords' arbitrariness and mistreatment of servants and peasants. Still, they also asked for servants' politeness to noblemen and asked noblemen to pay regularly their servants and service personnel (Barta 2004).

These works represent the beginning of descriptive science, partially statistical, and partially politico-economic 'in spirit' of works of famous Western authors as Francesco da Sansovino (1521–1586), Giovanni Botero (1544–1617), and Sebastian Münster (1488–1552). These works depicted the organization of the courts of leading aristocrats, improvements in administrative issues, laws, and customs valid in the lands, as well as observation on economic geography. All this lacked the system, so much required by modern times. Nevertheless, these works affected the educated readership, as multiple editions of these works document (Láng 1913, pp. 27–28). To this literature in the Hungarian Kingdom, we need to add also Johannes Honter (Joan Honteri) (1498–1549), who published in 1562 *Rudimentorum Cosmographicorum* in Tiguri (Zürich). Archbishop of Esztergom Nicolaus Olahus (Miklós Oláh) (1493–1568) had written *Hungaria* in 1536, which introduced a geographic and cultural description of the Kingdom. This work of Olahus was published only in 1736, by Matthias Bel. The famous House of Elzevir in Amsterdam published *Respublica et Status Regni Hungariae* in 1634 in the series Respublicae. These studies did not provide an in-depth discussion of a narrow set of issues, but they had an extensive grasp of a wide range of topics, especially agricultural work, husbandry, gardening, geography, and similar. These works were published in Hungarian, Latin, German, and rarely French (Láng 1913; Bekker 2008b; Dóczy et al. 1934).

In Poland, the authors discussed, among others, just price, usury prohibition, depreciation of gold and silver, the metal content of coins. Sources of these studies were works of Aristotle, Church Fathers, Saint Thomas Aquinas and other theological systems, and judicial collections. In the territory of today's Poland, one of the first writings on the broad economic issues was the work of a monk, Jakab from Pradyz (1380–1464), who studied at the University of Cracow. His work, Tractatus de contractibus (Disputation on Contracts), discussed different ways how in business activities individuals attempted to avoid usury laws (Horváth 2001, p. 142).

Nicolaus (Nicholas) Copernicus (1473–1543), in his work De revolutionibus orbium coelestium from 1543, transformed humankind's view of the universe. Besides, he has written *Monetae cudendae ratio* (On the Minting of Coin) published in 1526, which dealt with the decreasing value of money. Copernicus was born in Toruń (in German Thorn) and studied at the University of Cracow and the University of Bologna. He earned a doctorate at canon law at the University of Ferrara in 1503. Copernicus was answering a request of the Polish King Sigismund I, who attempted to tangle the issue of currency reform. Copernicus argues, in the spirit of Gresham law, that is, that money, the value of which is fixed at a cheap rate will tend to drive out the dearer money. In other words, it is challenging for a full-weighted coin and for a coin with less weight to circulate together. Copernicus is considered the first theorist, who argued that prices change in proportion with the supply of money.

Rothbard (1995) argues that Copernicus provides us with the first version of the quantity theory thirty years before Azpilcueta Navarrus and "without the stimulus of an inflationary influx of specie from the New World to stimulate his thinking on the subject." Copernicus realized that "the dearness of everything is the result of the cheapness of money." "'An excessive quantity of money', he opined, 'should be avoided'" (Rothbard 1995, p. 165). Similarly, de Soto (2008, p. 32) writes that Azpilcueta and

Copernicus were the first to present the mechanistic version of the quantity theory of money. In addition, Toporowski (2014) discusses Copernicus' articulation of a version of Gresham's Law.

Jan Ostroróg (1436–1501) considered middle nobility the healthiest base of society and wanted to reinforce the cities' inhabitants. He criticized usury and the worsening of the value of money, wanted lower tariffs and stronger Kingdom, and more healthy state finances. Similarly, Andrzej Frycz Modrzewski (1503–1572) was reform-minded in his work *O poprawie Rzeczypospolitej* (On Betterment of the State). According to him, the state should protect peasants from nobility's whims, and the law should hold for each individual. Calvinist Anselm Gotomski (1508–1588), in his work *Gospodarstwo* (Household Economy), presented views on the bettering of domestic agriculture and favored strict education, work, and personal discipline. Jan Grodwagner, in his work from 1632 *Discurs o cenie pieniedzy terazniejszej i niektórych skutkach jej* (A Treatise on Current Value of Money and Some of Its Implications) writes that restrictions on the export of bullion are ineffective. Instead, emphasis should be on a positive trade balance. For that reason, the state should protect the domestic industry, constrain the export of raw materials and import of finished products. He viewed the role of money as a motivation for economic activity (Horváth 2001, pp. 144–145).

Doležalová (2018) discusses the radical teachings of Jan Hus (1369 or 1371–1415) and some of his predecessors as the beginnings of Czech economic thought. John (Ján) Amos Comenius (Komenský) (1592–1670) was born in Moravia studied at German universities. In 1638 he left for England and other countries and settled in Holland. His pedagogical activities were highly acclaimed already during his lifetime. His famous works include *Všeobecná porada o nápravě věcí lidských* (General Advice in the Emendation of Human Matters) (1662), *Labyrint světa ráj srdce* (Labyrinth of the World and Paradise of the Heart) (1623), and *Gentis felicitas* (The Happiness of the Nation) (1659). "Comenius's legacy is latently present in Czech economic thought. Two hundred years later, we find Comenius's search for the harmonious organization of the world society in the work of František L. Chleborád" (Doležalová 2018, p. 18).

The celebrated polyhistor of his time was Martin Szentiványi (1633–1705). His name is also spelled as Szent-Iványi Márton in Hungarian, Martin Szentiványi or Sentiványi in Slovak, Martinus Szent-Ivany in Latin. In the print of his book Curiosiora et Selectiora, the author's name is P. Martino Szent-Ivanyi. Kirschbaum (2007) spells his name as Sentiváni (Szentiványi), and Zavarský (2011) as Sentiváni. Unčovský (2011) considers him of Slovak nationality, and Zavarský (2018) calls him a Slovak polymath. The Czech Wikipedia also counts him a Slovak, while the German edition considers him a Hungarian, and in the English edition, he is Hungarian or Slovak. Raymund Rapaics in *A természettudomány a nagyszombati egyetemen* (Natural Sciences at the University of Trnava), published in a journal Természettudományi Közlöny in June 1935, calls him the greatest Hungarian encyclopedist. Rapaics writes, "It is without a doubt that Szentiványi was not only of the seventeenth century but in general the greatest Hungarian polyhistor."

Szent-Iványi entered the Jesuit Order in 1653 and taught in Graz, Munich, and Trnava (Tyrnae in German, Nagyszombat in Hungarian, Tyrnaviae in Latin), where he was also the Rector of the University. He was a prolific author and published a large number of books, especially in natural sciences and theology.

In Trnava, he published his work *Curiosiora et Selectiora Variarum Scientiarum Miscellanea* (An Assortment of Interesting and Rather Select Items of General and Academic Knowledge) in 1689–1702. *Curiosiora et Selectiora* is a three-volume encyclopedic work that deals with questions in astronomy, meteorology, botany, zoology, geography, history, geology, and other fields. Kenny (2004, pp. 3–6) shows that in the context of the time, *Curiosiora et Selectiora* represented a keen and anxious desire for knowledge. A curious object could then be a useless or a useful object of interest, exclusive, and learned. Kenny (2004, p. 222) translates the title of Szentivanyi's work as 'Very Curious and Select Miscellany of Various Sciences.' Szentiványi himself writes about the Curiosiora: "curious, very curious, yet neither playful nor vain; curious because they are rare, because they are far removed from common knowledge, not because they are collected all at one go, but rather because they are selected one by one from the most select authors; not, admittedly, because they are wholly new or unheard-of, but because they have been arranged and collected with great labour from a huge number of extremely rare books in distinguished, famous libraries" (Kenny 2004, pp. 222–223).

From *Curiosiora et Selectiora*, a selection was published in Trnava in 1746, in Claudiopoli (Cluj-Napoca) in 1748, and Budapest in 1782. Unčovský (2011, p. 103) quotes from a selection published in 1746 titled *Oeconomia philosophica*, divided into five parts, most of which deal with agricultural issues. Szentiványi elaborates on domestic animals and plants, the schedule of agriculture works, agricultural laborers' problems, and similar. The fifth part is entitled *Variae Observationes Economis Utiles, Tum Physica, Tum Ethica* (Various Useful Economic Knowledge, both Physical as well as Ethical), where Szent-Iványi copes with agricultural advice, water and forest management, and management of meadows, cattle, and linden. Chapter eleven deals with the question of the longevity of human life. Chapter fifteen is entitled *Centum Observationes Oeconomico-Monarchicae* (One Hundred Observation on the Economy of Monarchy). This chapter consists of one hundred shorter and longer paragraphs dealing with a variety of political economy issues. Thus, this chapter is a short political economy treatise as it deals from comparative and historical perspectives with the national economic issues, as how money works or how taxes are collected (Unčovský 2011, p. 103).[8]

In the *Curiosiora et Selectiora*, a section entitled *Centum Observationes Oeconomico-Monarchicæ* appears in part two. The one hundred paragraphs provide treatment of different issues. For example, the first ten paragraphs deal with the principles of imposing the tax burden on the subjects. In particular, he states that it is the Prince and the Monarch's exclusive right to tax the subjects, but they have to attain necessary political support. Even increased taxes can be rational, and for the common good, if they preserve the economic activity. Prince imposing taxes should act as a shepherd who cares for sheep, enjoys wool and milk, and needs to defend the sheep from the cold and the heat. Also, a farmer does not cut all trees, just their branches, so new fruits could arrive in the spring. Prince can levy taxes, according to the necessity of time, but proportionately. God notices the unfair collection of taxes; besides, such a state of affairs is harmful and can stimulate riots. The imposition of taxes should follow the rules and should support the right causes. The imposition of taxes should not last beyond the time when their purpose is achieved. Prince should have moderate relations with his subjects to prevent rebellion. Szent-Iványi also dealt with the issue of tariffs, using examples across Europe and history.

The authors publishing before the eighteenth century were typically not fully aware of the modern concept of the economy. They investigated

[8] It contains paragraphs on Treasury under Emperor Augustus, the economy under Caligula and Tiberius. Szent-Iványi refers to the authors who inspired him. For example, he mentions the Politicorum of Aristotle; he quotes Diego de Saavedra Fajardo, Adam Contzen, and especially the Belgian Laurens (Laurentius) Beyerlinck. Szentiványi was also quoting French Honoratus Fabrius (1608–1888), a Jesuit theologian and mathematician, and also Athanasius Kircher (Kircherus) (1602–1680), a German Jesuit polymath, and the work of Christoph Fischer (1611–1680) *Opus oeconomicum* (Unčovský 2011, pp. 103–104).

particular issues, but not general economic concepts. Also, they did not consider that economic activity creates wealth; instead, wealth was a property of the land and could be achieved through political and military activities.

Significant changes in the development of economic thought happened in the eighteenth and early nineteenth centuries.

The Eighteenth and the Early Nineteenth Centuries

The Austrian's winning the conflict with the Turks led to Hungarian Protestants' persecution and a massive redistribution of land into Catholic loyalists' hands. This persecution gave rise to widespread anti-Habsburg insurgency in the early eighteenth century. In 1711 signed the Treaty of Szatmar, between the Habsburgs, the Hungarian estates and the rebels, gave Hungary a decentralized system of aristocratic self-administration, confirmed aristocratic privileges (called domestically liberties) of wealthy landowners as their exemption from taxation. This Treaty, in essence, till 1847, guaranteed Hungary's special status within the Habsburg Empire.

From 1711 till 1740, the Habsburg Empire was run by Karl VI, whose governments promoted the textile industry's development, provided subsidies to mining, metallurgy, and light industries as porcelain, and glassware, with production mostly in Austria and Bohemia-Moravia. Period of 1740 till 1790 was characteristic of reforms introduced by Maria Theresia and her son Joseph II. Taxes on the Catholic Church's wealth were increased, from 1773, the Jesuit order was dissolved, and gradually more practical state education was introduced. Joseph II, who governed in 1780–1790, suspended Hungarian aristocracy' privileges, and his administration promoted more productive utilization of human resources, away from restrictive ethnic and religious hierarchies. There was a strong opposition to these efforts as they would emancipate primarily those groups whose human talent was hitherto suppressed and restricted (Bideleux and Jeffries 2007, p. 174).

The outbreak of the French Revolution in 1789 and the death of Josef II in 1790 led to a substantial retreat from reform under the reign of Emperor Franz II (1792–1835). His reign began with a purge of reformers from the central imperial administration, a reaffirmation of traditional seigneurial and ecclesiastical privileges, and a substantial reversal of the enlightened reforms of Maria Theresa and Josef II.

During the late seventeenth and early eighteenth centuries gradually, the Polish-Lithuanian Commonwealth weakened. The Counter-Reformation curtail the participation of Protestants in the Commonwealth's life. This decreased the political pluralism and cultural diversity and brought about intellectual stagnation. The First Partition of Poland happened in 1772.[9] In 1792, the French Revolution had succeeded in uniting Europe's monarchies. Russia and Prussia agreed on a second Partition of the Commonwealth. In 1794, there was a Polish-Lithuanian insurrection against the Russian and Prussian forces led by Tadeusz Kosciuszko (1746–1817). However, the insurrection had been crushed by Russia, Prussia, and Austria. As a result of the Third Partition, Russia obtained around 60% of the former Commonwealth's territory, with the remaining part shared between Prussia and the Habsburg Empire.

From 1809 to 1848, Habsburg policy's conduct fell into Klemens von Metternich (1773–1859), who substantially increased the international importance of Vienna. Also, close cooperation between political police and censors organized the struggle against the internal political threats posed by nationalism, liberalism, and radicalism. Metternich's police powers, censorship, networks of police 'informers' created a modern police state.[10]

Economic Thought in the Eighteenth and the Early Nineteenth Centuries

Poland, as well as Hungary, lagged in agricultural developments as compared to some Western lands. Agricultural production was predominantly dependent on the less motivated work of serfs. Some economists living in Central Europe had pointed to the inefficiencies of the institution of serfdom. One of those was Stanislaw Leszczynski (1677–1766), another one was a noted physiocrat, Antoni Poplawski (1739–1786), an enlightened member of the Piarist order spreading the teachings of Quesnay and educational reform. Antoni Poplawski studied law and economics in Rome and Paris, was a professor at the Cracow Seminary, and later its Rector. He

[9] However, in 1773 the Sejm established a Commission for National Education entrusted with re-organizing schools into a single countrywide education system. The Commission was headed by a team of enlightened aristocrats, endowed with part of the wealth of the dissolved Jesuit Order dissolved.

[10] Still, by twentieth-century standards, it was a mild police state. The state kept relatively few political prisoners, made little (if any) use of torture, and kept no camps for its enemies.

was a member of the Society for Elementary Books from its establishment in 1775 through 1780. Together with other noted intellectuals as Hieronim Stroynowski and Hugo Kollatay, Poplawski was deeply concerned with the peasants' education and welfare. He urged the gentry to be more attentive to the needs of the peasants. "He argued that if the serfs were to receive instruction in various trades, in better methods of gardening, animal husbandry, and farming they would, in turn, become more productive, and thus improve and enlarge the wealth of the landowners" (Rackauskas 1977, pp. 145–146).

Hieronim Stroynowski (1752–1815) was a bishop and professor at Wilno. His influential book published in 1785 was entitled *Nauka prawa przyrodzonego, politycznego, ekonomiki politycznej i prawa narodów* (Natural and Political Law, Political Economy and International Law). He favored freedom for industry and trade, the abolition of guilds and monopolies. Walerian Stroynowski (1759–1834) criticized state policies supporting new manufacturing enterprises as he believed in the natural accumulation of capital and natural development. Influential economic and social thinkers were Stanislaw Wawrzyniec Staszic (1755–1826) and a member of the Piarist order Hugo Kollatay (1750–1812). Both were notable personalities of the Polish Enlightenment aiming to overcome the country's backwardness, primarily through educational reforms. Staszic has seen a perspective in a strong monarchy, while Kollatay formulated a program of new republicanism (Wandycz 2001; Horváth 2001, p. 146).

Some of the principal Polish thinkers in the period lived in foreign lands. One of the most noted was Count Fryderyk Skarbek (1792–1866), who is considered the father of Polish economic thought. Skarbek graduated in 1808 from Lyceum in Warsaw, in 1809–1811 studied in Paris, listening to lectures of Piotr Maleszewski (Maliszewski) (1767–1828). Between 1818 and 1830, was a professor at Warsaw University, and chaired the Department of Political Economy after Dominik Krysinski (1785–1830) (Litynska 2000). Later Skarbek was Minister of Finance in Warsaw. He published a textbook *Gospodarstwo narodowe* (National Economy) in 1820, and *Rys ogólny nauki finansów* (Foundations of Finance) in 1824. In 1829 in Paris, he published *Théorie des richesses sociales* (Theory of Social Wealth), which appeared in the Polish language in 1859. His book deals with the theory of exchange, income, and consumption, and applications for different strata in society (Horváth 2001, p. 148).

Both Maleszewski and Skarbek were active during the early time of the industrial revolution and held in admiration and distaste for its advancements. They understood that Europe begins to leave the feudal structures and enters the new epoch. They liked the results of the changes, but they liked less the new shape of this British-led civilization. Skarbek has written: "Putting aside our admiration for the progress of various industries and the development of arts and crafts, the state of the richest and the most enlightened nations of Europe makes every friend of mankind painfully sorry for the lot of a large proportion of inhabitants for whom destitution has become an inherited calling, as it were" (Jedlicki 1999, p. 76). Later in his life, he expressed concerns that the working-class desires for a better life might grow faster than the means assembled to achieve it, and such a situation could threaten the social order. He argued that people should not imitate the upper classes' lives since this breeds envy, which breeds rebellion. In other words, people were to know their place in society, and their aspirations were not to be too high (Jedlicki 1999, pp. 158–159). In the eighteenth century and the early nineteenth century, several great works also appeared in the Hungarian Kingdom. Among the early works, one finds István Hatvani's (1718–1786) writing on political arithmetic, *Introductio ad Principia Philosophiae Solidioris*, in Debrecen in the 1750s (Horváth 1960). In 1780, Samuel Tessedik (1742–1820) published writings on peasants' destiny entitled *Parasztember* (The Peasant) (Horváth 1963).

Miklós Skerlecz (Nikola Škrlec) (1729–1799) produced a series of works concerning economic and demographic matters. Skerlecz (1914) belonged to authors who had identified the reasons for backwardness compared to Western Europe in demographic developments, namely low population density, caused by the almost permanent state of war along the borders between the Habsburg Empire and the Sublime Porte. In this period, a number of scientists had identified an increasing population as a source of wealth. The more densely populated Western Europe put pressure on more intensive forms of agriculture. At the same time, in Central and also Eastern Europe, the "great quantity of arable land and the ease of population resettlement resulted in a repetition of traditional structures of production from one century to another, in Western Europe the peasants were obliged to ensure that a limited amount of land would be capable of supplying the needs of an increasing population" (Gunst 1991, pp. 53–54).

Michal Baludjanski[11] (1769–1847) was born in East Slovakia, in a Ruthenian family.[12] His father was a Greek-catholic priest. He studied at the gymnasium of Sátoraljaújhely then at the Royal Academy in Košice. At the faculty of law on Vienna University, he took courses for political and cameral sciences under Joseph von Sonnenfels. In Vienna, he learned several foreign languages and read the works of Adam Smith. Baluďanský defended his degree of doctor in law writing a Latin dissertation concerning safety stocks of grain and a system of warehouses for their storage. He began to teach at a new law faculty in Oradea (Grosswardein, Nagyvárad, Varadín). In 1802 he was elected as dean of the faculty. In 1804, he was appointed a professor of the pedagogical institute in Saint Petersburg, teaching political economy and commercial law. In 1819 the Pedagogical institute was transformed into Saint Petersburg University, and he became its first Rector until 1821, when he was dismissed. Afterward, Baludjanski, who belonged to a circle of reformers around Mikhail Speransky (1772–1839), worked as a legal expert. His main book *Izobraženije rozličnych chozjajstvennych systematov* (Analysis of different economic systems), remained only in the manuscript as well as other of his economic writings (Špirko 2009, p. 169). Baluďanský belonged to those personalities who opposed the serfdom as he considered freedom of peasants and laborers a pre-condition for capital creation (Unčovský 2000, p. 689). During his career in Russia, he participated in the organization of jurist education and in editing a collection of legal decisions, published in 1835.

In 1792, the Catholic priest, József Bencsik (around 1764–1827), anonymously wrote a study entitled *De Industria Nationali Hungariae*. He believed that nations' economy depended on a large and dense population, which would increase security and be the basis for a more significant labor force. Among the reasons for the small population, he listed

[11] Unčovský (2000), Hamza (2017), Baláži (2018), Ilina (2014), Špirko (2009), and Wortman (1976).

[12] The spelling of his name appears in various forms. In Russian, Михаил Андреевич Балугьянский, Mikhail Andreevitch Balugyanskij, Michal Baluďanský in Slovak, Balugyánszky Mihály in Hungarian. Also, the determination of his nationality is an intricate issue. The first Czech encyclopedia, *Slovník náučný*, edited by František Ladislav Rieger, 1860, volume 1, considers him of Slovak nationality and writes his name as Michal Baluďanský. Russian Enciklopeditcheskij Slovar, published in 1891 in Saint Petersburg, considers him a Carpato-Russian born in Hungary. Wortman (1976, p. 39) considers him a Hungarian scholar and spells his name as M. A. Balugianskii.

continuous warfare, religious intolerance, oppression of serfs, and the existence of sizeable unproductive labor (Kautz 1911, p. 164).

We observe national pamphleteers, the work which dealt in no small extent with improvements of the peasants and serfs' destiny and the general advancement of specific regions and peoples' economic situation. Some of this work formed the base of the national movements. One should mention the work of František Chleborád (1839–1911) and Ľudovít Štúr (1815–1856), Juraj Fándly (1750–1811), and lots of others. Chleborád had published Soustava národního hospodářství politického (The System of Political National Economy) in 1869. He was a proponent of the cooperative movement who stood at anti-socialist positions. His other works included Boj o majetek (Fight for Property) (1884), Hospodářství vlastenecké (Patriotic Economy) (1868), and Pomoc chudým dělníkum (Help to Poor Workers) (1868). Turnovec (2002, p. 51) writes about him that "his social and moral enthusiasm for the economic advance of the Czech nation outweighed specialized theoretical reflections."

A prevailing school of thought till the middle of the nineteenth century was the Austrian-dominated Cameralism. Cameralism was a state-centric administrative theory aimed at improving the level of development in the Austrian Monarchy. In the prevailing Cameralist view, the majority of the population lacked business spirit. Consequently, the state—as their guardian—was needed. Cameralist policies promoted industries' development, supporting detailed regulations of economic activities, and introducing restrictions on foreign commerce. Cameralists also supported abolishing medieval guilds, unifying laws for small principalities and municipalities, and a similar set of actions (Small 1909).

The Cameralist state bureaucrats had been trained in German universities or Austria and later in the University of Trnava, and shortly in Collegium Oeconomicum in Szempcz (Senec) (Fináczy 1899). Collegium Oeconomicum was founded by Empress Maria Theresia (1717–1780) in 1763. In 1769 the University of Trnava established the first Department of Political and Cameral Sciences in the Hungarian Kingdom. Joseph von Sonnenfels (1732–1817) recommended Anton Weisengruber as the first professor. After him, subsequent professors were Gaspar Paal Ehrenfels (?–1792) and Franz Giurkowitz. By comparison, the first Cameralist Department in Prague was founded in 1766; its first professor was another student of Sonnenfels, Josef Ignác Buček (Butschek) (1741–1821) (Unčovský 2011; Fináczy 1899).

Next, we present selected personalities from this period, namely Mátyas Bél, Gregorius Berzeviczy, and Marton Schwartner.

Mátyas Bél (Matej Bel, Matthias Bel) (1684–1749)[13]

Bel, who described himself as 'by language a Slav, by nation a Hungarian, by erudition a German' was a polyhistor who worked in different fields of study. He was born to a family of the protestant denomination. He had written in Latin and German, but also in Hungarian and translated some works into the Slovak language. His teachers, at an early age, recognized Bel's talent. He moved to study from his birthplace Ocsova (Očová) first to Lučenec (Losonc), then to Kalnó (Kalinovo), Alsó-sztregová (Dolná Strehová), Banská Bystrica (Besztercebánya), Pozsony, Veszprém, and finally Halle. In Halle, August Herman Francke (1663–1727), a Lutheran Pietist scholar, geographer, and theologian, influenced his thought. Bel became a pastor. However, his interest in science began to grow after his studies ended in Halle. After his university years, he spent one year close to Magdeburg and then moved to Besztercebánya, where he worked from 1710 as a Rector of Gymnasium. From 1714 he moved to an Evangelic Lutheran Lyceum in Pozsony and returned the former fame to this institution.

Bel was a universalist, one of the great scientists of the Baroque period. His intellect grasped in different languages large sections of the knowledge of that time in history, philology, literature, ethnography, geography, economy, and natural science. In Halle, in 1722, together with Daniel Krman (1663–1740), he published a translation of the Bible into the Czech language. Bel had written various articles for noted Western scientific journals; "Bel was a pioneer of the modern scientific method. He made use of a wide network of collaborators, drew on library and archival resources, and always drew up a rational plan before he set out to work; his writing is thus a very critical and judicious synthesis of the available sources" (Petro 1995, p. 38). His *Notitia Hungariae* is probably the first academic and scientific work based on other studies, facts, empirical observations, and similar methodology. For example, when students from Lyceum went home for holidays, Bel asked them to collect geographical, natural, ethnographic, historical, and other information about Hungarian

[13] Haan (1879), Deák (1984), Tóth (2017), Kirschbaum (2007), Láng (1913).

counties. In Central Europe, his work represented a sizable step forward toward publications containing original contributions.

His most famous work is *Notitia Hungariae novae Historico-geographica* (Historical and Geographical Knowledge about the New Hungary), published in 1735–1742. This book provides historical, political, natural, administrative, and other characteristics of the Hungarian Kingdom regions. Around a decade before Bel published the *Notitia Hungariae*, in 1723, he published an account that he wants to accomplish in his work entitled *Hungariae antiquae et novae Prodromus* (Norinbergae, 1723). Bel needed to overcome lots of difficulties when trying to publish this work. Individual counties did not like to share data. Initially, such endeavor met with suspicions: who would need complete information about different Hungarian counties if not representatives of a foreign power. Neither nobility wanted to share data about their property ownership, and noble family archives were not public, and so on. However, once the Imperial Court in Vienna and some enlightened members of the nobility encouraged and financed his work, some counties became friendlier and helped with data collection. Finally, the Notitia was a success. It was reviewed in Philosophical Transaction in London in 1744. Reviewer especially noted the book's elegant and expensive print, the quality of maps prepared by Samuel Mikovinyi (1698–1750), a noted cartographer.

Each part of the *Notitia Hungariae* is structured similarly. The general section (pars generalis) preceded a specific section (pars specialis). Pars generalis contained the physical, natural description of the area, followed by population and labor. Pars specialis included a description of towns, including their privileges, castles, and villages (Láng 1913, p. 37).

Bel expected to publish a detailed endowment description of all counties of the Kingdom. However, he fully finished only a part of it. The first volume appeared in 1735, presented the history of the county and the city of Pozsony, provided an account of its natural endowments, hydrography, agriculture, mining, political situation, economic geography, describing the soil, productions, rivers, temperature, agriculture, its inhabitants, nobility, and general characterization of this county. Also, this book describes different ethnicities living in the city, privileges awarded, its Churches, public buildings, and other vital characterizations. In 1736 the second volume describing the vicinity of Pozsony appeared. Then the third and other volumes followed. However, during his lifetime, Bel did not manage to publish studies of all royal counties of the Kingdom, as he originally intended. Description of some of them, altogether there were forty-eight, remained in manuscript, later bought from his wife by Cardinal József Batthyányi (1727–1799), and Adam Kollár (1718–1783). Unfortunately, the papers damaged when delivering to Cardinal Batthyányi and became hardly readable (Láng 1913, p. 36).

Haan (1879, p. 54) stressed that one of the most prominent aspects of Bel's work was that his writings were not biased toward any ethnic or religious persuasion. This aspect of the work of Matthias Bel was a source of inspiration to one of the founders of economic thought in Central Europe, whose work we discuss in the next segment.

Gregorius Berzeviczy (Gregor von Berzeviczy, Berzeviczy Gergely) (1763–1822)

In Central Europe, Berzeviczy belonged to the most significant scholars of the end of the eighteenth and the early nineteenth centuries.

Berzeviczy descended from an old noble family, who had moved to the Hungarian Kingdom from Tirol or Germany. The family was awarded the manor in Lomnicza as early as the beginning of the thirteenth century. Most of the family accepted the Lutheran faith. Berzeviczy's mother tongue was German. However, he learned Hungarian and Latin into perfection, and most likely understood Slovak.

In an excellent publication, Gaál (1902) reconstructs the life of Berzeviczy, whose family still living in the Tatras allowed Gaál access to the complete family archive. Balázs (1967) had also published concerning his life, his travels, and his early years.

In October 1784, he left for studies in Göttingen, where he stayed till 1786. In 1786/1787, he undertook a long journey through Germany, Holland, and France to Britain (Gaál 1902). In Berzeviczy times, maybe even today, travel to Western Europe changed Central Europeans. Jedlicki (1999, p. 6) nicely describes this situation in the case of Poland of the early nineteenth century. "Instructions issued by local diets for Seym deputies contain numerous demands for the estates to make it unlawful for young gentry to go abroad, since those who returned to Poland after their foreign travels seemed to belong to a different nation. They altered their manner of dress, pursuits, and way of thinking and showed a marked disrespect for everything in their own country and family home."

After returning from studies, he stayed for three years in a lower level administrative job. He felt alienated from the social life, and in 1795 returned to his birthplace, where he stayed till the end of his life. There he continued in a systematic study of economic matters.[14]

In 1797, Berzeviczy published *De commercio et industria Hungariae* (On Commerce and Industry in Hungary) in Lőcse (Leutschau in German, Levoča in Slovak). This book established Berzeviczy's position in the international scientific community as it brought him membership in the Göttingen University Royal Academy (Gaál 1902, p. 69).

In Berzeviczy's time, the landed aristocracy was able to prevail over the urban class, which permitted the consolidation of serfdom. The power of the landowners and the weakness of cities helped suppress the bourgeoisie formation, delayed abolition of serfdom, and weakened the nobility's liberal part (Bianchini 2015, p. 32). This situation guaranteed independence to the landed class. However, it also led to isolation from the more developed part of Europe and led to slower inflow of Western technical innovations into the domestic agriculture (Bianchini 2015, pp. 34–35). In 1804 Berzeviczy completed a work, which reacted to this situation. *De conditione et indole rusticorum in Hungaria* (On the Situation and Character of the Peasantry in Hungary) describes the serfs' situation in the Kingdom. He collected observations concerning the life and behavior of serfs during travels. This study received a warm welcome in Göttingen. However, at the same time, it was viewed with suspicion in domestic aristocratic circles.

De conditione et indole rusticorum in Hungaria discusses the rural areas' development and describes the peasantry's conditions in the Hungarian Kingdom. In this book, after discussing the rights of peasants and their work ethics, Berzeviczy argues against the system of serfdom. He recognizes that achieving national political aims might be challenged after abolishing the serfdom (Berzeviczy 1902, p. 160).

Berzeviczy's later books treated practical problems of improving Hungarian international trade during the Napoleonic Wars. His last, theoretical book on political economy, *Oeconomica Publico Politica*, was written in a Latin manuscript in 1819. Unfortunately, the manuscript was lost, and only after more than eighty years after Berzeviczy's death, Gaál (1902) found the manuscript. Gaál (1902) published the book in Hungarian,

[14] One of Berzeviczy's favorite topics is demography. Berzeviczy, similarly to Schwartner, discussed later, thought that the Hungarian Kingdom was under-populated. Both Schwartner and Berzeviczy believed in Smith's idea that the capitalist system with free capital and labor movement would provide the optimal population size. Horváth (1964), Unčovský (1956).

entitled *A közgazdaságról* (De Oeconomia Publico Politica), based on the Latin manuscript of 1819. In *De Oeconomia*, Berzeviczy pays respect to Adam Smith and Jean Baptiste Say. The book divides into sixteen chapters, which deal with needs, goods, wealth, production, value, price, money, and other economic topics. The way he deals with these issues is very modern. He objects economic policy based only on the nation's narrow interests, he criticizes conspicuous consumption and favors progressive taxation.

Only in retrospect was the importance of Berzeviczy understood. In 1877 Kautz has published in edition Nemzetgazdasági első remekíróink (Our First Great Writers on National Economy), Berzeviczy Gergely emlékezete (To Remember Gergely Berzeviczy), Pesti Könyvnyomda, and Nemzetgazdasági Szemle, 1877, IV, 1–22. He considered Berzeviczy a Hungarian classic and saw his contribution to economic theory and foreign trade policy. Kautz did not know Berzeviczy's work published in 1902. Kautz appreciated Berzeviczy's erudition and his foreign literature's knowledge combined with acquaintance with realities in his homeland.

Marton Schwartner (Martin von Schwartner) (1759–1823)[15]

Similarly to Berzeviczy, Schwartner belongs to those German mother tongue intellectuals of protestant origin who moved to the highest levels of intellectual and scientific life in the Hungarian Kingdom. These intellectuals typically studied history and political sciences in Göttingen (established in 1737) and Tübingen and were influenced by the freer intellectual environment.[16]

[15] Láng (1913), Lukcsics (1914).

[16] Hungarian, predominantly Catholic, students who studied outside Hungaria, peregrinatio academica, had studied already in the fourteenth century at the newly established universities in Prague (1347), Wien (1364), Cracow (1365), Heidelberg (1386), Leipzig (1409), or Tübingen (1477). Studying abroad became more widespread after the Reformation period. In the first one hundred years of Göttingen University, almost five hundred Hungarian students enrolled. This number was smaller than at Halle or Jena, but typically, the Göttingen studies were considered more serious and more progressive. Futaky (2007, p. 56). Lukcsics (1914, pp. 14–15) mentions that Schlözer criticized those sending their children to lower-level colleges instead of Göttingen as that influenced the intellectual level in the Hungarian educational institutions. Lukcsics adds that Hungarian students mostly followed where stipends were available, and those universities were cheaper than the elite German colleges.

Schwartner originated from Kežmarok (Késmárk in Hungarian, Käsmark in German), in Spiš (Szepes) region in the Hungarian Kingdom. Schwartner's family were wealthy textile traders, and originated from Germany, moved to the Hungarian Kingdom toward the end of the fourteenth and beginning of fifteenth hundreds. In 1741 Maria Theresia raised the family status into nobility.

Schwartner receives elementary education in German, learns Latin, and mostly writes in these languages.[17] Similarly to Berzeviczy, he learned Hungarian as a young man. Between 1772 and 1775, he studied at Lyceum in Késmárk. He continues his studies in Sopron and till 1779 in Pozsony, where his teacher was, among others, János György Stretskó, also a student in Göttingen and a Rector of Lyceum (Lukcsics 1914, p. 10). Schwartner studied in Göttingen from 1779 till 1782, listening to lectures of Schlözer (1735–1809), Gatterer (1727–1799), Pütter (1725–1807), and Spittler (1752–1810). Schwartner observed statistics in the making during his stay in Göttingen, where Achenwall (1719–1772), Gatterer, and Schlözer famously worked on descriptive and analytical statistics. Thanks to his family background Schwartner studied without receiving a scholarship. He originally wanted to study theology; however, under the influence of his professors began to study other subjects. Schwartner graduated with a license from Schlözer, which notified his qualities. In Göttingen, the English spirit, Hume, and the English constitution influenced young Schwartner.[18]

After the return from Göttingen, he works as a tutor in an aristocratic family, later accepts a teaching position at a Lyceum in Késmárk. In 1786 he was offered a position at Lyceum in Sopron, where he lectured on world history and statistics. In 1787 he accepted a position at Pest University at the Department of Diplomatika. Joseph II would nominate

[17] Schwartner, similarly to Berzeviczy, was under pressure by nationally oriented scholars who lacked in his work sufficiently blossoming national spirit. Historian István Horváth (1784–1846), initially Schwartner's student and admirer, performed this critique in the case of Schwartner. Schwartner suffered a great deal from these attacks (Lukcsics 1914). However, even Láng (1913, p. 32) criticizes Schwartner for critical remarks toward national endeavors.

[18] Schlözer's work *Kritische Sammlungen zur Geschichte der Deutschen in Siebenbürgen*, published in the last years of the eighteenth century, infuriated Hungarian national spirit. In 1781 Joseph II ruled that the three predominant peoples of Transylvania, the Saxons (Sachsen), the Hungarians, and the Szeklers (Székely), should become equal under the law. The representatives of Saxons protested as that meant the loss of privileges allocated to them centuries ago. They turned to Schlözer for help. He took the side of the Saxons, showing how much Hungarian culture owed to the German creativity (Futaky 2007, pp. 22–23).

him for this position even if Pest University suggested two other candidates for university professors' posts. This nomination was a surprising act as Pest University was predominantly a Catholic institution. Schwartner became a professor of Diplomatika, a scientific field dealing with critical analysis of historical documents. He published Introductio in artem diplomaticam praecipue hungaricam in Pest in 1790, with the second edition published in Buda in 1802. Inspiration for this work came from one of his Göttingen teachers, Gatterer. German and Austrian journals positively reviewed this work. Schwartner also worked in the field of genealogy, where he became famous taking the issue of the Crouy-Chanel family, which in the eighteenth century claimed to have ancestors in the Hungarian Royal family (Lukcsics 1914).

Schwartner, in 1789, asks for a permit to publish his work Freiműthige Gedanken über die Einfürung der deutschen Sprache in Ungarn (Frank Thoughts about the Introduction of the German Language in Hungary). However, he did not obtain a permit as censors objected to its French spirit and critical views on religion. Schwartner's political position was quite hostile to the growing national spirit in the Hungarian Kingdom. He was influenced by Schlözer, who supported central power, potentially putting under central control the small German states and municipalities. In Schwartner's view Hungary, a country lagging behind Western Europe, should not be continuously involved in political conflicts with the Austrian Emperors. Quite the opposite, Hungary should follow the rule of the Emperor (Lukcsics 1914).

His main work, *Statistik des Königreichs Ungern* (Statistics of the Kingdom of Hungary), was a continuation of the works in descriptive statistics mentioned earlier. Similar work appeared by Antal Bajtay (Antonii Bajtay) (1717–1775), Catholic bishop and teacher of Joseph II, entitled *Politico Statistica Regni Hungariae*. This work also provides information on history, public law, administration, politics, and the Hungarian Kingdom's inhabitants (Láng 1913, p. 40). *Statistik des Königreichs Ungern* was published first in Pest in 1798, and then in the second edition in 1809–1811.[19] The second edition emerged in the years of Napoleonic

[19] Schwartner finishes his statistical work in 1796 and subjects it to the censor, and he receives his manuscripts back after half a year. In this publication, the censor suggested making almost a hundred changes to alter the character of discourse, often reminding the reader of the spirit of Enlightenment. He was fortunate that the censor of this work was János Keresztély Engel (Johann Christian von Engel) (1770–1814), a famous Hungarian historian who finally recommended publishing (Lukcsics 1914, p. 52).

advancements, and also French translation appeared, under the title *Statistique du Royaume de Hongrie* par M. Schwartner, traduite de l'allemand sur la second edition de Bude 1809 par M. Wacken, Francfort sur le Mein, 1813.

Lukcsics (1914, p. 29) describes the spirit of his main work in the following way: Schwartner adores England, its freedoms and points to the backwardness of the Hungarian Kingdom. He always thinks about how to raise Hungary to the level of England. He fights for the equality of different religions, and individual liberties, and free speech.

The main work of Schwartner consists of three parts: Ungarns Grundmacht (Basic Structure of Hungary), Ungarns Staatsverfassung (Hungary's State Constitution), and Ungarns Staatsverwaltung (Hungary's state administration). The first part consists of four parts: Land, Leute, Producte und Handel (Country, People, Production, and Trade). Schwartner's book is full of remarks concerning the industry, trade, and agriculture. His view is that country is well endowed but needs the right policies. He criticizes the low level of trade, as the nobility and gentry want to isolate the country from foreign inflows of goods and ideas. He is in support of free trade and criticizes a high level of custom duties. He places Hungary between cultured Germany and non-cultured Turkey, between Enlightenment and the Empire of Darkness (Lukcsics 1914, p. 55).

In the first part, he presents the Hungarian Kingdom's basic geography with emphasis on rivers, weather, and forests. He complains about marshes and un-regulated rivers and mentions favorable weather conditions in the country.[20] In the second part, he discusses the population, languages, and employment. Initially, he estimates the population of the Kingdom to be around eight million. In the second edition, he provides more precise numbers due to the census of Emperor Francis. He also estimates the density of the population. He shares the opinion that a larger population increases the country's wealth and argues for the cultivation of the low-lying, often flooded areas. He estimates the number of market towns and

[20] He reviews different population birth registers and based on them, and different other data sources, he provides birth rates, death rates, and marriage statistics basically for all towns in the Kingdom. He provides detailed data about trade and different professions, and presents 'national characteristics' of different ethnicities as their high or low propensity to trade, save, avoid, or keep the work discipline, and similar. Note that Schwartner called Pest "das zukünftige London" when Pest inhabitants were less than 60,000, including Buda (Láng 1913, p. 68).

villages at around eleven thousand, from which in less than four thousand the Hungarians live, in almost six thousand the Slavs, in remaining the Germans, the Vlachs, and other ethnicities. He praises the demographic qualities of Slavs and the civilizational qualities of Germans. He describes the wages of priests and high religious authorities, writes about the poverty of many. He criticizes the mistrustful Hungarians that trade is not of their primary interest and praises Jews, Greeks, Serbs involved in the trade. He writes that Hungarian artisans do not perform much-refined work, and thus wealthy ladies order from Viennese tailors and shoemakers (Lukcsics 1914, pp. 58–60). In the first part of the third section, he discusses typical Hungarian quality products as livestock and wine. He provides a detailed description of economic life in Pest and Debrecen. In the last section, he deals with trade. The third part deals with the Hungarian Constitution, the coronation process, and the judicial system. This was an immense amount of work as Schwartner collected most of the data for his book himself as he traveled around in the Kingdom.[21]

In 1815, in Buda, his last work appeared *De scultetis per Hungariam quondam obviis*. He deals with a medieval institution that helped to provide social order, arrange for paying taxes, and generally servicing the ruler. This position was in Latin called scultetus, in German Schultheis, in Hungarian soltész. In 1222, Endre II in Golden Bulla accepted their rights, but these rights became limited after the 1514 rebellion. This institution disappeared during the reign of Maria Theresa. The sparsely populated land in medieval Hungary led the aristocracy to increase the population by inviting foreign settlers, most of them were Germans. Parts of the settlers assimilated to the Hungarian nation while some others kept their German identity. Their situation was always better than the conditions of serfs, as they received different privileges from the aristocracy as fewer restrictions on movement and lower fees and taxes. He discusses the character of the payments to the lords, that is, whether in kind or money. He argues that those villages, especially German villages in Spitzen, gradually developed into market towns where the payments were in the money and not in kind.

In 1801 Emperor Francis elevated Schwartner to Hungarian aristocracy.

[21] Foreign journals praised his work. Göttingische Anzeigen wrote a favorable review: “In this important work, Schwartner provides first systematic statistics of the Hungarian Kingdom. Already Engel had turned our attention to him, and as we see, he clearly overdid our expectations” (Lukcsics 1914, p. 51).

Early Influence of Adam Smith in Central Europe[22]

The universal history of economic theories puts into the vanguard analytical contributions that seem to have validity across borders. A contribution to the universal history of economic thought means that the author moves the frontier of economic theory with universal validity. A national and regional history of economic thought needs to cope with foreign thought transfer to domestic economic thinking.

Ideas travel from one country to another and gradually leak from one national tradition into another. The process of transformation is never entirely smooth as the transmission of ideas faces different constraints. One type of restriction is the limited availability of foreign books, journals, and un-familiarity with foreign languages. In the process of adaptation to the domestic economic and social reality, the national history of economic thought becomes genuine and innovative. It adds value to the national and regional culture, even if, in most cases, it adds little to the development of universal economic thought (Psalidopoulos and Mata 2002).

The ideas reaching Central Europe from the West (as mercantilism, classical and neo-classical theory, Austrian school, German historical school, and later the modern economic thought) were typically progressive compared to domestic political and economic reality. This progressivity would not guarantee the success of these ideas in Central European lands. For example, the early transfer of ideas of Adam Smith thought to Central Europe faced different obstacles as the liberal spirit of Smith encountered the predominantly non-individualist and non-liberal atmosphere in the region, even if with some national differences. However, Western ideas always found ways into Central Europe through the work of intellectuals and economists. In each period one finds eager proponents of the modern views as individuals from Central Europe—from basically seventeenth century—traveled and studied in Western Europe and acknowledged Western learning.

We map the period from *The Wealth of Nations*' appearance in 1776, until the first decades of the nineteenth century. In that period, in Central Europe, comparatively few scholars would be capable of reading English

[22] An extended version was written with Tomáš Krištofóry under the title *Early Influence of Adam Smith on the Economic Thought in Central Europe* and presented at the Smith's Society Conference at the University of Palermo in July 6–7, 2017. Conference title was From Scotland to the South of the Mediterranean, the Thought of Adam Smith through Europe and Beyond.

as knowledge of French, German, and Latin was more adopted. Thus, the implementation of Smith's ideas in the region depended on translations, especially German intermediation, as to our knowledge Central Europeans were not directly students of Smith. Two Russian nationals, Simon Jefimovich Desnitsky and Ivan Andreevich Tretiakov, were Smith's students at Glasgow University and later professors at Moscow University (Anikin 1993, p. 251).

For the most part, in the period under consideration, Smith's ideas moved into Central Europe through translations and studies at the University of Göttingen. When *The Wealth of Nations* first appeared, Smith's thoughts found its supporters in students at the University of Göttingen, where Smith's reception was positive. Göttingen was the right place for the transmission of the ideas of the Scottish economists. Theory of Moral Sentiments was translated into German in 1776–78 In 1777, Johann Georg Heinrich Feder (1740–1821) presented a favorable review of *The Wealth of Nations* in the Göttinger Gelehrten Anzeigen. There were further reviews by Jeremias Nicolaus Eyring (1739–1803) and Isaak Iselin (1728–1782). Feder and his colleagues, August Ludwig Schlözer and Ludwig Timotheus Spittler, subsequently taught Smith's ideas (Waszek 1993). Not only the new subject and modern teaching methods attracted students to Göttingen. Also, the academic freedom of the university was an asset in the eyes of students. Besides, professors at Göttingen were knowledgeable of the region's history and reality.[23]

In political terms, in Central Europe in the last third of the eighteenth century and the first third of the nineteenth century, the Smithian teaching was at odds with the prevailing feudal structure of rent-seeking of the aristocracy and the Church. For the diffusion of Smith's work, the political atmosphere inside the Austrian Empire was decisive. From the late 1770s to the early 1790s, there was a more enlightened atmosphere when the teachings of Physiocrats were also positively received. Physiocracy and Smith's thoughts could have some impact on Joseph II.

[23] We have already mentioned Schlözer's article. Spittler had published in his *Entwurf der Geschichte der Europäischen Staaten* (Draft of the History of the European States) a chapter on Hungary. He emphasized how fast the early Hungarian tribes accepted Christianity and became members of the European community. Interestingly Spittler's book became prohibited in the Habsburg Empire. As the censor emphasized, this book could harm those who are not well versed in the dominant ideas of the time (Futaky (2007, p. 29; Fata et al. 2006, p. 182).

After the death of Joseph II, university teaching tended to follow the older Cameralist textbooks, principally till 1848. Up to the 1840s, professors needed to balance the spirit of Smith's ideas with the overall political atmosphere. Bažantová (2007, p. 25) writes that "although Adam Smith's book was almost immediately translated into German, it remained unnoticed in the Habsburg Monarchy for quite a long time." Vencovský (2003, p. 32) argued similarly: "Czech economists became aware of Adam Smith only in the second half of the nineteenth century."

In his writings, one scholar who considered Smith was Wenzel Gustav von Kopetz (Václav Gustav Kopetz) (1781–1857). Kopetz studied at the universities of Prague and Vienna. From 1833 was a professor at Prague University. In his university lectures and publications, Kopetz presented a combination of Smith's and Cameralist ideas, and he dismissed Smith's work as a mere synthesis of mercantilistic and physiocratic doctrine (Doležalová 2018, p. 34). However, Kopetz inspired a new wave of enthusiasts in liberal economic thought. Czech followers of Kopetz wrote about Say and Bastiat in the late 1840s and the 1850s. František Ladislav Rieger and Karel Havlíček-Borovský (1821–1856) were the most active among them (Šíma and Nikodym 2015).

We mentioned the influence of the University of Göttingen as one factor that brought Smithian ideas to Central Europe. One should note that for several liberally minded young aristocrats and burghers, the inspiration was also the French Revolution. However, more crucial was the emergence of the British supremacy. Count Ferenc Széchenyi toured England in 1787 and met Adam Smith in person (Kosa 1954). However, the spread of English technological innovation in Hungary owes more to his son, Count István Széchenyi, who remarked in his diary "as if England were on another planet—one which God bestowed on his creatures less sun and more mental power (intelligence)" (Bán 2004, p. 5). Count István Széchenyi published in 1830 a book entitled *Hitel* ('Credit'), a critique of Hungary's feudal economy. "This is a book 'full of Bentham and Adam Smith' and general 'Anglomania'" (Nyíri 1986, p. 150).

As we have already mentioned, the spirit of Berzeviczy, his political inclination, made him close to Smith. Berzeviczy was less exposed to political influences as he resided in a small settlement in the High Tatras, far from Vienna and Buda. The spirit of *The Wealth of Nations* has genuinely influenced some elements of Berzeviczy's thought, especially the belief in freedom of trade and industry, and the abolition of serfdom. Berzeviczy's policy recommendations as the idea to increase the volume of trade by river traffic and using foreign trade to enhance overall economic expansion show the impact of Smith's work. Inspired by Smith, Berzeviczy suggested creating commercial canals system connecting the rivers as Danube, Tisza, and Dunajec, an idea that is close in spirit to *The Wealth of Nations*. "The navigation of the Danube is of very little use to the different states of Bavaria, Austria, and Hungary, in comparison of what it would be, if any of them possessed the whole of its course, till it falls into the Black sea" (Smith 1977, p. 40).

Berzeviczy's book *De conditione et indole rusticorum in Hungaria* concerns the social situation of peasants and serfs. In Book 3 of the Wealth of Nations, Smith mentions the lands of the Austrian Empire and their insufficient effort to lift peasants' level, insistence on maintaining serfdom, and the persecution of those who raise their voice against serfdom. Smith observes that "this species of slavery still subsists in Russia, Poland, Hungary, Bohemia, Moravia, and other parts of Germany" (Smith 1977, pp. 512–513).

Indeed, laws in Central Europe forbade peasants' mobility, introduced obligatory labor duty, tied the serfs to their landlords, brought back the escaped serfs, and deprived them of their right to own land. These restrictions were in stark opposition to the situation of nobility, representing the country and its freedoms (Hodos 1999, pp. 21–22). Berzeviczy opposed this type of exploitation on moral, as well as on efficiency grounds.

From the Middle of the Nineteenth Century till World War I

In the second half of the nineteenth century, the Austrian leadership decided to make a deal with the Hungarian nobility. In 1867 the Kaiser had signed the Ausgleich (Compromise), which transformed the Austrian Empire into an Austro-Hungarian Dual Monarchy. As a result, the Hungarian elite had received free hand over administrative, educational, and justice issues in the Hungarian part of the Monarchy. The Monarchy's two parts dealt with some other matters jointly, and the Kaiser retained control over the military and the foreign policy. There is still a discussion concerning the implications of this Compromise. It brought stability and an economic boom to the Hungarian Kingdom, but it might also lead to the ultimate collapse of the Monarchy as it undermined the Slavs' position. Slavic nationalists, with some degree of legitimacy, interpreted the

Compromise as an alliance against the Slavs (Maxwell 2009, p. 25; Tihany 1969).[24]

The long nineteenth century, especially the second half, also brought changes in the development of economic thought. This period represents a qualitative change in the sense that political economy problems begin to live their own life, that is, they do not represent a sub-field of a more extensive social science anymore. In the second half of the nineteenth century, one observes distinct advancements in the economic thought in the region. Erudite professors emerge with a vast knowledge of Western economic theory and an understanding of local issues. Among them, one should mention Czech nationals as Josef Kaizl (1854–1901) and Albín Bráf; Polish nationals as Leon von Bilinski (1846–1923), Julian Dunajewski (1822–1907), Włodzimierz Czerkawski (1866–1913) and Hungarians as Julius Kautz, and Béla Földes. Most of them also held high ranking governmental positions. There were also a large number of other contributions, which we do not discuss. Among others, Józef Supiński (1804–1893) has published *Szkola polska gospodarstwa spolecznego* (The Polish School of Social Economics), in the early 1860s (Jedlicki 1999, pp. 93–94).

Next, we present some of those economists who shaped economic thought in the region.

Gyula (Julius) Kautz (1829–1909)[25]

In the second half of the nineteenth century, Gyula (Julius) Kautz was one of the most admired economists in the Central European lands. The obituary of Lang (1909) in the *Economic Journal* only confirmed his high social and academic status.

Kautz was born in Győr to wealthy and cultured parents. His brother was a Rector of Law Academy in Győr. Gyula Kautz studied in Budapest

[24] The Czech historian Palacký, as well as other intellectuals, predicted the rise of pan-Slavism as a natural response to a dualistic agreement between Austrians and Hungarians. Some Hungarian historians saw it differently and emphasized that the Compromise secured the Hungarian constitution and independence. Some other historians observed that the Compromise by reducing Slavs to obedience might have negative consequences for the Hungarians and the Monarchy. Also, not everybody in Austria favored the Ausgleich and would rather see an alliance with Germany, which would allow the Germanization of the Slavs (Tihany 1969, p. 120).

[25] Bekker (1998, 2002, 2004), Harmat (1980), Lang (1909), Mátyás (2005).

and later in Berlin, Heidelberg, and Leipzig under a member of the German historical school Wilhelm Georg Friedrich Roscher (1817–1894).

Kautz began his academic career at the Royal Academy in Pozsony in 1851, he moved to teach to Nagyvárad, and from 1858 had taught at Polytechnic School in Buda. From 1863 he teaches at Technical University of Pest. In 1864 Kautz declined an offer of a chair at Prague University. At Pest University, he continues, works as a Dean, and in 1873/1874 as a Rector. In the 1890s, Kautz became a Governor of the Austro-Hungarian Bank. He was a member of the Hungarian Academy of Science from 1861. Kautz was also President of the Hungarian Society of Political Economy.

Since 1865 he was a member of the House of Deputies. Kautz also worked as Under-Secretary of State in the Ministry of Finance. From 1887 he was a Deputy in the Upper House. Kautz was active in the Reform process in the last decades in the nineteenth century and the beginning of the twentieth century. In the Austria-Hungarian Compromise of 1867, he was advising on economic matters. In Hungarian domestic politics, he belonged to Deák's supporters. In 1890 together with Menger, Böhm-Bawerk, Pantaleoni he is voted to be an external member of the Parisien Société d'Économie Politique.

In 1860 his first significant work, *Theorie und Geschichte der National-Ökonomie* (Theory and History of the National Economy) appeared. Roscher's thought influenced this work. The book received a great welcome. For example, Encyclopedia Britannica stated, "It is a book of high interest, being the result of philosophical as well as of extended researches" (Lang 1909, p. 485). This book made international fame for Kautz. Bekker (2004, p. 86) mentions that economists as diverse as Marshall, Marx, Jevons, Knies, Roscher, and Schumpeter quoted him or wrote a positive reception concerning his work.[26]

[26] Bekker (2004) mentions sources as Jevons, W. Stanley, *The Theory of Political Economy*, Macmillan, London, 1888. Preface, XXXI; Knies, Karl, *Politische Oekonomie vom geschitlichen Standpunkte*. Hans Buske, Leipzig, 1930. 522–523; Marshall, Alfred: *Principles of Economics*. 3rd edition, London, 1885, 54–55; Schumpeter, Joseph: *Epochen der Dogmen und Methodengeschichte*, Tübingen, 1924, I. volume, 20, and others. In the Introduction to the *History of Economic Analysis* by Schumpeter, Routledge 2006, Mark Perlman on page x—when discussing lines of thought which left to Schumpeter's versions of the history of thought—mentions Kautz in what he calls the German lineage: "There is a German lineage, as well. Wilhelm Georg Friedrich Roscher first brought out his *Geschichte der Englishen Volkswirtshaftslehre* (1851) and then later in 1874 his *Geschichte der Nationalökonomie* in Deutschland, and his student, Gyula Kautz, published in 1860 *Die Geschichtliche Entwicklung der Nationalökonomie und Ihrer Literatur*." What Perlman mentions is the second volume of

Politically Kautz was close in spirit to Széchenyi, under whose influence his worldview gravitates closer to the English classical thought.[27] "Professor Kautz penetrated successfully into the intimate conceptions of the great English philosopher of political economics. The first visible token of this transformation was that Kautz devoted his systematical textbook of political economy to the memory of Count Széchenyi. And in the same degree, as he engaged himself in the study of Széchenyi, he continued to come nearer to Adam Smith" (Lang 1909, p. 486). Kautz was dealing with Smith and Széchenyi's concepts of political economy and development throughout his life. He published his first study on Adam Smith in 1856 entitled *Smith Ádám és az újkori nemzetgazdaságatan* (Adam Smith and the New National Economy), in the journal Kelet Népe. Then in 1860, he published in *A nemzetgazdasági eszmék és elméletek története* (History of Ideas and Theories of National Economy), in volume 4, *Smith rendszere* (On System of Smith) in Budapesti Szemle, 1860. VIII. 357–388. In volume five of the same publication, he published *Smith utódai* (Smith's Successors) in Budapesti Szemle, IX. 17–49. Finally, in 1890 *Smith Ádám mint a közgazdaság-tudomány megalapítója* (Adam Smith as a Founder of the Economic Science), in Nemzetgazdasági Szemle, XI, 953–985, which

Kautz's book. Translation of this book appeared in Hungarian only at the beginning of the twenty-first century, in 2004, in Publishing House Aula, 628 pages, translated by Bródy András, Frenkel Gergely, Hild Márta, and Horváth László.

[27] Count Széchenyi (1791–1860) was an iconic figure of the Hungarian reform program. Together with other Hungarian liberals, he was aware of the Kingdom's relative backwardness. In the decades before 1848, typically called the 'Reform Epoch,' there were efforts to improve Hungarian agriculture, administration, transportation, and similar. Széchenyi personally played an essential role in these efforts, as he was involved in the building of the first Danube bridge, the first steamship line, helped to create the Hungarian Academy of Sciences and other great projects. Széchenyi advocated the abolition of serfdom, expansion of education, and facilitating the selling of land to encourage investment in a commercial-agricultural revolution. Besides, Szechenyi counseled against attempts to impose the Magyar language on the minorities. Contrary to his views, in 1844, the Diet declared Magyar to be the official language of the Kingdom of Hungary, even though Magyars comprised only 37% of the population (Janos 1982, p. 11). Also, Szechenyi preferred collaboration with the Habsburgs and the non-Magyar minorities. However, during the 1840s, the political initiative had passed to a more radical nationalistic gentry headed by Lajos Kossuth (1802–1894). In the economic sphere, Kossuth advocated industrial subsidies and an interventionist strategy of state-induced industrialization and emphasized that Hungary's relative backwardness stemmed from its dependence on Austria.

in 1891 appeared as an independent publication in the Pallas Publishing House in Budapest.[28]

German historical school, as well as the English classical political economy, influenced his book *A nemzetgazdaság és pénzügytan rendszere* (Political Economy and Financial System). Harmat (1980) observes that the early Kautz' inspiration is the Hungarian progressive thought represented by Berzeviczy, Széchenyi, and Kossuth. Kautz investigates society, which is under constant change. He does not hold the view that in each historical epoch, there are valid economic laws. He did not believe that the national economy investigations should be only descriptive. Instead, the way to go was in combining economic principles with historical analyses and empirical data.

Kautz was a 'Westerner' in his beliefs in individual liberty and individual responsibility. He stressed these elements in his Introduction to the Hungarian translation of the *Wealth of Nations* (*Vizsgálódás a nemzeti vagyonosság természetéről és okairól*), translated by Enyedy Lukács, published by Pólya Jakab, Pallas, Budapest, 1891–1894. Simultaneously, as mentioned already, the German historical school influenced his thought. This school did not put the individual economic subject into the forefront and emphasized the role of the social process and the building role of the state. This tradition also objected to a certain degree the deductive principles and generalization taken from these principles. They were skeptical about the notion of economic law, which some economists in the nineteenth century commonly assumed. Kautz inherited from the German historical school a view that one should look at the economy from the general societal point of view.

Kautz was concerned with the role of institutions in economic development. He favored industry to agriculture, while the latter supports the order in the society, the former shows the power of the humans and makes the feudal structure untenable. He also observed shadow sides of industrial development, but did not accept socialist views as a response to the ills of industrial development. He opposed socialist ideas as he believed the

[28] Kautz published different work also on Széchenyi. In 1904 he published *"Hitel" és a "Világ" méltatása* ("The Worthiness of Hitel" and "Világ") in *Gróf Széchenyi István munkái* (Works of Count István Széchenyi), MTA, Budapest. In 1905 he published *Politikai programmtöredékek A "Stádium", a' "Kelet népe" és a "Politikai programmtöredékek" méltatása* (The Worthiness of "Stádium," "Kelet népe" and of "Fragmentation of Political Programs"), in: *Gróf Széchenyi István munkái* MTA, Budapest. Also in 1905 he published *Széchenyi és Kossuth* (Széchenyi and Kossuth)), Franklin Nyomda, Budapest.

private property was the basis of a modern developed society. Harmat (1980, p. 25) praised Kautz's knowledge of socialist classics and considered him one of the first scholars with an in-depth understanding of socialist ideas.

Kautz published his work *A nemzetgazdasági eszmék fejlődési története és befolyása a közviszonyokra Magyarországon* (The History of the Development of the Economic Ideas and Their Influence on Public Life in Hungary) in 1868, and in 1911 it was reprinted, and in 1987 another reprint appeared. This book is an intellectual pearl. It is not only a study in the history of economic thought but also deals with the legal, political, and cultural issues. It appeared basically without antecedents in the Hungarian literature, and still, today remains an excellent source of ideas.

Kautz observed that the widely spread national spirit and over-blown national ambitions also helped create an atmosphere in contrast to the development aims. Hungary, historically continually felt under threat, and subordinated economic development objective to the national goal of survival. This perceived threat is probably what a prominent Hungarian statesman Ferencz Deák had in mind in his speech in Parliament on February 22, 1866, when he argued that historically the country could be more prosperous, but then surely it would not be Hungarian (Magyar) (Kautz 1911, p. 79). Surprisingly, this also seems to be Kautz's opinion when he writes that for the Hungarian state, it was characteristic to follow old national habits; otherwise, the nation would disappear. In other words, the political circumstances led the country to put its independence into the forefront. As a result, the government did not have enough strength to make the economy to develop. "With full confidence, we can state that the existence of the Hungarian state and its constitution could be saved only by giving up the economic well-being!" (Kautz 1911, pp. 78–79). Such views emerged in an international relations discourse, which meant more often conflict, including war, than peace. In other words, a constant threat of war created the framework for such a discourse coupled with the interests of the ruling classes.

In the Central Bank of the Monarchy, Kautz worked first as a Deputy Governor and in 1892–1900 as a Governor. Bekker (2004, p. 88) mentions that he left a study about the Austro-Hungarian Central Bank among the unfinished manuscripts. In this study, he writes that the Bank was the only joint Institution after the Compromise, a complete success, in which the Hungarian side did not come up with constant complaints against the Viennese power (Bekker 2004).

Citations of Kautz work abounded during his lifetime in the international literature. From Hungarian economists who stayed most of their life in Hungary, maybe only János Kornai received similar fame.

Béla Földes (Weisz) (1848–1945)

He graduated in Gymnasium in Temesvár and Pest, and studied at Law Faculty in Vienna, Pest, and Leipzig. From the beginning of the 1870s, he worked at Statistical Office, taught at Pest Kereskedelmi Akadémia, and from 1874 at Budapest University. In 1876 he became Secretary of the International Congress of Statistics. In 1880 became a Professor of the national economy and monetary affairs at Budapest Kereskedelmi Akadémia. From 1889 he chaired the Department of Statistics at Budapest University, later became a Dean of Law Faculty, and in 1917 Rector of the University. From 1901 he was a member of the Hungarian Academy of Sciences. In the last days of World War (from August 18, 1917 till May 8, 1918), he was a government minister without a portfolio. After 1920 he moved out of public life.

His main work is *Társadalmi gazdaságtan* (Societal Economics) in two volumes, which he published in 1893–1894 and was reprinted many times. German historical school influenced Földes; politically, he leaned toward social democracy. He was interested in statistics of criminal activity, collected data on commodity prices, and also in other aspects of his work, he was very modern. For example, he published in 1906 in the *Journal of the Royal Statistical Society*, an article titled *The Criminal*, still quoted in the literature concerning criminality (Bunn 2012). Földes tried to explore the social background of crime and developed a system of physical, economic, intellectual, moral, legal, and political factor categories affecting criminal activity (Domokos 2013, p. 33).

His works include, in addition to works written in the Hungarian language, also works written in German, which were reviewed in leading economic journals. We mention *Finanzwissenschaft*, published in Jena by Verlag von Gustav Fischer, reviewed in March 1922 by T.A. Smiddy in the *Economic Journal*, Volume 32, 125 pp. 96–98. Another book published in German was *Die Hauptströmungen der sozialistischen Gedankenwelt* published in 1923 in Berlin by Otto Eisner Verlagsgesellschagt, and reviewed by W. H. Dawson in the Economic Journal, Volume 33, 129, 1, March 1923, pp. 113–114.

Albín Bráf (1851–1912)[29]

Albín Bráf was a prominent representative of Czech national awakening and is commonly considered the founding father of Czech economic thought.

Bráf enrolled at Prague University in 1871. At that time at the Law Faculty, there had been already irregular lectures in economics in the Czech language. Albrecht (1992) reports that according to the university lecture list, Eberhard Jonák (1820–1879) offered a course in the Czech language in the academic year 1850/1851 but did not continue lecturing in Czech. At the Czech Technical University, there were lectures in Czech from 1869. However, only from 1882, Prague University was separated into Czech and German parts, which enabled regular lectures in Czech. Bráf was the first faculty member to lecture regularly economics in Czech from 1877 when he began his academic career at Business Academy and as a private teacher at Prague University, where from 1882 he became an assistant professor and from 1890 a full professor.

On the occasion of Bráf's sixtieth birthday, several former students published papers in Czech economic journals—as Obzor národohospodářsky—celebrating his contributions as a scholar and teacher. These authors included noted economists as Jan Koudela (1880–1935), Cyril Horáček (1862–1943), and Josef Gruber (1865–1925). Bráf helped to create from his students a group of economists, who later became influential representatives of the new Czechoslovak state. His students had open minds, were not driven to represent a unified view, and excelled in research output. The school of Bráf did not constitute a specific theoretical perspective but represented a robust group of economists, who later had a positive impact on society.[30]

Bráf formulated the basic ideas of national economic revival promoted by institutions as the Czech Academy of Sciences and Arts, National Economy Institute, Council of Agriculture, Prague Chamber of Commerce, and others. Bráf was active in the general society, popularized economic thought, and helped organize the Czech Academy of Arts and Sciences in the last decade of the nineteenth century. To decrease the lag in development compared to the German ethnic was one of the Czech

[29] Doležalová (2013, 2018), Albrecht (1992), Krameš (2014, 2016a, b).

[30] Josef Goldmann probably played a similar role in the 1970s and the early 1980s, when he built up a group of economists in the Economic Institute of the Czechoslovak Academy Science, who played a role in the transformation process.

national revival aims. To buy each other's products, hiring Czech staff and similar steps were to help to eliminate this lag (Krameš 2014, p. 780).

Albín Bráf married a daughter of František Ladislav Rieger (1818–1903) and was a part of the so-called Old Czech political movement. Bráf served as a member of the Czech Diet (Český sněm) from 1883 to 1895 and was a member of the upper house of the imperial parliament from 1905. While being strongly anti-socialist, he understood the need to integrate lower classes into the national societal life, for example, by helping to organize workers' insurance programs and improve their working conditions. He wanted to strengthen the autonomy of Bohemia inside the Austrian Empire. In 1909 he was appointed Minister of Agriculture in the government of Count Richard von Bienerth (1863–1918). He resigned from this position after less than a year but re-entered the government in 1911/1912.

Bráf combined in his thought ideas stemming from different schools of thought as English liberalism, classical political economy, German historical school, and Austrian marginalism. From each school, he appreciated what fitted the reality of Bohemia in the Austrian Monarchy. For example, he welcomed the emphasis on individual initiative and economic motivation but was not in favor of unlimited competition, and neither of the concept of homo oeconomicus. For him, societal aims—as the Czech national aims—had at least equal importance than building up wealth.

Early Transfer of Austrian Ideas into Central Europe[31]

From the early 1880s, followers of Carl Menger (1840–1921) developed his concepts, and this process led to the creation of the Austrian school. Members of the Austrian school dominated Vienna chairs since the 1890s basically till the end of World War I. Followers of Menger achieved prominent academic positions at different universities of the Habsburg monarchy. The fact that Carl Menger studied at the German university in Prague and the Jagellonian University of Cracow strengthened connections of the Austrian school to Central Europe.

Before World War I, Eugen Böhm-Bawerk (1851–1914) was at an academic position at Innsbruck. Friedrich von Wieser (1851–1926), Robert Zuckerkandl (1856–1926), Emil Sax (1845–1927), student of Wieser

[31] A more extended version of this topic was written together with Tomáš Krištofóry and presented at the yearly Conference of the European Society for History of Economic Thought in Antwerp in May 2017.

Hans Mayer (1879–1955), and Franz Xaver Weiss (1885–1956) held for shorter or longer period academic positions in Prague. Wieser was a full professor from 1889 and also a Vice-Chancellor in 1901/1902 at the University of Prague. In 1903 he succeeded Menger as a chair at Vienna University. Wieser's influence was dominant wherever he was teaching, as recollections of Hayek and Morgenstern document. Hayek mentions that students never forget Wieser's impressive personality (Higgs 1927, p. 152). Similarly, Morgenstern writes (1927, p. 674) "The completeness of his culture, the universal character of his interests, the position he occupied in science, politics, and social life, the admirable urbanity of the aristocrat, which he was par excellence, made him seem an ideal representative of the old Austro-Hungarian Empire."

In the world, the Austrian ideas were alive after World War I. However, in Vienna, the school's influence weakened as Menger left the University of Vienna in 1903, Böhm-Bawerk died in 1914, Eugen von Philippovich died in 1917, and Friedrich von Wieser died in 1926. Before World War I, Austria became a core country in terms of its economic research quality and remained in that position until the late 1930s when most of its distinguished representatives left Europe.

Ideas of the Austrian school began to spread in the German-speaking universities of the Austrian Empire. Until 1918 the economic education of Central European peoples was performed in institutions of the Empire, mostly in German language or in Hungarian. It helped the international diffusion of the Austrian economic thought that it faced low language barriers as it was common for educated classes to master the German language. Austrian thought's influence happens inside imperial boundaries and later spreads across national boundaries as some of these universities became situated in the newly independent states of Central Europe. However, this was not a one-direction passive process, and some non-Austrian Central Europeans helped develop the Austrian school of thought. Austrian economists themselves remind us about the contributions of economists from Central European (non-Austrian) ethnic to the development of the Austrian thought. Hayek (1992, p. 83) states that the school's ideas dispersed to other nations in the Monarchy. "In the following years, numerous adherents also appeared among the Czech, Polish, and Hungarian economists of the Austro-Hungarian monarchy." Mises (2013, p. 151) also points to non-German Central Europeans' participation and emphasizes the contribution of two Czech economists Franz Čuhel (1862–1914) and Karel Engliš.

For the general public, the information about different schools of thought was transferred by popular textbooks on the history of economic thought. Charles Gide and Charles Rist wrote one of the most popular, and Jan Koudela, a student of Albín Bráf, together with Milada Koudelová, translated it into Czech in the early years of the twentieth century. Wlodzimierz Czerkawski translated it into Polish at about the same time (Chodorowski 1997, p. 53). These textbooks functioned as an excellent introduction to the Austrian thought to the interested general reader.

Roman Rybarski published in 1922 a book *Wartóśc, kapitał i dochód* (Value, Capital and Income), which engaged with Böhm-Bawerk's theory of price. Adam Heydel (1928) published a paper in the Viennese Zeitschrift für Nationalökonomie. Klausinger (2016) describes Heydel's activity in Viennese Nationalökonomische Gesellschaft. In Vienna, Heydel got acquainted with Rosenstein-Rodan, who in Rosenstein-Rodan (1934) quoted Heydel in his article on the role of time in economic theory. One should mention notable contributions in the 1930s of Oskar Lange in the socialist calculation debate with the Austrians (Paryna 2011).

The influential Hungarian economists of the time Gyula Kautz,[32] Ákos Navratil, and Béla Földes inclined toward the German historical school (Balás 1927, p. 206). Bekker (2008a) writes that these economists instead preferred a midway between different schools of thought. Farkas Heller (1945) praised the abstract character of the Austrian school as compared to the German historical school. Still, he also perceived that both Roscher and Schmoller denied the abstract method with valid arguments as the economic life is a universal social life. He understood that the German historical school approach was competent only to an extent as descriptive studies provide a profound understanding of economic activities. In other words, Heller stands on the side of Menger but also learns from the teachings of the German historical school. Heller, in a sense, tries to create a synthesis of both schools (Mátyás 1995, p. 740; Madarász 2000). Heller considered applied economics a more general and ultimately more important than the theory.

[32] Implicitly, essential for the development of marginalism was the role of Kautz (1860). Jevons (1888, p. 15) has written that it was this Kautz's book, which got his attention to the work of Gossen. Daal (2012, p. 371) mentions that Kautz commented that Gossen built the theory of pleasure on a mathematical basis that raised the interest of Jevons. Kautz was also in the midst of the debates of the monetary reform of 1892, which sparked discussions concerning the theory of money, including Menger's view of money as spontaneous evolutionary order.

Slovakia remained until 1919 without a university in the Slovak language. The development of its economic thought lagged behind other Central European nations. In 1919 Comenius University was founded in Bratislava. As there were a small number of ethnic Slovaks who could take up the professors' positions at the new university, the first economics professors were ethnic Czechs nominated by the Prague's Ministry. The only erudite Slovak economist who found a job at the new university, soon after its establishment, was Milan Hodža (1878–1944). However, Hodža, who in the 1930s became a prime minister of Czechoslovakia, was deeply involved in politics, and his university post in Bratislava was merely formal. Baďurík (2009). One of the ethnic Czechs who began to teach in Bratislava was Antonín Basch, who joined the new Law faculty of Comenius University after studying in Vienna. Basch (1944) was close to Austrian thought, even his review of Mises' work for the American Economic Review is quite critical. In 1926, at Comenius University, Basch was succeeded by Cyril Čechrák, an institutionalist skeptical of Austrian teachings. He remained in Bratislava until 1938 when Slovakia expelled Czech professors (Bažantová 2009).

František Čuhel kept personal contacts with representatives of the Austrian school of thought. His book from 1907 examined the theory of needs, especially from a psychological point of view. Krameš (2016b, p. 928) writes that the book got published on Menger's recommendation to Böhm-Bawerk, who wrote a support letter to the publisher at Innsbruck, where he used to have an academic position. Čuhel (1907) was published in German and was an immediate success, and its fame went far beyond the borders of Austria. Čuhel's star soon faded away—mostly because of his health conditions. Hudík (2007) mentions that Čuhel's ordinal theory of needs without using indifference curves and his insistence on the interpersonal incomparability of utility represents a foundation of the modern microeconomics. A large number of noted authors quoted Čuhel, as Böhm-Bawerk, Eugen Slutsky, Wesley Clair Mitchell, Theo Surányi-Unger, Fritz Machlup, and others. Slutsky (1915) cited Čuhel in his famous paper on a consumer budget, published first in Italian. Wesley Mitchell quotes Čuhel in a survey article on human behavior and economics in the *Quarterly Journal of Economics* in 1914. Surányi-Unger, in his paper in the *Journal of Political Economy* in 1948, criticizes Čuhel's concept of state collective welfare and collective persons. Machlup quotes Čuhel in an article published in *Southern Economic Journal* in 1956.

In the Czech lands, Karel Engliš was in contact with the Austrian school representatives, who reacted to his work. Hayek refers to Engliš when discussing whether to consider social science as a teleological science. Hayek writes: "Some authors, particularly O. Spann, have used the term teleological to justify the most abstruse metaphysical speculations. Others, like K. Engliš, have used it in an unobjectionable manner and sharply distinguished between teleological and normative sciences. See particularly the illuminating discussions of the problem in Karel Engliš, Teleologische Theorie der Staatwirtschaft (Brünn: R. M. Rohrer, 1933). But the term remains nevertheless misleading" (Hayek 2010, p. 90).

Kirzner (1976), in his history of economic thought, written from the Austrian viewpoint, praised Engliš. He likened Engliš's approach to Mises' praxeology. "When Engliš defined economics as a teleological discipline, he was attempting to place his finger on the very nerve center of the subject. There is a place for a distinct science of economics only because the teleological quality of action makes possible a unique kind of explanation" (Kirzner 1976, p. 165).

Mises, in *The Human Action*, when discussing causality and teleology as the only two approaches provided to humans, also mentions Engliš's work published in Brno in 1930, entitled *Begründung der Teleologie als Form des empirischen Erkennens* (Mises 2004, p. 25). Mises (1951) understood economics as a part of a more general science of human action, which he called praxeology. He reasoned that one deduces the core of economics from some axioms concerning human purposes and choices. All events are either due to the intentions of subjects or reflect some law. In other words, it is teleology or causality. This point was close to the view of Engliš.

References

Albrecht, Catherine. 1992. Two Czech Economists: Albín Bráf and Josef Kaizl. *East Central Europe/L'Europe du Centre-Est* 19 (1): 1–15.

Anikin, Andrei. 1993. Adam Smith in Russia. In *Adam Smith: International Perspective*, ed. Hiroshi Mizuta and Chuhei Sugiyama, 251–260. London: Macmillan Press.

Anonym (Bencsik, József). 1792. *De Industria Nationali Hungariae.* Viennae.

Baďurík, Jozef. 2009. Zakladateľské a profilujúce osobnosti na historických katedrách Univerzity Komenského v Bratislave do roku 1950 k 90. výročiu jej vzniku (Founding and Important Personalities at Historic Departments of

Comenius University in Bratislava till 1950, For 90 Years of Its Existence). *Studia Academica Slovaca* 38: 29–38.

von Balás, Karl. 1927. Ungarn. In *Die Wirtschaftstheorie der Gegenwart*, Gesamtbild der Forschung in den Einzelnen Ländern, ed. Hans Mayer, vol. 1. Wien: Springer.

Baláži, Peter.2018. Komplexná historiografická analýza osobností dejín financií obdobia existencie Rakúsko-Uhorska (Complex Historiographic Analyses of Personalities in History of Finance During the Existence of Austria-Hungary). *Finančné trhy*, Bratislava, Derivat.

Balázs, H. Éva. 1967. *Berzeviczy Gergely a reformpolitikus, 1763–1795 (Berzeviczy Gergely a Reform Politician 1763–1795)*. Budapest: Akadémia Kiadó.

Bán, Imre. 1962. Melius Juhász Péter. *Orvostöréneti Közlemények* 23: 252–280.

Bán, D. András. 2004. *Hungarian – British Diplomacy, 1938–1941: The Attempt to Maintain Relations*. London: Frank Cass.

Barta, János. 2004. Az agrárirodalom kezdetei Magyarországon (Beginnings of the Agriculture Economics Literature in Hungary). In *Emlékkönyv Csetri Elek születésének nyolcvanadik évfordulójára*, Volume to Commemorate Elek Csetri 80th Birthday. Kolozsvár: Az Erdélyi Múzeum-Egyesület kiadása.

Basch, Antonin. 1944. Review of Omnipotent Government by Ludwig Von Mises. *The American Economic Review* 34 (4): 899–903.

Bažantová, Ilona. 2007. Vliv J. B. Saye na české ekonomické myšlení (Influence of J.B. Say on Czech Economic Thought). In *Jean-Baptiste say: 240 let od narození (Jean-Baptiste say: 240 years from his birth), Sborník textů*, 25–43. Praha: Centrum pro ekonomiku a politiku.

———. 2009. Cyril Čechrák. In *Antologie československé právní vědy v meziválečném období (1918–1938) (Anthology of Czechoslovak Legal Science in the Interwar Period)*, ed. Petra Skřejpková, 570–573. Praha: Linde Praha.

Bekker, Zsuzsa. 1998. Széchenyi és Kautz: A "helyes középút" tradíciója (Széchenyi and Kautz: The "Right Middle Way" Tradition). In *50 éves a Budapesti Közgazdaságtudományi Egyetem, (Budapest Economic University is 50 Year Old)*, ed. Temesi József, 430–449. Budapest: BKE.

———. 2002. *Magyar közgazdasági gondolkodás (a közgazdasági irodalom kezdeteitől a II. világháborúig) (Hungarian Economic Thought (From the Beginning till World War Two))*. Budapest: Aula Kiadó.

———. 2004. Kautz Gyula élete és munkássága (Life and Work of Kautz Gyula). *Hitelintézeti Szemle* III (5): 83–91.

———. 2008a. *Szakmai beszámoló, Magyar közgazdasági gondolkodás története c. project (Scientific Report for the Project About History of Hungarian Economic Thought)*. https://www.real.mtak.hu/826/1/42881_ZJ1.pdf.

———. 2008b. *Illik-e magyarhoz csalfa kereskedés? 17. és 18. századi magyar nyelvű gazdasági irodalom (Does Fraudulent Trading Suits a Hungarian? Economic Literature from 17th and 18th Centuries)*. Budapest: Aula Kiadó.

Berzeviczy, Gergely. 1902. *A közgazdaságról (On Economics)*, Originally Written in Latin in 1819 as Oeconomica Publico Politica.

Bianchini, Stefano. 2015. *Eastern Europe and the Challenges of Modernity, 1800–2000*. Abingdon and New York: Routledge.

Bideleux, Robert, and Ian Jeffries. 2007. *A History of Eastern Europe: Crisis and Change*. 2nd ed. Abingdon and New York: Routledge.

Bunn, Geoffrey. 2012. *The Truth Machine, Social History of the Lie Detector*. Baltimore: The John Hopkins University Press.

Chodorowski, Jerzy. *1997. Roman Rybarski (1887–1942): z historii polskiej myśli ekonomicznej i prawnoustrojowej pierwszej połowiny 20 wieku (Roman Rybarski (1887–1942): From History of Polish Economic and Legal Thought in the First Half of 20th Century)*. Wrocław: Wydawnictwo Uniwersytetu Wrocławskiego. Acta Universitatis Wratislaviensis. Prawo.

Csohány, János. 2013. Melius Juhász Péter. A Debreceni Kollégium 475 éves jubileumára (Melius Juhász Péter. Celebrating 475 Years of Collegium in Debrecen). *Egyháztörténeti Szemle* 14 (4): 100–106.

Čuhel, Franz. 1907. *Zur Lehre von den Bedürfnissen. Theoretische Untersuchungen über das Grenzgebiet von Ökonomik und Psychologie*. Innsbruck: Wagner.

Daal, van Jan. 2012. The Entwickelung According to Gossen (Chapter 14). In *Handbook of the History of Economic Thought. Insights on the Founders of Modern Economics*, ed. Jürgen Georg Backhaus. New York, NY: Springer.

De Soto, Jesús Huerta. 2008. *The Austrian School, Market Order and Entrepreneurial Creativity*. Cheltenham, UK; Northampton, MA: Edward Elgar.

Deák, András. 1984. *Bél Mátyás élete és munkássága – A magyarországi halakról és azok halászatáról (Life and Work of Bél Mátyás – On Fishing and Fish in Hungary)*. Budapest: Vízügyi Dokumentációs Szolgáltató Leányvállalat nyomdája.

Dobos, Irma. 2011. Georgius Wernher, Magyarország csodálatos vizeiről (Georgius Wernher, Wonderful Hungarian Waters). *Bányászattörténeti Közlemények* 11 (6): 3–14.

Dóczy, Jenő, Imre Wellmann, and István Bakács. 1934. *A magyar gazdasági irodalom első századainak könyvészete 1505–1805 (Hungarian Economic Literature 1505–1805)*. Budapest: M. Kir. Mezőgazdasági Múzeum Könyvtára.

Doležalová, Antonie. 2013. Od Albína Bráfa k Josefu Mackovi – příspěvek k výročí úmrtí dvou významných českých ekonomu (From Albína Bráf till Josef Macek – Contribution to Anniversary of Death of Two Important Czech Economists). *Politická ekonomie* (3): 428–438.

———. 2018. *A History of Czech Economic Thought*. Abingdon and New York: Routledge.

Domokos, Andrea. 2013. The Emergence of Criminology in Hungarian Criminal Sciences – Late 19th – Early 20th Century. *Acta Juridica Hungarica* 54 (4): 331–348.

Erdősi, Laura. 1963. Wernher: De admirandis Hungáriáé Aquis. Communicationes ex Bibliotheca Historiae. *Medicae Hungarica* 29: 103–168.

Evans, R.J.W. 2006. *Austria, Hungary, and the Habsburgs. Essays on Central Europe, c. 1683–1867.* Oxford, New York: Oxford University Press.

Fata, Márta, Gyula Kurucz, and Anton Schindling. 2006. *Peregrinatio Hungarica, Studenten aus Ungarn an deutschen und österreichischen Hochschulen vom 16. bis zum 20. Jahrhundert.* Stuttgart: Franz Steiner Verlag.

Fináczy, Ernő. 1899. *A magyarországi közöktatás története Mária Terézia korában (History of Hungarian Public Schools During the Time of Marie Theresia).* Vol. I–II. Budapest: Magyar Tudományos Akadémia.

Futaky, István. 2007. *Göttinga, A göttingeni Georg-August Egyetem magyarországi és erdélyi kapcsolatai a felvilágosodás idején és a reformkor kezdetén (Göttingen, Hungarian and Transylvanian Contacts with Georg-August Göttingen University during the Enlightenment Period).* Budapest: MTA Egyetemtörténeti Albizottsága: ELTE Levéltára.

Gaál, Jenő. 1902. *Berzeviczy Gergely élete és művei (Life and Work of Berzeviczy Gergely).* Budapest: Politzer Zsigmond és fia kiadása.

Gide, Charles, and Charles Rist. 1915. *Dějiny nauk národohospodářských od doby fysiokratů až po naše dny (History of Economic Thought from Physiocrats till Our Days).* Díl 1. Praha, 1915. Díl 2. Praha, 1917, Laichterův výbor nejlepších spisů poučných.

Gunst, Péter. 1991. Agrarian Systems of Central and Eastern Europe. In *The Origins of Backwardness in Eastern Europe: Economics and Politics from the Middle Ages Until the Early Twentieth Century*, ed. Daniel Chirot, 53–91. Berkeley, Los Angeles, Oxford: University of California Press.

Haan, Lajos. 1879. *Bél Mátyás, székfoglaló értekezés (Bél Mátyás, Inaugural Lecture).* Budapest: Magyar Tudományos Könyvkiadó Hivatala.

Hamza, Gábor. 2017. *Emlékezés Balugyánszky Mihályra (1769–1847), a kiemelkedő jogtudósra – adalék a magyar-orosz kapcsolatokhoz a jog területén (Commemoration of Mihály Balugyánszky (1769–1847), the Outstanding Legal Scholar – Contribution to the Hungarian-Russian Legal Relations).* https://mta.hu/data/dokumentumok/ix_osztaly/Jubileumi%20megemlekezesek/Balugyanszky%20Mihaly_2017.pdf. Accessed 2 March 2020.

Harmat, Zsigmond. 1980. Kautz Gyula Közgazdasági nézetei (Economic Views of Julius Kautz). *Egyetemi Szemle* 2 (2): 23–32.

von Hayek, Friedrich August. 1992. In *The Fortunes of Liberalism: Essays on Austrian Economics and the Ideal of Freedom*, The Collected Works of F. A. Hayek, ed. Peter G. Klein, vol. IV. London: Routledge.

———. 2010. In *The Collected Works of F.A. Hayek*, Studies on the Abuse and Decline of Reason: Text and Documents, ed. Bruce Caldwell, vol. XIII. Chicago: The University of Chicago Press.

Heller, Farkas. 1945. *A közgazdasági elmélet története (History of Economic Theory)*. Budapest: Gergely R. Könyvkereskedése.

Heydel, Adam. 1928. *Sprawodzanie z wyjazdu w celach naukowych za granice w okresie luty – kwiecień.* http://kwasnicki.prawo.uni.wroc.pl/pliki/HeydelSprawozdanieWieden1928.pdf. Accessed 19 June 2019.

Higgs, Henry. 1927. Friedrich von Wieser, 1851–1926. *Economica* 20: 150–154.

Hodos, George. 1999. *The East-Central European Region, An Historical Outline.* Westport: Praeger Publishers.

Horváth, Róbert. 1960. Hatvani István és a Magyar közgazdasági irodalom kezdetei (Hatvani István and the Beginnings of Hungarian Economic Thought). *Közgazdasági Szemle* 1: 74–91.

———. 1963. Tessedik a társadalomtudós (Tessedik a Social Scientist). In *Körös Népe IV*, ed. Eperjessy Kálmán. Békéscsaba: Békéscsaba Város Tanácsa VB.

———. 1964. Berzeviczy Gergely közgazdasági és népességi tanai (Economic and Demographic Teaching of Gergely Berzeviczy). *Acta Universitatis Szegediensis de Attila Jozsef Nominatae, Acta Juridica et Politica*, Tomus XI, Fasciculus 7, Szeged.

Horváth, József. 2001. A Lengyel közgazdasági gondolkodás rövid törtönete (Short History of Polish Economic Thought). *Society and Economy in Central and Eastern Europe* 23 (3/4): 141–157.

Hudík, Marek. 2007. František Čuhel (1862–1914). *New Perspectives on Political Economy* 3 (1): 3–14.

Ilina, Kira. 2014. *Academic Luck: General and Specific Scenarios of Academic Attestation in Russia in the 1830s.* Working Paper Series, Humanities, National Research University Higher School of Economics, Moscow. https://wp.hse.ru/data/2015/01/20/1106860887/81HUM2014.pdf. Accessed 19 February 2020.

Janos, Andrew. 1982. *The Politics of Backwardness in Hungary, 1825–1945.* Princeton: Princeton University Press.

Jedlicki, Jerzy. 1999. *A Suburb of Europe, Nineteenth-Century Polish Approaches to Western Civilization.* Budapest: Central European University Press.

Jevons, William Stanley. 1888. *The Theory of Political Economy.* 3rd ed. London: Macmillan. http://oll.libertyfund.org/EBooks/Jevons_0237.pdf. Accessed 3 January 2019.

Kautz, Gyula. 1860. *Die geschichtliche Entwickelung der National-Oekonomik und ihrer Literatur.* Wien: Gerold.

Kautz, Gyula. 1911. *A nemzetgazdasági eszmék fejľődési története és befolyása a köz-viszonyokra Magyarországon (History of Ideas of National Economy in Hungary and Their Influence on Public Relations)*. Pest: Heckenast Gusztáv. Originally Published in 1868.

Kenny, Neil. 2004. *The Uses of Curiosity in Early Modern France and Germany*. Oxford and New York: Oxford University Press.

Kirschbaum, J. Stanislav. 2007. *Historical Dictionary of Slovakia*. 2nd ed. Lanham, Maryland; Toronto; Plymouth, UK: The Scarecrow Press, Inc.

Kirzner, Israel. 1976. *The Economic Point of View*. Menlo Park: Institute for Humane Studies.

Klausinger, Hansjörg. 2016. The Nationalökonomische Gesellschaft (Austrian Economic Association) in the Interwar Period and Beyond. In *Research in the History of Economic Thought and Methodology*, ed. Luca Fiorito et al., 9–43. Emerald Group Publishing Limited.

Kosa, John. 1954. The Early Period of Anglo-Hungarian Contact. *American Slavic and East European Review* 13 (3): 414–431.

Krameš, Jaroslav. 2014. *Czech National Economy Revival in the Work of Albín Bráf and in Literature of His Pupils*. The 8th International Days of Statistics and Economics, Prague, September 11–13, pp. 776–784.

———. 2016a. *Profesor Albín Bráf a jeho žáci: (česká národohospodářská škola Bráfova) (Profesor Albín Bráf and His Students: Bráf's Czech School of National Economy)*. Prague: Národohospodářský ústav Josefa Hlávky.

———. 2016b. *Professor Albín Bráf, His Students, and the Austrian School*. The 10th International Days of Statistics and Economics, VŠE, Prague. https://msed.vse.cz/msed_2016/article/70-Krames-Jaroslav-paper.pdf. Accessed 22 April 2020.

Landes, David. 1998. *The Wealth and Poverty of Nations. Why Some Are So Rich and Some So Poor*. New York and London: W.W. Norton & Company.

Lang, Louis. 1909. Obituary, Professor Dr Julius Kautz. *The Economic Journal* 19 (75): 483–487.

Láng, Lajos. 1913. *A statisztika története, bevezetésül Magyaorszáq statisztikájához (A History of Statistics, as an Introduction to Hungarian Statistics)*. Budapest: Grill Károly könyvkiadóvállalata.

Litynska, Alexandra. 2000. Fryderyk Skarbek – tworca polskiej szkoly narodowej w ekonomii (Frederyk Skarbek – Creator of Polish National School in Economics). *Zeszyty Naukowe, Akademii Ekonomicznej w Krakowie* 555: 87–94.

Lukcsics, Pál. 1914. *Schwartner Márton élete és tudományos jelentősége (Life and Scientific Importance of Schwartner Márton)*. Veszprém Egyházmegyei könyvnyomda.

Machlup, Fritz. 1956. Rejoinder to a Reluctant Ultra-Empiricist. *Southern Economic Journal* 22 (4): 483–493.

Madarász, Aladár. 2000. Heller Farkas (1877–1955). *Közgazdász*, October, II.

Mátyás, Antal. 1995. Die Österreichische Schule der Nationalökonomie im Spiegel der ungarischen volkswirtschaftlichen Literatur. In *Krise und Exodus*,

Österreichische Sozialwissenschaften in MittelEuropa, ed. Kurt R. Leube and Andreas Pribersky, 62–77. Vienna: WUV Universitätsverlag.

———. 2005. 175 éve született a korszerû magyar közgazdaságtan elsõ nagy képviselõje, Kautz Gyula (175 Years from the Birth of Kautz Gyula a Great Representative of Modern Hungarian Economic Thought). *Közgazdasági Szemle* LII: 613–622.

Maxwell, Alexander. 2009. *Choosing Slovakia, Slavic Hungary, the Czechoslovak Language and Accidental Nationalism*. London, New York: I. B. Tauris.

von Mises, Ludwig. 1951. *Socialism: An Economic and Sociological Analysis*. New Haven: Yale University Press.

———. 2004. *Human Action*. Ludwig von Mises Institute.

———. 2013. *Notes and Recollections: With the Historical Setting of the Austrian School of Economics*. Liberty Fund.

Mitchell, Wesley C. 1914. Human Behavior and Economics: A Survey of Recent Literature. *The Quarterly Journal of Economics* 29: 1.

Morgenstern, Oscar. 1927. Friedrich von Wieser, 1851–1926. *The American Economic Review* 17 (4): 669–674.

Nyíri, János Kristóf. 1986. Intellectual Foundation of Austrian Liberalism. In *Austrian Economics, Historical and Philosophical Background*, ed. Wolfgang Grassl and Barry Smith. London: Croom Helm.

Paryna, Wojciech. 2011. *Obrona wolnósci, pokoju, kultury i postepu – Adam Heydel*. Wroclaw. http://kwasnicki.prawo.uni.wroc.pl/pliki/Paryna_Praca-mgr-Adam-Heydel.pdf. Accessed 3 January 2019.

Petro, Peter. 1995. *A History of Slovak Literature*. Montreal & Kingston, London, Buffalo: McGill-Queens University Press.

Psalidopoulos, Michalis, and Maria E. Mata. 2002. *Economic Thought and Policy in Less Developed Europe: The Nineteenth Century*. London: Routledge.

Rackauskas, John. 1977. *The Commission for National Education of Poland and Lithuania (1773–1794): A Historical Study of Some Aspects of Its Educational Reforms*. The University of Ottawa.

Rosenstein-Rodan, Paul. 1934. The Role of Time in Economic Theory. *Economica* 1: 77–97.

Rothbard, Murray N. 1995. *Economic Thought Before Adam Smith, An Austrian Perspective on the History of Economic Thought*. Ludwig von Mises Institute, Auburn Alabama with Edward Elgar Publishing Ltd.

Schwartner, Martin. 1798. *Statistik des Königreichs Ungern*. Pest: Ein Versuch.

Šíma, Josef, and Tomáš Nikodym. 2015. Classical Liberalism in the Czech Republic. *Econ Journal Watch* 12 (2): 274–292.

Skerlecz, Miklós Baró. 1914. *Művei (Works)*. Budapest: Magyar Tudományos Akadémia kiadása.

Slutsky, Eugen. 1915. Sulla teoria del bilancio del consumatore. *Giornale degli Economisti e Rivista di Statistica* 51 (July): 1–26; English Translation on the

Theory of the Budget of the Consumer; Translated by G.J. Stigler and K.J. Boulding, Homewood, III.: Richard D. Irwin, Inc., 1952, pp. 27–56.

Small, Albion W. 1909 (1st ed.). 2001 (Republished). *The Cameralists*. New York: Franklin. Kitchener: Batoche Books.

Smith, Adam. 1977. *An Inquiry into the Nature and Causes of the Wealth of Nations*. University of Chicago Press. Originally Published in 1776.

Špirko, Juraj. 2009. O jednom z najvýznamnejších absolventov našej univerzity (About One of the Most Important Graduates of Our University). *Acta Iuridica Cassoviensia* 26. https://www.upjs.sk/public/media/4021/AIC26.pdf. Accessed 22 March 2020.

Surányi-Unger, Theo. 1948. Individual and Collective Wants. *Journal of Political Economy* 56 (1): 1–22.

Tihany, C. Leslie. 1969. The Austro-Hungarian Compromise, 1867–1918: A Half Century of Diagnosis; Fifty Years of Post-Mortem. *Central European History* 2 (2): 114–138.

Toporowski, Jan. 2014. The Polish Contribution to Economics. *Royal Economic Society, Newsletter Online*, April.

Tóth, Gergely. 2017. Vestigia Barbarae Gentis, Mátyás Bél on Ottoman and Post-Ottoman Hungary. In *Identity and Culture in Ottoman Hungary*, ed. Pál Fodor and Pál Ács, 367–386. Berlin: Klaus Schwarz Verlag.

Turnovec, Frantisek. 2002. Economics – Czech Republic. In *Three Social Science Disciplines in Central and Eastern Europe: Handbook on Economics, Political Science and Sociology (1989–2001)*, ed. Max Kaase and Vera Sparschuh, co-ed. Agnieszka Wenninger. Berlin: GESIS/Social Science Information Centre (IZ) and Budapest: Collegium Budapest Institute for Advanced Study.

Unčovský, Ladislav. 1956. *G. Berzeviczy*. Martin: Vydavatelstvo Osveta.

———. 2000. Michal Baludanský, ruský ekonóm rusínskeho pôvodu zo Slovenska (Michal Baludanský, a Russian Economist of Russinian Origin from Slovakia). *Ekonomický časopis* 48 (5): 676–693.

———. 2011. Niektorí ekonómovia na Slovensku pred rokom 1848 (Some Economists in Slovakia Before 1848). *Ekonomické rozhľady* 40 (1): 102–126.

Vencovský, František. 2003. Echo of Adam Smith Among the Czech Economists. In *Adam Smith Semper Vivus*, ed. Josef Šíma, 32–44. Prague: Liberální institut.

Wandycz, Piotr S. 2001. *The Price of Freedom, A History of East Central Europe from the Middle Ages to the Present*. 2nd ed. London and New York: Routledge.

Waszek, Norbert. 1993. Adam Smith in Germany, 1776–1832. In *Adam Smith: International Perspective*, ed. Hiroshi Mizuta and Chuhei Sugiyama, 163–180. London: Macmillan Press.

Wortman, Richard. 1976. *The Development of a Russian Legal Consciousness*. Chicago: The University of Chicago Press.

Zavarský, Svorad. 2011. Martin Sentiváni Dissertatio cosmographica seu de mundi systemate (Martin Sentiváni the System of World, a Cosmological Study). *Slavica Slovaca* 46 (3): 1–154.

———. 2018. Between the Universe and Universal Knowledge: Martinus Szent-Ivany's Curiosiora et selectiora variarum scientiarum miscellanea (1689–1709). In *Astrid Steiner-Weber and Franz Römer edited Acta Conventus Neo-Latini Vindobonensis.* Proceedings of the Sixteenth International Congress of Neo-Latin Studies (Vienna 2015): Brill.

CHAPTER 3

The Interwar Period

The growth of nationalism in the second half of the nineteenth century culminated with the creation of nation-states after World War I.[1] However, it was not only the nationalism, but also the Monarchy was not prepared to manage such a massive war as occurred in 1914–1918. Habsburg armed forces counted 2.3 million men in 1914, compared with 5.3 million for Russia and 3.8 million each for Germany and France. Austro-Hungarian armies were underfunded and ill-equipped for war. Bideleux and Jeffries (2007, p. 304). Austria-Hungary before 1914 was not anymore a significant power, not because of its economics, but because the Habsburgs, the Austrian Reichsrat, and the Hungarians did not progress with a military re-organization, due to political tensions among them. "The reason for the shortage of funds was political or, better to say, national. Deák (1990, p. 64)."

World War I changed the map of Central Europe.[2] Poland again re-emerged as an independent state, similar to Czechoslovakia. Hungary

[1] Edvard Beneš was well aware of the dangers of nationalism after World War I, when he said: "The war caused the nationalism of all the different peoples there to expand to such a degree that any attempt to suppress it would lead to another terrible war ." Berman (1995, pp. 619-620).

[2] After World War I, John Maynard Keynes got involved in a discussion about the future of Central Europe. Keynes has seen in Central European nationalist endeavors—representing for him a destructive energy—an enemy of post-war reconstruction. Besides, he has consid-

J. Horvath, *An Introduction to the History of Economic Thought in Central Europe*, Palgrave Studies in the History of Economic Thought, https://doi.org/10.1007/978-3-030-58926-4_3

became independent but on smaller territory than the semi-independent Kingdom as the Trianon Treaty significantly reduced Hungary's territory and population.[3]

In the new arrangements, the state's importance increased as states led the post-war re-organization. Governments began to support domestic industries with subsidies, tax exemptions, tariff protection, import controls, and similar at levels unseen in the Monarchy. After World War I, these countries were pulled into the international economy and exposed to more fierce competition than before the war. Before 1918 they were part of Empires (Habsburg, Ottoman, Tsarist, Wilhelmian), which protected their economy, to an extent, from the overall effects of the international competition.

Once these nations moved out from the protection of the Empires, they became much more vulnerable to large neighboring states. Fehér (1989, p. 439) writes that the Third Reich exploited "the often legitimate grievances of the German ethnic minorities in the new nation-states created by Versailles, and used them as a fifth column in its campaign of colonization." Especially Poland and part of former Czechoslovakia became full dependencies. Once the Germans lost World War II, a new power almost immediately rushed in and tried to re-make it to its image.

Before World War I, Central Europe was predominantly in the sphere of Austrian and German influence. In the 1920s, when German, Austrian, and Russian impact was minimal, a political vacuum appeared. As a result of World War I, Entente Powers should have a dominant position in this territory. However, the French and English influence was in education, but less in military affairs and trade. France was unable to provide the protection that some Central Europeans expected from her, as

ered the potential connection between nationalists and the anti-market forces of societal and economic planning. He presented these ideas in the Economic Consequences of Peace, which criticized the Treaty of Versailles, arguing that Europe's rebuilding after World War I without Germany was an impossibility. The good times in Central Europe were in Keynes' eyes, connected with prosperous Germany. Keynes understood that Europe's economy was highly interdependent, and weakening Germany could also make the European continent economically weaker with further political repercussions, another war, and revolutions. That is why he proposed revising of the Treaty, especially reducing the reparations demands and moderation of coal and iron deliveries. Berman (1995).

[3] The additional difficulty was that the leading sector of the Hungarian economy, agriculture, was before World War I, to no small extent oriented toward the Austrian and Czech markets. Thanks to the Monarchy's high import tariffs, the Hungarian agricultural producers faced no real competition outside the Monarchy. Berend and Ránki (1972).

documented by the late years of the 1930s. Thus, these countries were again gradually incorporated into German influence.

After World War I, Czechoslovakia became the prosperous state of Central Europe. "Masaryk's success was due in significant measure to the existence of middle-class norms of democratic behavior that had been tested by Czech participants in Habsburg politics. Strong parties, all committed to national democracy, provided the creators of the Czechoslovak state with the raw material of democracy." Stokes (1991, p. 218). This arrangement's weakness was that the new country did not manage well the treatment of the formerly ruling nationalities. However, not only the German and Hungarian question remained open. The ethnic nationality principle, which allowed the Czechs and the Slovaks to form a new state, did not make the Slovaks entirely enthusiastic. The Czechoslovak nation's concept, with two different peoples, reminded Slovak nationalists' Hungarian ideas during the Monarchy.[4]

In Hungary, Mihály Károlyi, after World War I, attempted to formulate a moderate democratic society close to the West, but "he received almost no support from the public or Hungarian political elites." Stokes (1991, p. 219). Under pressure from leftist revolutionaries, Károlyi resigned in March 1919. After the short-run Soviet Republic, Admiral Miklós Horthy consolidated society and his power. This process continued with Count Stephen Bethlen as premier till 1931. Afterward, the Hungarian government came increasingly into the hands of more radical movements. Stokes (1991, p. 219). Domination of Hungarian political reality by landowning aristocracy, highly stratified property relations with a small class owning the majority of agricultural wealth characterized the Hungarian society in the interwar period. Ownership of land provided substantial political power and allowed the landowning class to influence the political process. Land reform was needed to get the talent from the lower strata of rural society to improve their and society's living conditions.

Transfer from the war economy into a civilian economy was difficult as financing of the war created pre-conditions for post-war inflation. In the early after-war years, the economy was supply-determined as the war

[4] "In 1922, Hlinka wrote an anti-Czechoslovak manifesto whose English title captures its hysterical tone: 'A Country Doomed to Death, A Nation in her Last Agonies Implores the Civilized World for Help.'" Maxwell (2009, p. 176). Czechoslovak leaders attributed Slovak-Czech tensions to Slovak economic backwardness; they believed that the Slovak society's economic development and modernization would erase those tensions. Maxwell (2009, p.184).

destroyed productive capacities, and the civilian demand differed from the war-time demand. After the war, these countries faced problems of substantial and often increasing budget deficits as it was difficult to contain the costs of building a new state administration. Social payments significantly increased due to war casualties.[5] Weak governments, together with uncertainties of the new political organization, also intensified inflationary pressures. Printing money typically financed the deficits with the potential for this situation to explode.

Indeed, one of the tragic economic events after World War I was some countries' inability to contain inflationary pressures. Hyperinflation erupted in Germany and Austria as well as in Poland and Hungary.[6] Hyperinflation contributed to the horrors of the war and helped the emergence of authoritarian regimes in the 1930s. Only Czechoslovakia avoided the inflationary spiral, into which most of the others fell in.[7]

It seems a complex issue why Hungary was not able to control inflation after World War I. Lost war, short-run Bolshevik revolution, together with the governments not able to manage the political situation. The government financed huge expenditures by borrowing from the State Note

[5] For Hungary, there were additional reparation costs to be paid. "The prospect of having to pay reparations increased already existing uncertainties, made it almost impossible to balance the budget of the respective states, and to obtain foreign financial help to curb the inflation." Ránki (1983a, pp. 476-477).

[6] Berend and Ránki (1972, p. 121) show the effect of hyperinflation by providing data on the value of the Hungarian crown vis-à-vis the Swiss franc. The value of hundred Hungarian crowns in Swiss franc was in June 1914, 104.28; in March 1919, 22.46; in December 1919, 3.20; in December 1920, 1.24; in December 1921, 0.76; in December 1922, 0.23; in December 1923, 0.03; and in May 1924, 0.0065. The tragic destiny of the crown ended by 1927 when the pengő replaced it. Teichova (1983, p. 537) provides data on the adequate gold cover of selected note-issuing banks. Thus, comparing July 22, 1914, with September 23, 1919, the Austro-Hungarian Bank had 58% cover before the War and 0.6% after the War. The data for Reichsbank was 71.8% and 3.9%, for Bank of France 69.4% and 10.0%, and the Bank of England 137% and 108%. On the situation in Poland, see Landau (1968) and Landau (1983).

[7] When the War ended, the notes issued by the Austro-Hungarian Bank were to finance government expenditures, and the Bank was discounting the war loans near par, even if the market rate was well below. Czechs initially got a membership on the Board of this Bank but pulled out. The Czechoslovak National Committee in early November 1918 prohibited branches of the Austro-Hungarian Bank on the territory of Czechoslovakia to accept war loan securities; also, taxes could not be paid by war loans by the decision of the Committee. Consequently, these securities moved to Austria, Hungary, and other places and pushed the inflation upward. Teichova (1983, p. 544).

Institute, which also made loans and discounts to private agents, politically close to the after-revolutionary government. Sargent (1982, p. 61) writes that "These private loans account for a much larger increase in high-powered money in the Hungarian than in the other three hyperinflations we shall study." In early 1921 the minister of finance Lóránt Hegedüs attempted to halt the inflation. Initially, he was able to decrease the printing of notes. Consequently, the interest rate had risen, an outflow of foreign currencies and gold halted, and the Hungarian crown strengthened. Hegedüs intended to achieve a balanced budget by introducing a capital levy of less than 20% on wealthy individuals, financiers, industrialists, and around 5% on land and cash value. Propriety classes opposed, especially the landowners, and the amount raised was insufficient to impact budget balancing. Finally, in summer, the currency began to weaken again, and the stabilization attempt failed. "He resigned, and his successor based his monetary policy on the banknotes press." Ránki (1983b, 527). The inflation accelerated to the hyperinflationary level, and this process ended only in March 1924. Berend and Ránki (1972) and Pécsi (1985) argue that the economic policy after World War I had become consciously inflationary. Inflation decreased the tax burden and helped cut the real costs for the wealthy landowners who got rid of their debt.

In the interwar period, there were vast differences between the relatively well industrialized Czech lands and Poland, Hungary, and Slovakia. In the Czech lands, most of the industry was owned by the private sector, while primarily in Poland the state sector's role was prevalent.

In Hungary, the state controlled approximately one-quarter of the national product. However, Hungary, in fundamental difference to other countries of Central Europe, "essentially preserved the semifeudal system of large estates." Hodos (1999, p. 65). Hungarian government tried to overcome dependence on agriculture. Till the Great Depression, the industrial production massively increased, the number of factory workers nearly doubled, and the industry share in the gross national product increased from one-fifth to one-third. Hodos (1999, p. 65). Still, over half the population remained occupied in agriculture. The Great Depression profoundly affected Hungarian agriculture as the export products' prices collapsed, and export volume fell.

The arrangements after World War I made it difficult for the new states to create viable economic units as the resource endowments and industrial capacity—which evolved more naturally in the pre-war period—were redistributed based on the political preferences of the winning powers.

Economic regional cooperation between the new states was on a low level, as each state was building foundations for its economic and political independence. All these adverse effects were multiplied by the Great Depression, which strengthened those who would envisage Central Europe future in radical political options. Intellectuals and economists felt that something was vitally wrong with capitalism. Fascism gained popularity in some places as well as Soviet-type central planning as both of these new organizations of society were less exposed to recession and unemployment than the traditional capitalist market societies. Economic difficulties mounted and created the backbone for introducing authoritarian systems in Central Europe, which were still less radical, in the interwar period, than the reality in Germany and the Soviet Union. Aldcroft and Morewood (1995), and Aldcroft (1997).

Economic Thought in the Interwar Period

In the period after World War I, institutionalization and professionalization of economics as an academic discipline happened. Improving the quality of the universities and their scientific produce was considered an essential factor in the respective countries' nation-building process. After 1918, the new nations began to build modern universities where the language of instruction was predominantly the native language of the majority of the population.[8] In the interwar period, state institutions were re-built with the need for many experts into the state bureaucracy. That led to the foundation of new universities and research institutes as Szkola Glówna Handlowa in Poland, Comenius University in Bratislava, and others.

[8] In the pre-World War I period, German or Hungarian speaking universities made it more difficult for a nationally oriented Czech and Polish economists to be awarded the university professorship. For instance, Krameš (2016) mentions the story of František Ladislav Rieger and Maximilian Wellner in Prague in the 1860s. Rieger, known as the Czech Bastiat, was a Czech journalist and writer. Rieger and Wellner were Czech nationals who felt strongly about their national identity and were denied university positions. The situation in Prague changed once in 1882, the Austrian government re-established the Karl-Ferdinand Prague University as a bilingual twin university, that is, a Czech as well as a German university. From 1882 almost every unit of Prague University was divided into its separate Czech and German language section. Havránek (1997). This division also continued in the period 1918–1939. In 1939 the Nazi occupation forces closed Czech universities, and from May 1945, German education at Prague University terminated.

Similarly to the second half of the nineteenth century, we observe the influence of erudite university professors as Karel Engliš, Ákos Navratil, Farkas Heller, Imrich Karvaš, Edward Lipiński, and others. Some of them had achieved high governmental positions. In Poland, Michal Kalecki and Oskar Lange began their career in this period. Other eminent economists of the period included Wladyszlaw Marian Zawadzki and Aleksy Wakar (1898-1966), both known for their contributions to mathematical economics. Another noted economist of the period is Edward Lipiński (1888-1986), founder of the Institute of Business Cycles in 1928 and the founder of Ekonomista, a leading Polish economic journal from 1929.

In this period, one observes the emergence of different schools of thought in individual countries. For instance, one can distinguish three schools representing the Czech economic thought. The first school was represented by Alois Rašín, who prevented the rise of hyperinflation in the early 1920s and pushed for deflationary policies in the framework of strict gold standard principles with a balanced state budget. Karel Engliš is the renowned representative of the other school. He was the founder of the teleological theory of the national economy, which was "based on the idea that the cognition and understanding of all economic processes should reflect the purposefulness, intentionality, and choice of aims and means in the behavior of all economic subjects." Turnovec (2002, p. 52). The third school was more Keynesian in its spirit, and Josef Macek was its renowned representative.

The break-up of Austria-Hungary was felt most negatively in Hungary. For example, in four volumes of *Review of the Contemporary Economic Theory,* Hans Mayer edited in the second half of the 1920s—only a Hungarian academician, Balás (1927), regretted the developments after the break-up of the monarchy. Czech and Polish nationals welcomed the post-World War I developments, especially concerning the educational institutions in their respective countries. Both Engliš (1927) and Zawadzki (1927) valued highly the new freedom to establish universities with instruction in their languages.

Next, we mention the work and life of some Central European economists active in the interwar period.

Rosa Luxemburg (1871–1919)[9]

Rosa Luxemburg (1871–1919) was born in Polish territory under Russian rule and was murdered during the German revolution in Berlin. She had received a doctoral degree in 1897 in Zurich for a work Die industrielle Entwicklung Polens (The Industrial Development of Poland). Between 1907 and 1914, Luxemburg was lecturing political economy in the German Social Democratic Party school. She was one of the founders of the Social Democratic Party in the Kingdom of Poland under Russian rule. However, her widely known activities included her involvement in the German Social Democracy movement.

Similarly to Lenin, Tugan-Baranovsky, and others, she attempted to develop those aspects of Marx's theory that dealt with the modern capitalist economy of the beginning of the twentieth century. Her starting point was not the individual commodity and capital, but she put a more macroeconomically oriented approach into the forefront. Her book *Die Akkumulation des Kapitals* (The Accumulation of Capital) deals with the issue of interest of Marxists in the first half of the twentieth century, that is, how to define and understand imperialism. For her, imperialism was "the political expression of the accumulation of capital in its competitive struggle for what is still left of the non-capitalist regions of the world." Amsden (2018, p. 6132). Luxemburg (1913) has written about the existence of a new phase in the development of capitalism characterized by monopoly and imperialism.

For her, an under-consumption theorist, the answer to reasons for capitalists to invest when facing weak demand was to be found in the context of the world economy: exports to underdeveloped and less developed countries were providing markets for capital goods. This imperial relation, coupled with state expenditure on armaments were to overcome the weak demand. She argued that the mostly agricultural periphery's proletarianization was a vital activity for keeping the capitalist order. According to her, the accumulation of capital depends mainly on the non-capitalist social strata. "The solution envisaged by Marx lies in the dialectical

[9] Kowalik (2003), Amsden (2018), Van Duin (2018), Dellheim and Wolf eds. (2016), Kowalik (1987). We include Rosa Luxemburg into this period, as it was the interwar period in which her influence was dominant in internal socialist discussion in the Central European lands concerning their vision of socialism. For a similar reason, we also mention in the text Mikhail Tugan-Baranovsky, who was of Ukrainian-Tartar origin and had written in Russian but impacted Central European socialist thought. We thank a reviewer for these suggestions.

conflict that capitalism needs non-capitalist social organisations as the setting for its development, that it proceeds by assimilating the organizations which alone can ensure its own existence." Luxemburg (2003/1913, p. 346). Her historical analysis led to the thesis about the impossibility of capitalism's existence without the pre-capitalist environment. She has seen this relationship between the imperialist and colonial countries as a primary source of wars and revolutions.

Marxists observed that the living standard of the proletariat was rising in leading Western countries. That needed an explanation, so the dogma about exploitation should remain alive. The new culprit was imperialism and its economic consequences, that is, exploitation of colonial lands by the Western capitalist countries. In a stylized way, Marxists could then argue that Western bourgeoise was buying their labor class and social peace by exploiting the surplus from the colonies.

She was a revolutionary socialist, but not of a Bolshevik style. The discussion evolved after the Bolshevik revolution in 1917 among the socialist camp. For Lenin and Trotsky, the socialist revolution meant abolishing legality, parliamentary institutions, restrictions on the flow of information and press, and suppression of political opponents. Luxemburg writes in a completely different spirit. "Freedom only for the supporters of the government, only for the members of one party—however numerous they may be—is no freedom at all. Freedom is always and exclusively freedom for the one who thinks differently" Van Duin (2018, p. 31).

She disagreed with Lenin's model of the communist revolutionary vanguard party. The Lenin-Luxemburg confrontation became a significant issue in the Marxist and international socialist movement between the 1920s and 1960s. Van Duin (2018).

Wladyslaw Marian Zawadzki (1885–1939)[10]

He was born in Vilno and studied in Moscow, Leipzig, and Paris. As a young scholar, in 1914, published *Les Mathématiques appliquées à l'économie politique* in Paris. He became one of the first members of the Econometric Society. He became a professor of Political Economy at the re-opened Vilno University from 1919. There he began his work on economic sociology, which culminated in the book *Theory of Production*. "Zawadzki distinguishes five types of environments in which regular

[10] Swianiewicz (2008).

production can take place: primitive, patriarchal, individualistic, based on compulsion and collectivist." Swianiewicz (2008, p. 1). He is skeptical about the Marxist view, "but he admits the possibility of a revolutionary transition to collectivism as preached by George Sorel and the French syndicalist revolutionaries." Swianiewicz (2008, p. 2).

Zawadzki was the Polish Minister of Finance for half a decade in the early 1930s. In the last years of his life, he worked at the Central School of Commerce in Warsaw.

Alois Rašín (1867–1923)[11]

Rašín belonged to the core group of politicians considered founders of the Czechoslovak state. As a Minister of Finance, he prevented hyperinflation, when all the neighboring states lived through a monetary ruin. Berlin, Vienna, Budapest, and Warsaw were in monetary destruction when the actions of Rašín provided monetary stability to Prague. Furthermore, his tragic end in the hands of the young radical makes his life story quite distinctive.

Rašín was born in a small city of Nechanice. His father began his career as a baker, successful in business and local politics, became mayor of Nechanice, and later a member of the Parliament in Vienna. Rašín studied in Broumov, Hradec Králové, and began to study medicine, which he interrupted for health reasons and finally settled for studying law in Prague. As a university student, he was active in the student movement, participated in Adam Mickiewicz re-burial in Cracow, and at Congress of Slavic students who hoped for a Monarchy's federalization. As a young student, he published a book on the subject of Czech state law, which led to his arrest and first prison sentence. He left the prison in 1895. In the 1911 elections, Rašín became a member of the Parliament as a politician for the Mladočeská strana (Party of Young Czechs). In Parliament, he worked in different committees oriented toward financial issues.

During World War I, his publishing and political activity became less and less loyal to the Monarchy.[12] It became apparent to the Austrian

[11] Šiková (2017), Drápela (2007), Bažantová (2003), Holman (2003).

[12] Rašín was critical to the concept of Mitteleuropa, which was emerging into discourse at that time. He, in Národní Listy, on October 21, 1917, had published the following: "Herr Naumann may for a time cease roaming over Central Europe, public agitation for 'Mitteleuropa' may diminish, but in reality no new idea, no program has been offered which would make amends for centuries of oppression. … All the pronouncements of the Austrian

authorities that the Czechs do not intend to struggle to preserve the Austro-Hungarian Empire. As a reaction, the authorities initiated waves of arrests of public figures. Klima (1993, p. 243). In summer 1915, the authorities arrested Rašín together with the future Prime Minister Karel Kramář, Václav Klofáč, and others. Rašín and Kramář were accused of treason for their pan-Slavic and other political activities and sentenced to death. The appeal court confirmed the decision in November 2016. However, the ailing Emperor did not sign the sentence, and the new Emperor Karl changed the decision to fifteen years of prison for Kramář and ten years for Rašín. In July 1917, the Kaiser called for amnesty, and both politicians could leave the prison.

Rašín was a disciplined personality who used his prison terms for writing studies. In 1916, he completed writing his book *Národní hospodářství* (National Economy). This book consists of five sections: The Basic Conditions of Development; Production and Wages; Value, Price and Credit; Creation and Distribution of Income; and Consumption. Rašín held strong views about the character of money. He was a metalist who believed that gold is a basis of a healthy financial system. Also, he was not a supporter of the quantity theory as he emphasized the role of credit's adjustment to the requirements of the trade. Rašín argued that as the level of credit reacts to the economic activity, it does not necessarily transfer into movements in prices.

After leaving prison, he fully entered political life. In his wartime speeches, he has already foreseen the chaos of the post-war state of affairs, which a firm economic policy should help avoiding. Preparations for the after-war period included possible separation from the Monarchy, liquidation of the Austria-Hungarian central bank, new tax regime, land reform, and other policy steps. In these discussions, the idea of monetary separation from the Monarchy's other countries was at the forefront.

In November 1918, Rašín became a member of the new Parliament (Národní zhromáždění), and also became the Minister of Finance. The financing of expenditures of the new Czechoslovak state became a priority of the new government. There was a conscious effort to achieve financing

and Austro-Hungarian governments have been designed to conceal the real intentions." Meyer (1955, p. 189). A similar position was of Masaryk, who also rejected Naumann's framework and saw the concept of Central Europe as a German domination tool. Trencsényi (2017, p. 169). During World War I, Tomáš Garrigue Masaryk (1850–1937) and Robert Seton-Watson (1879–1951) established a journal in London titled a 'New Europe' to counteract the influence of the concept of Mitteleuropa.

of the state expenditures from loans provided to the new Czechoslovak state by the domestic economic subjects, either in the form of the Loan of Freedom (Pujčka Svobody), or loans from commercial banks. In November 1918, the new Parliament decided to disallow 'economic agents' to pay taxes by Austrian government bonds.

At the Ministry of Finance, Rašín adopted conservative fiscal and monetary policies. Neighbors of Czechoslovakia adopted similar policies, but only after their currencies had significantly depreciated. Even before the Peace Treaties required it, Czechoslovakia marked the Austro-Hungarian notes circulating within its border with a unique stamp. Stamping of notes was prepared by Vilém Pospíšil (1873-1942), later the first Governor of the Czechoslovak Central Bank. At midnight on February 25, 1919, the Currency Separation Act came into force, and from February 26 to March 9, 1919, the country's borders closed for movements of goods, people, and money. The government retained part of the notes in the form of a forced loan. "Fifty percent of privately held banknotes as well as of bank and savings accounts were withdrawn and converted into a one percent compulsory loan." Teichova (1983, p. 538). Bankovní úřad ministerstva financí (Banking Office of the Ministry of Finance) took over the administrative control of currency from the former Austro-Hungarian Bank. A new monetary law of April 10, 1919, limited the fiduciary or unbacked note circulation. This law forced the government to finance its expenditures by levying taxes or issuing debt. From April 10, 1919, the stamped notes became legal tender, and only later, gradually, the new Czechoslovak notes were issued.

Rašín associated the prestige of the new country with the stability of the currency. Rašín and his collaborators prepared the stamping old Austro-Hungarian notes located at the Czechoslovak Republic territory. During this process, Rašín initiated to withdraw 80% of the notes from circulation. Under the pressure of other parties and the Parliament, he agreed finally to 50% withdrawal in the form of a forced 1% loan to the new state. Rašín initially favored obtaining international loans, which would allow restoring the prewar parity of the crown. However, other political parties opposed such a plan. At the beginning of the 1920s, obtaining a loan of such a volume to keep koruna's value at the prewar rate turned out politically difficult. Also, the government introduced taxes on the increase in wealth obtained during the war.

The election in June 1919 weakened Rašín's position, and he had to leave the post of the Minister of Finance. In opposition, he criticized the new government for inserting massive financial injections to ease social tensions. His credentials increased as once he left the minister's position, the Czech currency was losing value. In a couple of months, it heavily depreciated vis-à-vis the Swiss currency. In the early 1920s, Rašín, together with industrialists and bankers around Živnostenská Banka, began to propagate deflationary policies together with a strengthening of the value of the Czech currency. His insistence on deflation policy reflected the prevailing discourse of the time, much alive until the emergence of modern Keynesianism. The Group of Five and Eduard Beneš supported his policies, but he faced opposition from export interests and labor.[13] In October 1922, in the new government led by Švehla, Rašín again became Minister of Finance.

Rašín attempted to make koruna stronger also during his second term as the Minister of Finance. Koruna naturally strengthened as hyperinflation in the neighboring countries increased the demand for stable currencies. In this period, "Rašín differed from the wisdom advocated by Ralph Hawtrey at the British Treasury, who argued that stabilisation must be achieved at existing depreciated levels. In Rašín's view, this was good for the hyper-inflated currencies, but not for the healthy Czechoslovak economy." Lojkó (2006, p. 211).

Deflationary effects with declining prices of produced goods and increased debt value led some manufacturing companies into bankruptcy. On the other hand, financial institutions, especially banks, were strengthened by acquisitions of these industrial and trade units. Rašín claimed that companies' bankruptcies were not a consequence of deflationary policies but of a non-competitive situation in the heavily regulated coal markets, which led to higher coal prices and higher production costs. Also, Rašín believed that deflation weakens speculation. He understood deflation as a moral issue: those who save are to receive premium as they prepare resources for future investments. In October 1922, a middle-sized commercial bank bankrupted in Brno, which led to panic in the market and a substantial weakening of his position. All in all, his opponents hit back. There was a witch-hunt by the leftist press, and the representatives of minorities, irritated by his nationalist policies. On January 5, 1923, he was

[13] Rašín was part of the influential Group of Five, consisting of representatives of essential democratic parties. This group included Antonín. Švehla from the Agrarians, Rudolf Bechyně from Social Democrats, Jiří Stříbrný from National Socialists, Jan Šrámek from People's Party, and Rašín from National Democrats.

shot by a nineteen-year-old anarcho-communist and died on February 18, 1923.

His slogan "work and save" reflected his vision that one should work for the new republic and not ask for benefits guaranteed by the state. It did not help his popularity that Rašín confronted the Czech Legions, that is, those who returned with Masaryk from the Soviet Union and had achieved an influential position in the new Czechoslovak state. In his speech, in December 1922, he praised their fight for the new republic but criticized them as excessively interested in receiving privileges.

His readings made him close to the Austrian school of economics. Throughout his life, he always stood on strong anti-socialist positions. He rejected social experiments and viewed the protection of private property as a moral duty. Nevertheless, after the war, he supported social reforms and some active social policies. However, he opposed the law to introduce eight hours working day, arguing that this would make sense only if all countries competing with the Czech exports would introduce it. He was a conservative-liberal with strong Czech nationalist inclinations, preferred traditional conservative values dressed in a Czech garb.

Rašín's name as a successful policymaker emerges when one discusses how—after the free trade area and a monetary union of the Austro-Hungarian Monarchy collapsed—Czechoslovakia, Hungary, and Poland managed their new currency. Rašín was able to push his policy through, while "in Hungary, Hegedüs looked much like Rašín, for a while, and then failed." Dornbusch (1992, p. 405).[14]

Holman (2003, p. 38) writes that as Rašín's contribution was less in a theoretical field, reviews of Czech economic thought at times did not consider him. However, he remains a national economic legend. Klaus (2003,

[14] Lóránt Hegedüs (1872-1943) studied law in Budapest and graduated in 1895, sub auspiciis regis, awarded to those students who received the best marks for all exams. He continued in Berlin studying finance, where one of his teachers was Adolph Wagner. He also studied sociology under Herbert Spencer in London. From 1898 Hegedüs was the youngest member of Parliament. In the first ten years of the twentieth century, he edited Hungarian economic journal *Közgazdasági Szemle* and from 1905, he was Director of the Association of Hungarian Industrialist, and from 1913 Director of Hungarian Commercial Bank. In 1919 he was arrested by the revolutionary socialist government. He was a member of the Hungarian delegation at the Peace Treaty negotiations in Paris. From December 16, 1920, until September 27, 1921, he was Minister of Finance. Hegedüs' stabilization plan did not succeed; he suffered from it personally and spent years hospitalized after a nervous-breakdown. Rab (2017), and https://novekedes.hu/elemzesek/arckepek-a-magyar-panteonbol-hegedus-lorant-a-reneszansz-penzugyminiszter-5ce0665011324, accessed 22 April 2020.

p. 11)—who sees familiarity in economic policymaking in 1919 and 1989—considered Rašín a grand Czech politician. In the words of a British diplomat and author Robert Bruce Lockhart (1887-1970), Rašín "stood out among the Finance Ministers of Central Europe like a giant in Lilliput." Lojkó (2006, p. 209). Similarly, high respect was provided by the interwar journalist Ferdinand Peroutka (1895-1978), who lauded Rašín insistence on revaluing the country's finances "as an example of quiet heroism, an unpopular but desperately necessary step. A long chapter depicts Rašín himself as an energetic man of action for whom the republic should have been grateful." Orzoff (2009, p. 192).

In summary, he was an economic and political authority who influenced the modern Czech state and left the heritage of stable currency, the role the Czech koruna keeps till today.

Karel Engliš (1880–1961)[15]

He was born in a small village near the city of Opava, into a poor family. He studied at the Law Faculty of the Charles University under Albín Bráf, where he graduated in 1904. He continued at the University in Munich, where he accompanied a young count from the Czernin family. In Munich, he listened to lectures of Ludwig Joseph Brentano (1844-1931), a representative of the younger German historical school.

After doctorate, Engliš became a senior lecturer at the Czech Technical University in Brno, and in 1911 became an associated professor at Brno University. In Brno, he also entered political life and was elected into the Moravian Provincial Assembly. In the last days of World War I, he was in Prague to represent Moravian interests. He was involved in forming a new political party (National Democratic Party) and was delegated by this party to the Revolutionary National Assembly and later became a member of the first Czechoslovak Parliament.

Even after Rašín's death, the Czech governments continued with the deflationary policy and faced a business slump. In the government of Jan Černý (1874-1959), Engliš became the Minister of Finance. He resigned from this position as he opposed deflationary policies, arguing that the appreciated Czechoslovak crown led to a weakening of the economy in the mid-1920s. At the end of 1925, he again became a Minister of Finance. He stayed in

[15] Doležalová (2018), Koderová (2011), Paulík (2004), Vencovský (1990), Vencovský (1997), Vencovský (2000), Bažantová (2016).

this position till 1931, except for 1928–1929. During these years, he favored weaker domestic currency, which was opposed by the more conservative central bank leadership. After the resignation of Vilém Pospíšil, Engliš was appointed the Governor of the Czechoslovak Central Bank. During the Great Depression, Engliš preferred that the country abandons the gold standard and devalues its currency. However, he also opposed an active central bank policy supporting economic growth. Engliš supported the devaluation of koruna in 1934, which led to the resignation of the leadership of the Central Bank, including the Governor, Vilém Pospíšil. Koderová (2011).

In 1919, after the establishment of the Masaryk University in Brno, Engliš became one of its professors and the first Chancellor. Later he was appointed as a professor of the Faculty of Law of Charles University. He worked there till the Nazis closed Czech universities in 1939.

After World War II, Engliš continued his work at the Faculty of Law and became a Rector of Charles University in 1947. After February 1948, the new regime forced him to resign and to leave the University. Communists stopped to pay out a pension to him and ordered Engliš to move out of Prague to his native village. He died forgotten entirely in the new socialist reality. Similar destiny waited for the members of the Brno School of Economics, Miloš Horna (1897–1958), Vladimír Vybral (1902–1980), and Alois Král (1902–1991), of which Engliš was the founder. The communists destroyed the school Engliš attempted to build, persecuted its members, removed their books from libraries, and closed in 1950 the Law Faculty of Brno University. Bažantová (2016, p. 236). Rehabilitation of Karel Engliš happened after the break-up of socialism, he had received the Order of T.G. Masaryk in memoriam, and in his native village, his statue was unveiled. [16]

His teaching and contribution were besides other topics, also in developing teleological economic theory. He argued that one could grasp economic phenomena conditioned on the ability to identify purpose or objective in economic agents' behavior. Engliš' approach to economic theorizing was unique in the emphasis on the philosophical aspects.

[16] A student of Engliš, František Vencovský, tried to rehabilitate Engliš already in the late 1960s, Koderová (2011, p. 82). Vencovský succeeded after the fall of socialism when Engliš' work became again discussed. A university was established in Brno and named after Karel Engliš. In the 1990s, Vencovský also published manuscripts of Engliš, and have published studies on the work of Engliš, for example, Vencovský (1990).

Namely, he wanted to build economic theory closely related to Kant's noetics. Engliš recognized not only the positive world (as it is) and the normative world (as it should be) but also the world as wanted by economic participants. Engliš summarized his teleological ideas in different works, one of them was *Malá Logika* (Small Logic) published in 1947 by the Prague publishing house Melantrich. His book consists of six parts. Only the last two deal with specific economic topics as value and rationality. The first four parts present Engliš' theory of knowledge, logical propositions, the system of logic, the order of thought, and methodology of science. In the introduction, Engliš mentions that this work pre-empts the more extensive work, *Velká Logika* (Large Logic), expected to appear in Spring 1948. Unfortunately, the Communist coup d'etat took place in February 1948, and they liquidated this work of 1600 typewriter pages. Vencovský (1990, p. 899).

Among his significant works, one finds *Soustava národního hospodářství* (System of the National Economy), published in 1938 in Praha by Melantrich. Engliš argued that an economic system is never purely individualistic or purely solidaristic. However, he considered the economic system based on individualism as a natural one. As people are not primarily solidaristic, then an economic system based on solidarity would need to be introduced into existence only by force, thus "longing for freedom is the strongest opponent of communism."[17] The introduction of the founding elements of one system into the other might prove disastrous. For example, the right to employment would prove disastrous in a capitalist system. Engliš developed his position on this issue not only on the abstract level but also on the practical steps of economic policy. For example, he argued that the role of equilibrium prices determined by supply and demand is crucial for attaining high labor productivity. Consequently, systems with controlled prices would lead to distortions to productivity and, as such, would survive only as a temporary system. His critique of the solidaristic system also presented after World War II undoubtedly irritated communist ideologues.

The conflict between Rašín and Engliš reminds similar controversies in England after World War I between Churchill and Keynes concerning the

[17]This citation follows Vencovský (1990, p. 902); the original work of Engliš is Hospodářské soustavy (Economic Systems), Prague Všehrd 1946, page 148.

reconstruction of the gold standard.[18] Rašín, similarly to Churchill, represented directly or indirectly, the interest of the financial sector. Rašín argued that a new republic needs a commitment to gold, which should be entirely credible. He would prefer an overvalued currency and attempted to drive the price level somewhat to a lower level. Engliš was closer to viewpoints of export and manufacturing capital, facing the negative consequences of deflationary policies.

Karel Engliš was a renowned economist, known to his peers and involved in discussion with them concerning his work. Bažantová (2016) documents the sources of Engliš' polemics with Emil Lederer, Walter Weddigen (1895–1978), Oskar Engländer (1876–1937), Aleksander D. Bilimovich (1876–1963), Hans W. Ritschl (1897–1993), Ludwig von Mises (1881–1973), Arthur Spiethoff (1873–1957), and Oskar Morgenstern (1902–1977).[19] Most of these polemics happened in German language scientific journals, as *Österreichischer Volkswirt*, *Jahrbücher für Nationalökonomie und Statistik*, *Zeitschrift für Nationalökonomie*, and *FinanzArchiv*. Engliš also published in the Czech language, especially in *Obzor národohospodářský*.

Imrich Karvaš (1903–1981)[20]

Karvaš was an influential Slovak researcher, professor of the Comenius University in Bratislava, Governor of the Central bank (Slovenská národná banka), and a political prisoner of both the fascist and communist totalitarian movements. His life story is distressing, even if typical of social scientists and intellectuals who faced the radical political mass movements.

Imrich Karvaš was born into a notary family in Levice district, which today belongs to the southern part of Slovakia. From 1921 Karvaš began

[18] This does not mean that we consider Karel Engliš a Keynesian, clearly not, as during his career, he faced disputes with important Keynesians as Josef Macek and Jaroslav Nebesář (1882-1958). Engliš was a strong supporter of liberal economic policies, possibly, with some state interventions.

[19] For example, Bilimovich (1931) and Bilimovich (1933) did not agree with the position taken by Engliš that the main difference between natural sciences and economics lies in the fact that the former belongs to the causal sciences while economics belongs to the teleological sciences. Bilimovich's critical review of the work of Engliš sparked a polemic between them. Bilimovich argued that despite the teleological character of economic activities, it might not be accurate to claim that economics is not a causal science. Sušjan (2010, p. 211), Engliš (1932), and Engliš (1933).

[20] Tkáč (2005), Leková (2008), Hlavatý (2003), Horváth (2002), Horváth (2011).

his studies at the newly established Law Faculty of the Comenius University in Bratislava. During his studies, he visited the French universities of Grenoble in 1923 and Sorbonne in 1924. In 1925 he graduated with the law degree and continued to study in Strasbourg during the academic year 1926–27. In the early 1930s, Karvaš visited as researcher Berlin and London. In 1934 he became a member of the Econometric Society and defended his habilitation; in 1937, he visited Stanford university. In 1937 Karvaš was promoted to an extraordinary professor at Comenius University, and in 1940, he became a full professor.

Between 1926 and 1938, he was editor of *Hospodárske rozhľady* and co-founder of the bi-weekly *Politika*. Between 1926 and 1930, Karvaš worked as general secretary of the Chamber of Commerce and Industry in Bratislava, and in 1930–33 he was secretary of the Union of Slovak Banks. Furthermore, in 1932–38 Karvaš was the general secretary of the Institute of National Economy of Slovakia and Ruthenia (Národohospodársky ústav Slovenska a Podkarpatskej Rusi). He participated in the fourth Congress of Pan European Union in Vienna. In 1932 Karvaš co-organized the meeting of young social activists in Trenčianske Teplice. Karvaš remained far from the rising radical Slovak nationalist movement but shared nationalists' dissatisfaction with Czechoslovakia's economic developments.

After the Munich agreement, Karvaš joined the government of General Syrový as a minister representing Slovak ethnic, functioned as Minister of Industry and Commerce. After Germany militarily occupied Bohemia, Karvaš moved back to Slovakia. In March 1939, after the break-up of Czechoslovakia, the new Slovak Minister of Finance Mikuláš Pružinský (1886–1953) began preparations for establishing the central bank. Karvaš, while staying in Bratislava, was asked to participate as an expert and joins the meeting at Reichsbank in Berlin in March 1939. In April 1939, he became the Governor of the Central Bank. Schvarc and Schriffl (2010) and Karvaš (2001)

During the war, Karvaš tried to support Slovak national interests against the interests of the Reich. Furthermore, he was involved in the preparation of the Slovak national uprising, technically by helping to move currency reserves from Bratislava to Banská Bystrica, the center of the uprising. He also kept contacts with the Czechoslovak government in emigration in London. As a result of these activities, the German security service arrested him. The military court sentenced him to death in February 1945. He is moved to Dachau and later to Flossenburg, where he survived the end of the war.

After World War II, the Czechoslovak court evaluated Karvaš' activity during the war and found him not guilty of crimes of collaborations with occupying forces. In 1946 he became a Dean of the Law Faculty of the Comenius University.

After communists took power in 1948, Karvaš was arrested in 1949 and sentenced by a military court for a two-year prison term. In 1953 the communist authorities forcibly moved him from Bratislava to a hilly town in the High Tatras. He was again arrested in 1958 and sentenced to seventeen years in prison and property loss in a fabricated case of espionage and treason. During this last prison term, his health significantly deteriorated. The reforms of the Prague Spring led to his rehabilitation in 1968.

Karvaš began to publish at a young age. In 1929 he published a study of the international monetary order with particular emphasis on French inflation and stabilization in the 1920s. In 1929 he published a more detailed study discussing on what conditions countries returned to the gold standard in the 1920s.

From the early 1930s, we see a gradual movement of Karvaš from liberal belief toward belief with emphasis on the role of the state as a crucial player in the economy. One observes this change, already in Karvaš (1932) dealing with the cartels' impact on the business cycle. Karvaš (1933) is an influential study comparing the Czech and the Slovak development paths. Karvaš (1937) is a theoretical survey on the role of time in economic theory. From 1939 through 1944, Karvaš published a variety of short studies on monetary policy and the role of the central bank during the war, for example, Karvaš (1940). His final academic publication appeared in 1947. It was republished in Karvaš (1999) as a two-volume book titled *Základy hospodárskej vedy* (The Foundations of Economics). Together with Briška (1943), this book represents the foundation of Slovak economic thought as these were the first-quality economic textbook published in the Slovak language from domestic authors.

Elemér Hantos (Hecht) (1880–1942)[21]

Hantos was an economist, politician, and a prolific writer on Central European economic affairs. He was born in Budapest, graduated from Lyceum in Sopron, studied Law at Budapest University, and later at Leipzig and Cambridge. He was a member of the Hungarian Parliament in 1910–1918 and worked as a Secretary of State at the Ministry of Trade before the end of World War I. Hantos also edited Hungarian monetary review, *Pénzügyi Szemle*. Also, for a short period, he was the president of a private Post Office Saving Bank. He earned a doctorate in public administration and law and became a university professor from 1929.

After World War I, Hantos was disappointed by the situation in which the newly emerged Central European and Balkan states raised barriers to trade and decreased cooperation. Hantos began to organize different activities which potentially were to improve collaboration between these states. In this spirit, he later founded Central European Institutes in Vienna, Brno, and Budapest. In Hungary, Hantos participated in the democratic opposition. This political position made his efforts more difficult as foreign government representatives typically pointed out that he had little domestic support. Piahanau (2018, p. 46). Hantos was also a supporter of Hungarian-Czechoslovak reconciliation. Piahanau (2018, p. 45)

Furthermore, Hantos founded in Geneva Centre d'Études de l'Europe Centrale. Hantos was also one of the representatives of Mitteleuropäischer Wirtschaftstagung, with members including Richard Dolberg (1888–1972), Governor of the Austrian National Bank Richard Reisch (1866–1938), or the Czech economic minister Rudolf Hotowetz (1865–1945). These activities aimed to improve economic and trade cooperation among countries of Central Europe, or on a broader scale among the Danubian nations. Hantos, in his work, addressed a variety of economic, monetary, and political issues, but also he cared for sectoral issues, especially for agriculture and transportation. He has written a large number of books, some of them were translated into different languages as Hantos (1904, 1925a, 1925b). Besides, Hantos participated in different movements to dismantle customs barriers. Other known personalities involved were Charles Gide

[21] Németh (2010), Jeřábek (2011), Piahanau (2018), Zsugyel (2009), http://www.hantosprize.org/biography.htm, accessed 14 October 2019. We quote Németh (2010) from the English translation of his article available on the internet.

(1847-1932), later Belgian Prime Minister Paul van Zeeland (1893–1973), and Edmond Giscard d'Estaing (1893–1981). At one of these events, the first Central European Economic Conference (I. Mitteleuropäische Wirtschaftstagung) on September 8–9, 1925, in Vienna accepted the resolution criticizing the isolation of small national economies.

During the war and especially in the early interwar period, his activities point to a thoughtful economist who understood that the weakening of the Central European space might lead to the loss of sovereignty of these states in the subsequent developments. From a different ideological position, Milan Hodža proposed increased cooperation of Central European nations to contain economic nationalism. Hodža considered federation as a measure to resist pressure from larger countries, from the West as well as the East. Hodža, while in support of the principle of the national sovereignty of small Central European nations, argued that this should not mean their isolation, but, a basis for cooperation. Hodža summarized his ideas for cooperation among Central European nations in his book, Federation in Central Europe, published by Jarrolds in London, 1942. Múdry-Šebík (1968).

Hantos visited Central European countries and had discussions, for example, with leading Czech politicians Eduard Beneš and Kamil Krofta. Piahanau (2018, p. 46). The new states which emerged after the end of the world war—even if based on national sovereignty principle—were still left with significant minorities, especially Germans, Hungarians, and others. There was an accepted mechanism for the protection of minorities accepted in Versailles to which countries subscribed in principle. However, there were constant problems with its implementation. (Németh, 2010). Hantos was not a representative of the interest of minorities (as majority nations often considered him) but had in his vision a general improvement of the destiny of Central Europe.

Hantos believed in one form or the other that cooperation and even confederation among Central European states is vital for their independent survival.[22] He acknowledged that the Monarchy provided

[22] In the 1920s, Hantos accepted an active role in elaborating on the economic program of the Pan-European Union by Coudenhove-Kalergi. He submitted a draft recommendation to the first Pan-European Congress in Vienna in October 1926, concerning the importance of transportation. Németh (2010, p. 3, we follow the English translation of this paper). Trencsényi (2017, p. 171) writes that Hantos' efforts to reconstruct economic cooperation among countries of Central Europe and beyond "was a step toward Paneuropa that is a broader framework of economic and political integration."

economically stable conditions for the development of these nations, but in the interwar period, power politics prevailed, and advantages offered by the organizational structure provided by the Monarchy were lost. He believed that Central Europe should provide foundations for an economic unit representing economic, currency, and transportation union, which would endure the pressure of large states. Hantos understood that the basis of the collaboration should be economic interests as those persuade people in the best way that solidarity among Central European nations is possible.

Hantos considered a failure to abandon the unified monetary policy, which was successful in Monarchy times. Replacing the Monarchy's monetary stability, followed by the introduction of new currencies, brought devaluation and instability to most post-Habsburg lands. He also suggested establishing a cartel of central banks for a common currency with leaving the treasury activities in the hands of sovereign states. He also called for the re-organization of transport in Central Europe by proposing railway alliances and other forms of transport cooperation. "The system of commercial contracts in Central Europe, the Central-European transport network, the Central European credit system, and the Central European currency system has been destroyed. Central Europe has survived only in geographical terms, and its present national, economic, and social fragmentation requires an organization more than ever before." Hantos wrote in spring 1926 in his work *Das Kulturproblem in Mitteleuropa*. Verlag F. Enke, Stuttgart, 1926 p. 32, (quotation based on Németh 2010, p. 7).

Jeřábek (2011, p. 129) describes Hantos as a Central European per se, who felt nostalgia after the Monarchy but also wanted to sustain the economic power and the culture of Central Europe. Jeřábek, analyzing Hantos' lectures and activities in Brno and Prague, writes that Hantos emphasized that the Central European states must introduce and put into action the project of regional integration without the support of large countries. Also, in a lecture in Brno in October 1933, Hantos said that Danubian states could not remain the territory for conflicts among large nations. Jeřábek (2011, p. 130).

Hantos believed that there were historical-cultural ties among these nations that—despite strong nationalistic tendencies—could provide a basis for their economic cooperation. In this spirit, he founded institutes in different cities to provide research output, which would help to strengthen common economic and cultural features in these lands. "The resources to make the Central European Institute into a valuable, unifying organization are: vivid exchange of ideas at conferences, as in the press, and in literature; closer relations in all scientific and technical fields; exchange of teachers in the different disciplines, and the involvement of students in their mutual educational institutions." *Das Kulturproblem in Mitteleuropa*. Verlag F. Enke, Stuttgart, 1926 p. 35 (quotation based on the English translation of Németh, 2010, p. 8). Hantos wanted to take measures to guarantee personal contacts between scientists and scientific institutions and different societal and professional groups. His idea was that the Central European Institute's headquarter would rotate among different cities and that there would be branch offices in principal cities of Central Europe.[23]

Németh (2010) discusses the first World Economic Conference organized by the League of Nations in May 1927 in Geneva. At this Conference, Hantos delivered a text dealing with economic issues in Central Europe in which he concluded that "no intelligent person would think any more of restoring the former Central European political system. However, given the current situation, any reasonable person must raise the question, whether it was right to destroy the economic community forged together by generational traditions and by the powerful forces of nature, because of power interests" *Die Weltwirtschaftskonferenz. Probleme und Ergebnisse*. G. A. Gloeckner, Verlagsbuchhandlung in Leipzig, 1928 p. 131 (quotation based on the English translation of Németh, 2010, p. 9).

Hantos' efforts run against the interest of large countries. England and France, who were 'in charge' of Central Europe in the first decade after the war, did not have developed economic relationships with the region and never became decisive trading partners. Thus, space was emptied for Germany to enter, which from the early 1930s happened through bilateral clearing account trade agreements. With the consequent emergence of Germany and the Soviet Union as world powers, the small countries—defended so vehemently by Hantos—entered into political projects they could not resist. Suddenly, it was not only the nationalism of individual new states that opposed collaboration among Central European economies, but such collaboration went against large countries' interests. Any

[23] Spirit of Hantos is somehow alive in the Central Europe Foundation, which values those who worked to improve Central European nations' cooperation. Jeřábek (2011, pp. 130-131) considers Hantos a forerunner of George Soros with his emphasis on education in the Central European region and the creation of educational institutions and cooperation. The Central European Foundation, which keeps alive the spirit of Hantos, awarded its prize to different intellectuals, including George Soros.

form of Danubian cooperation would counteract military interests of Germany, and later of the Soviet Union. His attempts to re-create Central European states' economic cooperation failed as political powers entered the Central European space, and found weak, fragmented, non-cooperative small states.

Ákos Navratil (1875–1952)[24]

His father was an eminent surgeon who, in the 1890s, elevated the family into the aristocratic status. Also, his younger brother became a famous surgeon. His older sister married Lóránt Hegedüs, an influential economist and member of the government after World War I, whom we have already introduced.

Navratil studied at the Law Faculty of Budapest University, where he obtained a doctorate in 1899. Among his professors, one finds Béla Földes, Gyula Pikler, and Lajos Láng. In 1895/1896, Navratil also studied at Berlin University, where he listened to Gustav von Schmoller, Adolph Wagner, and Georg Simmel lectures.

From 1903 he was a professor at the Law Academy in Kassa, where he taught economics, finance, and Hungarian commercial law. From 1905 he took on a position at Kolozsvár (Cluj-Napoca). During Kolozsvár years, he visited Wieser, and Böhm-Bawerk. From 1918 he returned to Budapest University (Budapesti Királyi Magyar Tudományegyetem, later named Budapesti Pázmány Péter Tudományegyetem), where he took the position of Béla Földes. Navratil applied for a vacant position after Béla Földes became a provisional minister of economy in 1917. As Láng Lajos (1849–1918) passed away, there were two open positions, and Navratil and Károly Balás (1877-1961) promoted to these positions. Hild (2007, p. XV). At Budapest University in two academic years, he served as a Dean, and in the academic year 1941/1942, he was the Rector of the University. Hild (2007). In 1939 he became a member of the Hungarian Academy of Sciences. His inaugural lecture to the Academy of Sciences was entitled *Régi igazságok és új elméletek* (Old Truths and New Theories).

Navratil is one of the influential representatives of the Hungarian economic thought after Berzeviczy and Kautz. He was a deep thinker who tried to incorporate different social concerns into the economic theory, especially moral, political, and legal aspects. These days, historians of

[24] Hild (2007), and various.

economic thought still quote Navratil's work, primarily when dealing with the emergence of legal order and its connections to economic development. Pearson (1997, p. 40) quotes Navratil's work from 1905: "One of the most important facets of economic life … is the influence by means of which the economic phenomenon cultivates—or at least contributes to the development of—the external order of social collaboration, i.e., to the legal order. … Society intends either to enforce the laws that are favorable to a particular course of economic development, or else to use the legal order to obstruct the advance of a different course of economic development." This work is entitled *Wirtschaft und Recht: Ein Beitrag zur Theorie der sekundären wirthschaftlichen Erscheinungen*, (Economy and Law: A Contribution to the Theory of Secondary Economic Phenomena), published in *Zeitschrift für Ungarisches Offentliches und Privatrecht* (Journal for Hungarian Public and Private Law) 11, pp. 273-305.

In the German-speaking lands, Navratil belonged to the line of thought that included Menger's call for social science of institutions and Böhm-Bawerk's work on the connection of legal and economic issues. These continental developments in both legal and economic scholarship entered later into the British political economy. Pearson (1997). Surányi-Unger (1927, 2013, p. 47), in his monumental review of the history of economic thought, also cited Navratil's paper from 1905 discussing Navratil's classification of economic phenomena based on the fact whether they were independent of the legal order or originated from it.

Navratil was a subtle thinker who accepted new views only after substantial scrutiny. He would stay at the position of suspicion to new theories, during his lifetime, including socialist views. However, he published on topics that were typically on socialists' agenda as labor's welfare, insurance of workers, cooperatives, and other socio-political issues.

In 1898 he published his first longer study on Adam Smith entitled *Smith Ádám rendszere és ennek bölcseleti alapja* (System of Adam Smith and Its Philosophical Foundation). In 1901 he published the book *A gazdasági élet elemi jelenségei* (Basic Phenomena of Economic Life). In 1918 at Grill Károly publishing company, he issued a volume entitled *Valutánk helyreállítása* (Restoration of Our Currency), where he warned against an increase of the state's role in the after-war period.

In 1933 he published the first volume of *Közgazdaságtan* (Economics), and in 1939 he published the second volume. Navratil was an admired teacher, one finds among his students Tamás Balogh and Miklós Kaldor, who later gained eminence in emigration.

Farkas (Wolfgang) Heller (1877–1955)[25]

Heller was born in Budapest. In 1895, Heller enrolled into the Faculty of Law of the Budapest University (Királyi Magyar Tudomány-Egyetem Jog- és Államtudományi Kara). He received his doctorate in 1900. At the university, he was influenced by Béla Földes and Lajos Láng, an author of a widely used book on the history of statistics. From 1898 he worked at the Chamber of Commerce in Budapest, from 1901 till 1914 at the Ministry of Agriculture.

Heller struggled to achieve appointments at scientific or academic institutions. The Law Academy in Košice (Kassai Királyi Jogakadémia) rejected his application. Also, at Cluj Academy (Kolozsvári Ferencz József Tudományegyetem), they postponed his application for habilitation for an extended period. At that time in Cluj, Navratil was in charge. It seems he opposed Heller's application. Sipos (1990, p. 31). It appears that the more conservative Navratil considered Heller a progressive, but that was only one aspect of this issue. Sipos (1990, p. 37) writes in detail about the appointment procedure. He describes the influence of large aristocratic families and members of the Church hierarchy who influenced the Minister of Education, who had the right to make such appointments.

He prepared a detailed study about the marginality concept for the Hungarian Academy of Sciences, and he won the competition with this work in 1903. He published this work in 1904 as *A határhaszon elmélete* (The Theory of Marginalism). As an applied economist, Heller was trying to create a synthesis between the Austrian and German schools. Madarász (2000). There is the view in Hungarian economic thought represented, for example, by Bekker Zsuzsa that influential representatives of economic thought in Hungary in most cases did not belong to a particular school, but rather were 'középutas,' which means they followed the middle way among different economic theories. Such an approach puts additional pressure on the economist as he needed to be deeply involved in different

[25] Sipos (1990), Mátyás (1998), Madarász (1980/2000), Sipos (2005). His family originated from Prussia and Silesia. His father, August (Ágost) Heller (1843-1902), whose mother tongue was German, became a member of the Hungarian Academy of Sciences in 1893. His work *Geschichte der Physik von Aristoteles bis auf die neuste Zeit*, Stuttgart 1882-1884, was reprinted in 1965 in Wiesbaden by Sändig Verlag, and in 2013 in Hamburg by Severus Verlag. His younger brother Erik Heller (1880-1958) was a lawyer and a member of the Hungarian Academy of Sciences from 1934. A relative from his mother's side is Pál Bolberitz (1941-), an eminent Hungarian professor of theology.

methodological approaches to walk the subtle middle way. Surányi-Unger (1927, 2013, p. 67) nicely documents this point when discussing Heller's contribution: "Although he resembles Wieser in his insistence on the theory of marginal utility and in the formal structure of his doctrine, he is also anxious to do justice to the tenets of other schools. He resembles Spann in his emphasis on organic thought at the expense of atomism. Like Diehl, Amonn, and Oppenheimer, he stresses the social, legal, and authoritative elements of economics. Following Cassel, he bases his theory of distribution on his theory of price; and he resembles some of the American writers in his conception of capital. By reconciling such different tendencies and by some of his own researches, Heller manages to produce a well-rounded system."

Heller was also a noted historian of economic thought. In 1943 he published, by Gergely R. in Budapest, *A Közgazdasági elmélet története* (History of Economic Thought). Botos (2019, p. 1392) mentions that the book's English translation, together with the translator, fell victim to bombing during World War II. This work bases its structure, in the first sections, on differences among specific schools of thought. Later in the book, different economic fundamental concepts are explained through the eyes of history of thought as value, price, income distribution, money, trade, and cycles. Also popular was his *Közgazdasági lexikon* (Lexicon of Economics) published in 1937 by Grill Károly in Budapest, and translated into several languages.

References

Aldcroft, Derek, and Steven Morewood. 1995. *Economic Change in Eastern Europe since 1918*. Aldershot: Edward Elgar.

Aldcroft, Derek. 1997. *Studies in the Interwar European Economy*. Aldershot: Ashgate.

Amsden, Alice H. 2018. *Imperialism, in The New Palgrave Dictionary of Economics, The Third Edition*. London: Palgrave Macmillan.

von Balás, Karl. 1927. Ungarn. In *Die Wirtschaftstheorie der Gegenwart*, ed. Hans Mayer. Wien: Springer.

Bažantová, Ilona, ed. 2003. *Alois Rašín ˇceský politik, právnik a národohospodář, (Alois Rašín, Czech Politician, Lawyer and Economist)*, 24. Praha: CEP, Centrum pro ekonomiku a politiku.

———. 2016. Czech Economist Karel Engliš and his Relation to the Austrian School in the First Half of the 20th Century. *Prague Economic Papers* (2): 234–246.

Bideleux, Robert, and Ian Jeffries. 2007. *A History of Eastern Europe: Crisis and Change*. 2nd ed. Abingdon and New York: Routledge.

Bilimovič, Aleksandr. 1931. Begründung der Teleologie als Form des empirischen Erkennens. *Zeitschrift für Nationalökonomie* 2: 296–301.

———. 1933. Meine Antwort an Herrn Prof. Dr. Karel Engliš. *Zeitschrift für Nationalökonomie* 4 (4): 521–526.

Berend, Iván T., and György Ránki. 1972. *A magyar gazdaság száz éve.(Hundred Years of Hungarian Economy)*. Budapest: Kossuth Könyvkiadó és Közgazdasági és Jogi Könyvkiadó.

Berman, Nathaniel. 1995. Economic Consequences, Nationalist Passions: Keynes, Crisis, Culture, and Policy. *American University International Law Review* 10 (2): 619–670.

Botos, Katalin. 2019. 20. századi híres magyar közgazdák (Famous Hungarian Economists of the 20th Century). *Magyar Tudomány* 180 (9): 1390–1395.

Briška, Rudolf. 1943. *Národné hospodárstvo: Teória a politika (National Economy: Theory and Politics)*. Bratislava: Družstevné vydavatelstvo a kníhkupectvo.

Deák, István. 1990. *Beyond Nationalism: A Social and Political History of the Habsburg Officer Corps, 1848-1918*. New York: Oxford University Press.

Dellheim, Judith, and Frieder Otto Wolf eds. 2016. *Rosa Luxemburg: A Permanent Challenge for Political Economy. On the History and the Present of Luxemburg's 'Accumulation of Capital'*. London: Palgrave Macmillan.

Doležalová, Antonie. 2018. *A History of Czech Economic Thought*. Abingdon and New York: Routledge.

Dornbusch, Rudiger. 1992. Monetary Problems of Post-Communism: Lessons from the End of the Austro-Hungarian Empire. *Weltwirtschaftliches Archiv* 128 (3): 391–424.

Drápela, Martin. 2007. *Život Aloise Rašína a jeho přínos pro stabilizaci a rozvoj české ekonomiky (Life of Alois Rašín and his Contribution for Stabilization of the Czech Economy)*. Brno: Masarykova Univerzita, Pedagogická fakulta.

Engliš, Karel. 1927. Tschechoslowakei, in Hans Mayer ed. Gesamtbild der Forschung in den Einzelnen Ländern. In *Die Wirtschaftstheorie der Gegenwart*, ed. Hans Mayer. Wien: Springer.

———. 1932. Bilimovičovy námitky proti teleologické teorii národohospodářské (Bilimovič's Objections to the Teleological Theory of National Economy). *Obzor národohospodářský* 37: 585–609.

———. 1933. Zum Problem der Teleologischen Theorie Der Wirtschaft. *Zeitschrift Für Nationalökonomie Journal of Economics* 4 (2): 220–242.

———. 1938. *Soustava národního hospodářství: věda o pořádku, v kterém jednotlivci a národové pečují o udržení a zlepšení života. (System of National Economy: Science about the Order in Which Individuals and Nations Care for Improving Their Life)*. Praha: Melantrich.

Fehér, Ferenc. 1989. On Making Central Europe. *Eastern European Politics and Societies: and Cultures* 3 (3): 412–447.

Hantos, Elemér. 1904. *The Magna Carta of the English and Hungarian Constitution: A Comparative View of the Law and Institutions of the Early Middle Ages*, Kegan Paul, Trench, Trubner and Co. (reprinted Lawbook Exchange Ltd in 2005).

———. 1925a. *Das Geldproblem in Mitteleuropa*. Jena: G. Fischer.

———. 1925b. *Die Handelspolitik in Mitteleuropa*. Jena: Verlag von Gustav Fischer.

———. 1926. *Das Kulturproblem in Mitteleuropa*. Stuttgart: Verlag F. Enke.

Havránek, Jan. 1997. *Ďejiny Univerzity Karlovy III (1802-1918). History of Charles University III (1802-1918)*. Praha: Karolinum.

Hild, Márta. 2007. Bevezető Navratil Ákos válogatott tanulmányaihoz (Introduction into Selected Studies of Navratil Ákos). In *Régi igazságok és új elméletek a közgazdaságtanban*, ed. Navratil Ákos, VII–XLVII. Budapest: Aula Kiadó.

Hlavatý, Egon. 2003. Profesor Imrich Karvaš—vedec, národohospodár, politik a pedagóg. (Professor Imrich Karvaš—Scientist, Economist, Politician and Educator). *Ľudia, Peniaze, Banky, Zborník z konferencie*, NBS: 475-482.

Hodos, George. 1999. *The East-Central European Region, An Historical Outline*. Westport: Praeger Publishers.

Holman, Robert. 2003. Alois Rašín, konzervativní ekonom (Alois Rašín a Conservative Economist), in Bažantová, Ilona (ed)., 33-38.

Horváth, Július. 2002. The State of Economics in Slovakia. In *Three Social Science Disciplines in Central and Eastern Europe: Handbook on Economics, Political Science and Sociology (1989-2001)*, edited by Max Kaase and Vera Sparschuh, co-edited by Agnieszka Wenninger. Berlin: GESIS/ Social Science Information Centre (IZ) and Budapest: Collegium Budapest Institute for Advanced Study.

———. *2011*. Imrich Karvaš. Life and Work. *Lecture at the Slovak Central Bank*.

Jeřábek, Miroslav. 2011. Spiritus agens středoevropského hnutí Elemér Hantos a jeho publicistika—"Das Schicksaal des kleines Staates" (1939), (Spiritus Agens of the Central European Movement: Elemér Hantos and His Publication—"Das Schicksaal des kleines Staates" (1939)). *Slavica Litteraria* 14 (1): 127–135.

Karvaš, Imrich. 1932. *Vliv kartelov na konjunktúru. (On the Influence of Cartels on the Business Cycle)*. Bratislava: Knihovňa Právnickej fakulty Univerzity Komenského, Sväzok 38.

———. 1933. *Sjednocení výrobních podmínek v českých zemích a na Slovensku. (On Equalization of Conditions for Production in the Czech Lands and Slovakia)*. Praha: Sbor pro výzkum Slovenska a Podkarpatské Rusi.

———. 1937. *Problematika času v hospodárskej teorii. (Problem of Time in the Economic Theory)*. Bratislava: Práce Učené společnosti Šafaříkovy v Bratislavě, Svazek 24.

———. 1940. Slovenská národná banka vo svetle funkcie cedulového ústavu. (Slovak National Bank in Light of the Functions of Central Bank) Zvláštny odtlačok z časopisu (Special Imprint of the Journal). *Právny obzor* XXIII (1): 1–16.

———. 1999. *Základy hospodárskej vedy*. (Foundation of Economic Science) Bratislava. 2nd edition, first published in Martin 1947. Veda.

Karvaš, Milan. 2001. *Môj otec Imrich Karvaš. Život a dielo národohospodára, ktorý dosiahol na vrchol i celkom na dno, (My Father Imrich Karvaš. Life and Work of an Economist.)*. Budmerice: Rak.

Klaus, Václav. 2003. 80 let od smrti Aloise Rašína (Eighty Years from the Death of Alois Rašín) in Bažantová, Ilona (ed)., 11-13.

Klima, Arnošt. 1993. The Czechs. In Teich and Porter (eds), 228-247.

Koderová, Jitka. 2011. František Vencovský a Karel Engliš—dvě významná výročí (František Vencovský and Karel Engliš—Two Important Anniversaries). *Český finanční a účetní časopis* 6 (1): 81–93.

Kowalik, Tadeusz. 1987. Luxemburg, Rosa (1870–1919). In *The New Palgrave Dictionary of Economics*, ed. John Eatwell, Murray Milgate, and Peter Newman. London: Palgrave Macmillan.

———. 2003. *Introduction into Rosa Luxemburg (1913) The Accumulation of Capital*. London; New York: Routledge.

Krameš, Jaroslav. 2016. *Profesor Albín Bráf a jeho žáci: (česká národohospodářská škola Bráfova) (Profesor Albín Bráf and His Students: Bráf's Czech School of National Economy)*. Prague: Národohospodářský ústav Josefa Hlávky.

Landau, Zbigniew. 1968. The Reconstruction of Polish Industry after World War I. *Acta Poloniae Historica* 18: 1.

———. 1983. Inflation in Poland after World War I. In *Inflation through the Ages: Economic, Social, Psychological, and Historical Aspects*, ed. Nathan Schmukler and Edward Marcus, 510–523. New York: Brooklyn College Press.

Leková, Andrea. 2008. Prejavy slovenských regionalistov na stránkach časopisov Politika a Zem v 30. rokoch 20. Storočia. (Speeches and Opinions of Slovak Regionalist in Journals Politika and Zem in the 1930s). *Historický zborník* 19 (2): 35–50.

Lojkó, Miklós. 2006. *Meddling in Middle Europe, Britain and the 'Lands Between' 1919-1925*. Budapest, and New York: Central European University Press.

Luxemburg, Rosa. 1913. *The Accumulation of Capital. First published in Routledge Classics 2003*. London, New York: Routledge.

Madarász, Aladár. 2000. Schumpeter's Theory of Economic Development. *Acta Oeconomica* 25: 337–356.

Mátyás, Antal. 1998. Adalék Heller Farkas elméleti munkásságához (Contribution to Heller Farkas Theoretical Work). *Közgazdasági Szemle* XLV: 738–746.

Maxwell, Alexander. 2009. *Choosing Slovakia, Slavic Hungary, the Czechoslovak Language and Accidental Nationalism*. London, New York: I. B. Tauris.

Meyer, Henry Cord. 1955. *Mitteleuropa in German Thought and Action 1815-1945*. The Hague: Martinus Nijhoff.

Múdry-Šebík, Michal. 1968. Milan Hodza and Federation in Central and Eastern Europe. In *Czechoslovakia Past and Present*, Volume II, Essays on the Arts and Sciences, ed. Miloslav Rechcigl Jr. The Hague and Paris: Mouton.

Németh, István. 2010. Hantos Elemér közép-európai alternatívája az 1920–1930-as években, (Central European Alternatives by Hantos Elemér in the 1920 and the 1930s). *Valóság* 1: 35–50.

Orzoff, Andrea. 2009. *Battle for the Castle, The Myth of Czechoslovakia in Europe, 1914–1948*. Oxford; New York: Oxford University Press.

Paulík, Tibor. 2004. Karel Engliš. *BIATEC* 12 (8): 21–25.

Pécsi, V. 1985. A Few Problems of Financing Economic Development in Hungary before 1945. In *Economic Development in Hungary and in Finland: 1860-1939*, ed. Tapani Mauranen, 121–142. Helsinki: University of Helsinki.

Pearson, Heath. 1997. *Origins of Law and Economics, The Economists' New Science of Law, 1830-1930*. New York: Cambridge University Press.

Piahanau, Aliaksandr. 2018. Unrequited Love? The Hungarian Democrats' Relations with the Czechoslovak Authorities (1919–1932). *Hungarian Studies Review* XLV (1–2): 21–60.

Rab, Virág. 2017. A családi kapcsolatok reprezentációja Zsindely Sándor Hegedüs Loránt élete és munkássága című tanulmányában (Representations of Family Relations in Sándor Zsindely Work on the Life and Work of Loránt Hegedüs). In Hild M, and A. Madarász edited, *Az "ezüst pillanatok" nyomában: tanulmányok Bekker Zsuzsa emlékére* (The 'Silver Moments', Essays to Honor Zsuzsa Bekker). Pécs: Kronosz Publishing pp. 57–80.

Ránki, György. 1983a. Inflation in Post-World War I East Central Europe. In *Inflation through the Ages: Economic, Social, Psychological, and Historical Aspects*, ed. Nathan Schmukler and Edward Marcus, 475–487. New York: Brooklyn College Press.

———. 1983b. Inflation in Hungary. In *Inflation through the Ages: Economic, Social, Psychological and Historical Aspects*, ed. Nathan Schmukler and Edward Marcus, 524–530. New York: Brooklyn College Press.

Sargent, Thomas. 1982. The Ends of Four Big Inflations. In *Inflation: Causes and Effects*, ed. Robert E. Hall, 41–98. Chicago: University of Chicago Press.

Schvarc, Michal a David Schriffl. 2010. Vznik Slovenskej národnej banky a konštituovanie slovenskej meny vo svetle nemeckých dokumentov (Establishment of Slovak National Bank and Slovak Currency in Light of German Documents). *Historický časopis* 58 (1): 99–121.

Šiková, Kateřina. 2017. *Alois Rašín a jeho role v rámci první republiky* (Alois Rašín and His Role during the First Republic). Západočeská univerzita v Plzni, Fakulta filozofická.

Sipos, Béla. 1990. *Heller Farkas*. Budapest: Akadémiai Kiadó és Nyomda Vállalat.

———. 2005. Heller Farkas tudományos pályafutása és irodalmi munkássága. (Scientific Career and Literary Work of Heller Farkas) http://mek.oszk.hu/05400/05405/html/kozgazfirkak0004.html, accessed 03 January 2019. In *Közgazdaságtani (f)irkák, 68. Magyar közgazdászok arcképvázlatai: Karvasy Ágoston, Kautz Gyula, Heller Farkas, Háy László,* edited by István Mihalik. Budapest: Neumann Kht.

Stokes, Gale. 1991. The Social Origins of East European Politics. In *The Origins of Backwardness in Eastern Europe: Economics and Politics From the Middle Ages Until the Early Twentieth Century*, ed. Daniel Chirot, 210–251. Berkeley, Los Angeles; Oxford: University of California Press.

Surányi-Unger, Theo. 1927. *Die Entwicklung der theoretischen Volkswirtschaftslehre im ersten Viertel des 20. Jahrhunderts.* Jena: G. Fischer. English translation 1932 (1st edition). London: George Allen & Unwin. 2003 (republished). Economics in the Twentieth Century, edited by Edwin Seligman. London and New York: Routledge.

Sušjan, Andrej. 2010. Historicism and Neoclassicism in the Kiev School of Economics: The Case of Aleksander Bilimovich. *Journal of the History of Economic Thought* 32 (2): 199–219.

Swianiewicz, Stanislaw. 2008. Wladyslaw Marian Zawadzki. In *The New Palgrave Dictionary of Economics*, ed. Steven N. Durlauf and Lawrence E. Blume, 2nd ed. London: Springer.

Teichova, Alice. 1983. A Comparative View of the Inflation of the 1920s in Austria and Czechoslovakia. In *Inflation through the Ages: Economic, Social, Psychological, and Historical Aspects*, ed. Nathan Schmukler and Edward Marcus, 531–567. New York: Brooklyn College Press.

Tkáč, Marián. 2005. Imrich Karvaš. *Národná banka Slovenska BIATEC XIII* 4: 29–34.

Trencsényi, Balázs. 2017. Central Europe. In *In European Regions and Boundaries, A Conceptual History, edited by Mishkova, Diana and Balázs Trencsényi.* New York and Oxford: Berghahn Books.

Turnovec, František. 2002. Economics—Czech Republic. In *Three Social Science Disciplines in Central and Eastern Europe: Handbook on Economics, Political Science and Sociology (1989-2001)*, edited by Max Kaase and Vera Sparschuh, co-edited by Agnieszka Wenninger. Berlin: GESIS/ Social Science Information Centre (IZ) and Budapest: Collegium Budapest Institute for Advanced Study.

Van Duin, Pieter C. 2018. Political Life is Dying Out': Rosa Luxemburg's critique of Bolshevism and the Bolshevik Revolution. *Studia Politica Slovaca* 11 (1): 20–34.

Vencovský, František. 1990. Englišovo teleologické pojetí národohospodářské vědy (Engliš's Teleological Understanding of Economic Science). *Politická ekonomie* 38 (8): 897–908.

———. 1997. *Dějiny českého ekonomického myšlení do roku 1948. (History of Czech Economic Thought till 1948)*. Brno: Nadace Universitas Masarykiana, Nauma.

———. 2000. Z vědeckého odkazu Karle Engliše. K 120. výročí narození (From Scientific Message of Karel Engliš. 120 Years from His Birth). *Finance a úvěr* 50 (7-8): 430–444.

Zawadzki, Ladislaus. 1927. Polen, in Band 1., Gesamtbild der Forschung in den einzelnen Ländern. In *Die Wirtschaftstheorie der Gegenwart*, ed. Hans Mayer. Wien: Springer.

Zsugyel, János. 2009. Hantos Elemér útja a Nagytér-gazdaság eszméjétől a Közép-európai országok átfogó együttműködésének gondolatáig. *Polgári Szemle* 5 (6): 78–93.

CHAPTER 4

The Socialist Period

After World War II, gradually, Central European lands got under the influence of Soviet Russia. After the war, for some years, the alliance of the West with the Soviets continued. It was important for the Soviets as they suffered substantial labor and assets losses during the war. To pressure the introduction of socialist regimes in Central Europe immediately after the war seemed hazardous for the Soviets as it would break up the cooperation with the West. However, the Soviets needed guarantees that after World War II, the new Central European governments would be acceptable to both sides of the alliance. West accepted this Soviet request, which for all practical purposes, meant that the weight of the local Communist parties radically increased, and the position of the pre-War anti-communist parties considerably weakened.[1]

In Central Europe in the interwar period, the local communist parties were not part of governments, except the short period after World War I in Hungary. In other words, in the interwar period, the Soviet export of revolution was not successful. Only in Czechoslovakia, the Communist Party had a relatively stable position in the Parliament. After World War II,

[1] Volokitina, Murashko, Noskova, and Pokivailova (2002) write that "Building its foreign policy, Moscow relied on the idea of spheres or zones of influence. Eastern Europe was in the sphere of special interests of the Soviet Union. ... Moscow considered the Eastern European region mainly as a security belt of the Soviet state." (pp. 28–29).

J. Horvath, *An Introduction to the History of Economic Thought in Central Europe*, Palgrave Studies in the History of Economic Thought, https://doi.org/10.1007/978-3-030-58926-4_4

a different atmosphere arose concerning the advancements of Soviet socialism. In Czechoslovakia, especially the Czech part, many intellectuals have seen socialism as a natural choice seeing their country as a bridge between West and East. The situation was different in Poland, as Connelly (2000, p. 78) observes: "For most Polish intellectuals, by contrast, the Bolshevik Revolution and its aftermath had represented an existential danger."

After World War II, but before the communist coup d'etat, these economies became primarily state-controlled with a large share of state ownership. Illusions in the potential future triumph of collective economy were widespread. The process of gradual destruction of the institution of private property has begun. Dissatisfaction with liberal democracy and the market economy made it easier to prepare for the change in society's power structure. Before the Communist take-over, the prevailing societal atmosphere favored the pursuit of policies as planning, nationalization, and government intervention. The pressure from Communists make this trend to accelerate.[2]

After the Great Depression and World War II, the prevailing perception was that liberal capitalism and liberal democracy did not deliver sufficient social progress. Such a view was typical not only of the radical communists but generally of the political left. The Soviet victory over Nazism helped to increase the prestige of Marxist teachings, which seemed like an alternative to liberal capitalism.[3]

From the early 1950s, Central Europe's economic processes began to resemble the Soviet experience with forced industrialization, preferences for heavy industrial sectors, and increased military production. These

[2] Also, illusions concerning the cooperation of the new socialist countries emerged when an international organization for trade and economic cooperation, Comecon (Council for Mutual Economic Assistance), was founded in the late 1940s. After the war, the economic cooperation between the Soviet Union and an individual small country in the Soviet orbit was provided mainly on a bilateral basis. The Soviet leadership was interested in the creation of such an organization, as Comecon, to have more leverage over the management of the economy of the emerging "world socialist system." Orlik (2015). According to Nekipelov (2000, p. 275), in memoirs of Nikita Khrushchev, it is stated that economic aid to these countries served advertising purposes and aimed to demonstrate the infinite possibilities of the Soviet Union.

[3] However, after these societies embraced the Soviet type of communism large number of intellectuals would potentially agree with the opinion of George Kennan (1979, p. 423): "The Austro-Hungarian Empire still looks better as a solution to the tangled problems of that part of the world than anything that has succeeded it."

investments pooled a large number of unemployed and rural underemployed to higher productivity sectors, and also increased substantially the educational level. Besides, these countries, initially, had access to low-priced Soviet natural resources and achieved in the first decade of socialism high growth rates.[4]

The reform's idea was to change the model of the economy introduced in the first years after the socialist revolution. There was a constant tension between Party orthodoxy and economic experimentation. Webb (2008, p. 250) The continuous reform of the socialist economic mechanism was an essential part of the discourse, which served as a pretext for political changes. Direct discussion of the political order was a taboo for most of the times. Adibekov (1994).

Economists played a role in these discussions and implementations of these reform plans. In the following sections, we say a word about these efforts and later present the life and work of some influential personalities.

Economic Thought During Socialism

Political autocratic regimes restrict the space of economic thought and analysis. The autocratic socialist ideology complicated the picture as it was challenging for economists to link analytical patterns of thought with ideological devotion. One finds among economists different levels of ideological devotions to socialism. In rare cases, there were those dedicated to the teachings of the founders of communism. However, understanding the socialist reality was not helped by such a dedication as Marx's teachings did not concern with the economies' actual working after the socialist revolution. For Marx, these were to be happy times, which would unleash the people's productive potential.

[4] A stylized description of the socialist economy's original model includes national (socialized) ownerships of means of production and collectivization in agriculture. Other features of this model were the concentration of decision making at higher levels of hierarchy, central plan oriented toward quantities as opposed to prices, and monopoly of foreign trade. Local and firm initiatives were suppressed, especially in the beginning of the socialist period. The inefficiency of these economies became a fundamental issue, symbolized by low technical sophistication, quality of the products, high consumption of energy, and growing pollution. According to the socialist ideology, the central planning system was to prevent the occurrence of inefficiencies. Except, possibly, of hard-core revolutionary communists, most felt a persistent need to reform the socialist economic model.

For one group of economists, the commitment to the socialist revolution meant social mobility upward. For another group, the devotion to the socialism originated in the search for an antagonistic answer to fascism. The scientific pretensions of communists influenced both the faithful and the opportunists. These scientific pretensions permitted them to weaken their doubts concerning the autocracy and provided emancipation from the traditional morality's restraints.

Socialism brought discontinuity of economic thought to these countries. In the early years—in all countries—the old generation of erudite professors was replaced by young devotees of the new regime. The former renowned economists lost their jobs, emigrated from their native country, or were forced out from positions guaranteeing research and teaching. Such destiny did not await only for anti-socialists, who, in the communist jargon, represented the theoretical expression of the bourgeoisie. However, these regimes also persecuted socialist economists, especially in purges in the late 1940s and the early 1950s. These purges were a part of the general policy to weaken political rivals, strengthen the inner-party discipline, and undermine party and society's dissent.

Intriguingly, positions of individual economists changed in time concerning their devotion to the communist orthodoxy. For example, some of the young communist economists who moved upward in the 1950s later took the positions in favor of the reform vis-à-vis the communist power orthodoxy. A typical example could be Wlodzimierz Brus (1921–2007), who stood on orthodox positions in the early 1950s. Later, in Brus (1961), he compared the two socialist models, the orthodox and the market-oriented. Brus considered the market-oriented model based on the Lange-Lerner approach as more efficient, for which the official orthodoxy heavily criticized him, and after some time, he left Poland.

The Appendix collected information about economists who left their country of birth for the West. However, others had similar stories as Brus, and remained in internal, domestic emigration. We shortly present the story of Vladimír Kadlec (1912–1998), who belonged to those young people, who without teaching and research background, after 1948, replaced the economic and law professors. His story began when the authorities expelled prominent professors from the law faculty of Charles University, "the law faculty's action committee scrambled to cover the gaping vacancies by appointing Communist officials from the ministries who had no experience in university teaching." Connelly (2000, p. 128). One of those was Vladimír Kadlec, who joined the law faculty from the

Economic Department of the Presidential Chancellery. Intriguingly, Kadlec got utterly transformed. As a Rector of the Economic University in Prague and a Minister of Education became an influential supporter of the Prague Spring, was expelled from the Communist Party, became a signatory of Charter 77, and converted to a dissident intellectual.

The socialist period brings a new face to economic thought. Publications appear, which serve a purely apologetic role. Primarily, professors of the political economy of socialism and capitalism publish works without individual spirit, responding to the political regime's requirements. These authors were not scientists of integrity who wrote what they thought was the truth. However, even in these writings, the reader, from time to time, encounters cunning observations. Interestingly some of these writers did not agree with what they had written and published. Such publications helped the spiritual decline of the message of the socialist revolution.

At economic universities, both in Prague and Bratislava, the presentation of capitalist economies' functioning was quite at a low level. One of the reasons for such a state of affairs was that economic universities in Prague and Bratislava were under robust ideological scrutiny. In the 1970s and the 1980s, the university education of economics in Czechoslovakia provided students with a light-weight comprehension of Marxist doctrines with limited vocabulary not sufficiently complex to understand the behavior of economic agents under both socialism and capitalism. These schools did not teach authors who had a deeper understanding of the socialist reality as Kornai, Kalecki, Goldmann, and others. Instead, the teaching of the political economy of socialism and capitalism prevailed, full of inferior concepts. Aligica and Evans (2009, p. 28). The situation was different in Warsaw and Budapest.

One distinguishes reputed theoreticians of the socialist economies who were knowledgeable of the mainstream economic thought and understood the workings of the socialist economies. Also, there were personalities with an impact on the reform discourse of the socialist economic mechanism and policy. Among them, we point out scholars and policymakers as János Kornai, Oscar Lange, Michael Kalecki, Josef Goldmann, Karel Kouba, Cezary Jozefiak (1932–2007), Jozef Pajestka (1924–1994), Zdzislaw Sadowski (1925–2018), Kazimierz Laski, Edward Lipinski, Ota Šik, György Péter, Rezső Nyers (1923–2018), András Köves (1938–), László Antal (1943–2008), Márton Tardos (1928–2006), and a large number of others. Such lists are entirely subjective as one would need to consider a particular historical situation in which these reform and theoretical works happened. Wagener (1998a) and Wagener (1998b).

In Czechoslovakia, the 1960s economic reform was a vital part of political awakening but was interrupted after the 1968 invasion. In Hungary and Poland, a more reformed atmosphere prevailed until the end of the socialist system. Hungary introduced the New Economic Mechanism in the late 1960s, and it progressed—at times regressed—but still made out of Hungary a relatively thriving socialist economy. Czechoslovak political leadership was, except for the second half of the 1960s, always more orthodox than the Communist Party leadership in Budapest or Warsaw. During the 1970s and the 1980s, the Polish and Hungarian economic thought was more in line with what the Czechoslovak orthodox officials called a 'revisionist thought.' In this period, socialist orthodoxy prevailed in Czechoslovakia, but stimulating work on socialist reality emerged under the surface. Interestingly, orthodox Czechoslovak policymakers had a higher resentment to open inflation and were more reluctant to take up debt denominated in hard currencies, as policymakers in Poland and Hungary's reform-economies.

Reforms in the Framework of Czechoslovakia of the 1960s

After February 1948, the radical Soviet model did not fit the Czech industrial lands even if it was a bit closer to the under-industrialized Slovakia's needs. In this early communist period, revolutionary politics dominated economic policy discussions. Communist Party tried to establish its legitimacy to the general public with social policies guaranteeing full employment, especially welcomed by the lower classes, and persecution of some segments of the former upper classes and free-minded intellectuals. In this period—maybe until the second half of the 1950s—one cannot see any substantial attempt to reform the economic system. Later, when the dominance of the revolutionary politics weakened, attempts of economic policy reforms emerged.

In Czechoslovakia, the early pressure for reform emerged when other Central European countries introduced first reform-minded steps in the middle of the 1950s. However, in this period, the Czechoslovak orthodoxy was able to control the potential reform forces, except for some mild reform measures around 1958. In the 1950s, the national product's high growth rates characterized the Czechoslovak economy and made the orthodox thought foundation. It seemed that the mobilization of factors of production and high rates of investment guarantee high growth rates. However, from the early 1960s, the labor productivity and later the growth slowed down, and the first evident crisis emerged. Such a situation provided a stimulus for reform. The reform period begins and culminates in the activities of 1968.

In the early 1960s, a discourse controlled by the party orthodoxy differentiated between the extensive and intensive periods of socialist development. Official rhetorics interpreted the reform steps that emerged in the 1960s as a need to improve the extensive system, which has supposedly fulfilled its historical role of introducing a higher societal order. This concept of development allowed to avoid criticism of the policies pioneered in the 1950s.

In the Czechoslovak context, the main characteristics of the extensive system were forced industrialization with the development of backward regions (mostly in Slovakia), ideological appeals to mobilize resources, a complete change of foreign trade relations, changes in income and wealth distribution, monetary reform, and introduction of mandatory labor employment. The reform ideas concentrated on incentives to structural adjustments to achieve greater efficiency in the use of inputs. Also, reform steps were to shift the policies toward consumer-oriented sectors. Still, in the 1960s, the reform discourse did not question the priority of central decisions. However, it was possible to think about a mix in which the central authorities make the crucial planning decisions, and enterprises and customers are guaranteed more autonomy.

The orthodox interpretation of the early 1960s considered officials' incompetence and external shocks as factors that led to the crisis.[5] The orthodox ideology rested on the idea that socialist production should not be governed by markets but by planning. The orthodoxy made this view a dogma as this way of thinking was connected with the argument that economic reform, that is, weakening of central planning, undermines the communist party's political power. The reformers needed to address these issues so that such dogmas were not seen as endangered. The reformers proposed to increase the autonomy of managers of socialist enterprises.

[5] Such views were close to Kurt Rozsypal (1916–2013), the former first Deputy Head of the State Planning Committee, whom the government removed from his job as a reaction to the crisis of 1962. Rozsypal explained the low performance of the economy by domestic and external factors. Domestic factors included non-realistic plan figures and the inertia of old ways of thinking about a central plan, while as external factors, Rozsypal mentioned worsening of trade relations with China, the Berlin crisis of 1961, and adverse weather conditions.

However, the managers did not welcome such ideas as they could circumvent regulations to their advantage even under the conventional system. The central planners often prescribed the output targets based on enterprises' data, which quickly learned the mastery of providing information for their advantage. Managers of enterprises were aware of real facts of socialist economies, for example, that material deliveries did not arrive in time. "So they would respond by bargaining their plan: demanding more investments and raw materials than the amounts necessary for their targets." Verdery (1996, p. 21).

In the 1960s, the political class eased the pressure on research institutes, and their staff began to present more freely results of their analysis. Thus, one observes a young generation of economists writing with less ideological prejudice, studying Western economic textbooks. Advancement in the Western economic theory affected some economists of socialist persuasion. For example, work that pointed out that it might not be possible to derive collectively rational decisions from individual preferences might not have much impact on revolutionaries who wanted to push their preferences on society. However, it could impact those who believed that the socialist system attempts to implement the "will of the people."

Once the reforms of the 1960s failed, the orthodoxy fiercely criticized the economist reformers and researchers as they took over the discourse and received the support of the public and some sections of the press. Orthodoxy blamed the reform economists for winning the debates.

The late-1980s reformers wanted to re-establish the market economy. The late-1960s reformers wanted to introduce market socialism. In the 1960s, the goal was not a capitalist market system but a combination of the economy's planning character with spontaneous market forces. Planning would lead the economy toward politically agreed social aims, while the market would motivate coordination of economic processes to achieve these social aims. For the socialist firm, that would mean an increase in its autonomy. Firms would still receive planning numbers, but should be motivated to search for different factor combinations of output-mix than those in the plan.

What did the reform process achieve until August 1968? Approximately from 1967 in most firms, targets, that is, suggestions to produce, replaced the old command planning style. The government published guidelines with parameters for sectoral output, export, investment, and wages. There was also a price reform, which led to reduced state subsidies. Wholesale prices were centrally controlled (sectoral price indexes could rise within some pre-specified range) but not necessarily fixed. Kýn (1970, p. 303) mentions that market conditions at the end of 1968 guided around 4% of wholesale prices and 20% of retail prices. The remaining retail prices stayed fixed. In the late 1960s, to a large extent, retained profits and state bank loans financed investments, and investment subsidies declined. There was also some weakening of the monopoly of foreign trade. On the short history of Czech market reforms during socialism. Šulc (1998).

Nevertheless, all of this was interrupted after the invasion of August 1968. This interrupted reform process represented a fabulous cultural, societal period that again made Prague and the whole society, an open European space full of exciting people and events. The socialist market reform process was not an economic success but civilized the rhetorics and space. The reform atmosphere was a positive step toward the development of civil society.

Next, we present some observations concerning the prominent personalities of this period.

Ota Šik (1919–2004)

Šik joined the Communist Party of Czechoslovakia in 1940. Between 1941 and 1945, he was a prisoner in a concentration camp. After 1948 Šik studied at the College of Political and Social Studies in Prague. In the early 1950s, he worked at the Central Political School of the Communist Party, where he translated Marx's Capital into the Czech language. He became a full professor in 1957. Šik (1990), Kosta (2005), Vančura (2014), Šulc (2007), Chytil and Sojka (2003), Horváth and Sommer (2018).

Vančura (2014) describes Šik's work in 1953–1955 at the Political School of the Communist Party. At this time, his work is full of citations of the founders of communist thought (Marx, Engels, Lenin, and Stalin), and it is challenging to differentiate his writings from general communist propaganda. He writes, "It is proven, Comrade Stalin says, that the society is not powerless against the economic laws and that the sphere of action of these economic laws, when recognized, can be limited and used in the interest of society and be adapted like natural forces and their laws." Šik (1953a, p. 31). Even worse, "We planned to manufacture a huge amount of goods in the heavy machinery sector, which completely corresponds to the objective requirements of the development of our economy. However, traitors Slánský et al. managed to plan inadequate, or too low production of heavy metals, castings made of cast steel and heavy plates, essentially needed for the development in heavy industry. Then, necessarily a disproportion had to come." Šik (1953b, p. 9). Both quotations follow Vančura (2014, pp. 6–7). Vančura (2014, p. 6) shows that in these early writings, Šik labels markets as instruments of chaos and anarchy and considers capitalism a lower socio-economic form that suffers from a recurring business crisis. He also considers the Great Depression a natural breaking point documenting the lower status of the capitalist system compared to the Soviet system.

In the 1950s, Šik self-educated himself, especially with a detailed study of Marx. A large number of Marxists who competed with Šik in the political arena never read Marx's works. In interwar Czechoslovakia, the study of Marx's work was minimal, as documented in Nikl (1961). In the ideological discourse, the ease with which Šik quoted the Marxist literature made him a competitive debater in orthodoxy's eyes mostly trained on booklets of Institutes of Marxism-Leninism.

In 1958 he became a candidate member of the Central Committee of the Communist Party of Czechoslovakia, and in 1962 he became a full member of the Central Committee. From 1961 he was the Director of the Economic Institute at the Czechoslovak Academy of Sciences. In 1963, the party leadership commissioned him to design the economic reform with his team from the Economic Institute. The Communist Party officially acknowledged *A New System of Planned Management* (Nová soustava plánovitého řízení) in January 1965. Šik played the central role in developing the economic reform of the Prague Spring, with the contribution of researchers as Karel Kouba, Čestmír Kožušník (1928–2010), Bohumil Komenda (1925–1985), Jiří Kosta, Otakar Turek (1927–), and others.[6]

From April 8, 1968, to September 3, 1968, he was the Deputy Prime Minister responsible for economic reform in the government of Oldřich

[6]Among the leading reform-oriented publications of that time consider Komenda et al. (1963), Komenda (1964), Kožušník (1964), Komenda and Kožušník (1964), and Komenda (1969). Richterková (2013) discusses the contribution of Kožušník to Czech economic thought. Also, already from the late 1950s, quality publications appear based on mathematical optimization, mathematical analysis, output-input analysis, and similar. Among them, we mention Habr (1959), Habr and Korda (1960), Korda (1960), Toms and Hájek (1965), Bouška, Skolka, and Tlustý (1965), Kýn and Pelikán (1965), Toms and Hájek (1967), Korda et al. (1967), Rychetník and Kýn (1968), Rychetník (1968), Toms (1968), Kýn, Sekerka and Hejl (1969), Habr and Vepřek (1972), and Walter and Lauber (1975). Walter (1981) and Habr (1981) provide illustrative thoughts about early development in economic modeling using mathematical techniques. In addition, in the middle of the 1960s, Rumler (1965) published an interesting book on Keynes. Besides, Kaplan (1966) provided an excellent description of the political events.

Černík (1921–1994). After the Prague Spring suppression, the new regime forced him to withdraw from political life; he emigrated to Switzerland. Between 1970 and 1989, he was a professor at St. Gallen. In 1983 he was granted Swiss citizenship. Šik (1990).

In the work Economics, Interest, and Politics, published in 1962, he began to move away from the Stalinist concepts. This book initiated a wave of critical reformist approach toward the dogmatic ideology. He combined Marxist opinions with knowledge of the socialist economic reality to a level that, besides the argument's virtuosity, it was almost impossible for the reader to grasp the main point. In the book, he also included long passages of colorful critique of capitalism, making an impression on the superficial reader that the book belongs to what was otherwise conventional in the socialist Czechoslovakia of the early 1960s. Šik was making the point that interests are antagonistic under the capitalist system, but one can still identify their remnants in the socialist Czechoslovakia of the 1960s. Šik also identifies as one of the sources of the socialist economy's problems, underestimating of the "commodity relations," a concept used by the orthodox ideology to describe the traditional work of the market. Methodologically he contrasts arguments of Marx with arguments of Stalin. Šik (1962 and 1965a).

In the second half of the 1960s, Ota Šik developed a celebrity status. His life story and the changes in his intellectual development characterize the Czech society's encounter with the Soviet influence and document the search for a socialist model, which would reflect the traditions of that society, especially Prague's intellectual milieu.

Šik had become one of the most known proponents of the new economic model and led its implementation in the second half of the 1960s. He also succeeded in popularizing the economic reform. His ability to persuade the country communist orthodoxy to introduce the new economic model at the Communist Party Congress in June 1966 and later at meetings in June and July in 1968 is remarkable. In the struggle with the party orthodoxy, he was quite modern. For instance, he appealed to the general public to receive additional support for his economic reform plans. He appeared on national television and traveled across the country, addressing large meetings, especially with industry workers. Šik supported the introduction of workers' councils, but with substantially less power than was the case in Yugoslavia. He envisaged workers councils' role in choosing an upper-level enterprise management and voting on profit distribution.

He was able to combine his position in the elite party circles with popularity in the general public. Šik gained national fame in a television series documenting the Czechoslovak economy's low economic performance compared with Western countries. Šik (1972) presents his television lectures in the English language. He criticized the extensive growth of the early 1950s as inefficient, characterized by misallocation of resources and restrained consumption. As a result, he argued, West German workers needed much less working hours to buy basic foodstuffs. Even if not entirely correct from the economic point of view, such arguments resonated positively with the public and created the backbone of support for his reform ideas.

One of his principal works written in Prague was *Plan and Market under Socialism*, published in 1965 in the Czech language as *K problematice socialistických zbožních vztahů* (On Socialist Commodity Relations). In 1967 an English edition, translated to different languages, was published under the title *Plan and Market under Socialism*. The book had several editions that were gradually more critical of the authoritative central planning in socialist Czechoslovakia. Šik in the book supports replacing the strict central economic command by the system of material incentives with strengthening the allocative functions of markets. In this books, Šik (1965b, 1967 and 1968) is critical of Stalin's understanding of the working of the socialist economy. Šik presents this critique in the socialist jargon without questioning the existence of the socialist order. He accepts the thesis that the 1950s represented extensive development, which laid the socialist order's foundations. In the 1960s, however, this system was not to continue in the old form. In other words, the extensive development meant capital accumulation through forced savings and increased labor input, but both of these factors later faced decreased productivity. Consequently, intensive development should substitute the extensive development. An additional reason for intensive development is the massive increase in the extensive period's capital/output ratio. All of this led to a waste of valuable inputs, a rise in intermediate and final products' inventories. In the intensive pattern, the productivity of factors and efficiency should improve, which was to be achieved by decentralization and relying on socialist market relations within the framework of more flexible central planning.

In the 1967 edition of the book, he presents market relations as necessary for further development of productive forces under socialism. He does accept planning as, in principle, a better allocation mechanism than the market but criticizes the forms of administrative control peculiar to the Czechoslovak reality of planning. Also, in this work, he implicitly brings the idea of profit motivation of socialist enterprise into the forefront. In his jargon, he observes conflict between value and use-value, which means conflict between the enterprise's production costs and demand for the product. He also criticizes the planners' low level of expertise and the low level of computational ability to handle complex planning problems.

The review of his book in the June edition of the *American Economic Review* in 1968 was favorable. However, the reviewer, Jan M. Michal, remarked: "Those readers versed in the quantitative economic analysis will feel somewhat frustrated by Professor Šik's vague, non-interrelated theorems, his failure to define clearly the parameters and the variables of his model, and his apparent lack of profound knowledge of modern Western theory." Other parts of the review are devastating: 'Šik seems to have no clear concept of production and consumption functions. He also seems to make no clear distinction between static partial market equilibria, a general equilibrium, and an insufficiently identified concept of optimality. What is especially surprising in his discussion of the blessings of (hopefully competitive) socialist markets is the virtual absence of inquiry into the problems of external economies and diseconomies.' (p. 600). This review article supports the point that in a specific historical national context, the author's contribution is not to the development of the universal theory of economic science but the development of the quality of domestic discourse.

In the 1970s and the 1980s, Šik became a symbol of revisionism in different socialist countries, much criticized by the official orthodoxy. Katsenelinboigen (1980) writes about an episode at the Soviet Institute of economic and mathematical modeling at the end of 1971. Associates from the Central Committee of the Communist Party arrived at the Institute and emphasized the need for a stronger ideological front of Soviet economic thought. They condemned researchers from the Soviet Academy for not criticizing sufficiently hard the Czech economists' ideological mistakes, notably of Šik. Even in March 1988, the Hungarian Academy of Sciences organized a conference *Alternatives of the Socialist Economic Reforms*. Ota Šik was invited to this conference and accepted the invitation. However, he was later disinvited by the Hungarian organizers who did not wish to offend the Czechoslovak authorities who protested Šik's presence.

The public considers the liberal Czech reformers of the early 1990s as radicals and the reformers of the 1960s as moderate. However, one finds unexpected radicalism in the reform of the second half of the 1960s. For example, Ota Šik questioned the legitimacy of the Communist Party's rule if better living conditions and solutions of social contradictions were not guaranteed. Šik argued that if the Communist Party did not succeed in these tasks, the danger existed "that the people would begin to turn their backs on socialism." To prevent this, he demanded that "the Party should give up its monopoly on power" and fundamentally change its work style. One cannot consider such views as moderate. Wilke (2010, pp. 343–344)

Ota Šik progressed from Stalinist young intellectual to a mature leader of the Czech reform and established Western professor of the 'third way' of societal order. His views evolved as increasingly critical of what he called 'bureaucratic economy,' unable to respond to technological and other modern consumer society requirements. In his later writings, he—in opposition to the 'bureaucratic economy' model—presented the 'new economic model.' During his stay in Switzerland, Šik has published a variety of books, which sought a "third way" between the imperfections of both statist Marxism and neoclassical mainstream, or between socialism and capitalism. Šik became one of those economists who sought to combine markets' allocative efficiencies with social, planned, and more equitable milieu. Such an approach was his 'third way.' Somehow he remained close to the socialist ideal, even if the real socialist life was further from it. After the break-up of communism, Šik appeared in Prague, was positively welcomed. However, his economic proposals, as that privatization should introduce worker/employee stock ownership, were forcefully condemned by the new liberal elite, who have seen him as a symbol of the old world.

Jozef Goldmann (1912–1984)[7]

Goldmann was born in Karlové Vary. In 1931–1934, he studied economics at University in London and law at a German-speaking university in Prague. In 1936 he received a doctorate in law at the Law Faculty of Charles University. During World War II lived in Great Britain, first as a worker later as an assistant in the Oxford Institute of Statistics, where

[7] Čihák (1997), Doležalová (2018), Turnovec (2002), Havel, Klacek, Kosta, Šulc (1998), Šulc (2007), Klaus (1984). Biographical data follow Zdeněk Doskočil Biografický slovník českých zemí, (Biographical Dictionary of the Czech Lands) Praha 2017, pp. 670–671.

Kalecki was employed. After World War II, the Oxford Institute of Statistics published *Studies in War Economics*, which included four articles of Kalecki and one article of Goldmann. Toporowski (2018, p. 47).

Goldmann belonged to the generation experiencing the Great Depression of the 1930s, the break-up of Czechoslovakia, and the family's death during the occupation. He, similarly to Kalecki, considered socialism as a viable social project. In 1937 he joined the Communist Party, and till 1945 worked in the Sudeten-Deutschen section of the Communist Party of Czechoslovakia. After World War II, Goldmann worked on the two-year Plan (1947–1948) and the Five-year Plan (1949–1953). In Goldmann (1947), he presents the Czechoslovak post-war experience as a possible socialist roadmap for more developed countries. Goldmann, in his 1949 work, argued that "Czech planners were learning by doing, that planning mistakes had to be corrected permanently in terms of real results, that bottlenecks should be overcome by using reliable statistics" Havel, Klacek, Kosta and Šulc (1998, p. 218). One can hardly imagine such a formulation about central planning written by an insider from 1950 onward.

In 1949 he became a Deputy Minister in the State Planning Committee and became Czechoslovakia's representative in the Comecon. He was arrested in 1952 and sentenced in 1954 for twenty years of prison for treason and espionage. The prison term shortened in 1958 to twelve years, and he received an amnesty in 1960. From 1960 till 1963, Goldmann worked as a manual worker in a state auto-parts production company. In 1963 he was rehabilitated.

After rehabilitation, he joined the Economic Institute of the Czechoslovak Academy of Science, where he stayed until his death. His contribution had two different qualities, depending on the context in which the Institute worked. In the first period, basically, until the end of the Prague Spring, Goldmann was active in research of business cycles of socialist economies. This research became widely known and cited. The most known contribution of this period is Goldmann and Kouba (1967)[8],

[8] Karel Kouba (1927–2013) studied at the 1950s at Vysoká škola hospodářskych věd and in 1957 obtained a doctorate (candidate of economic sciences) in political economy. His publications at the beginning of his career included Kouba (1964). From 1964 he worked at the Economic Institute of the Czechoslovak Academy of Sciences, where his leading publications included Kouba (1966), Kouba et al. (1968), and Kouba et al. (1968). In 1969, Kouba became a Director of the Economic Institute. However, as the political atmosphere completely changed, he resigned. From the early 1970s till 1988, he was forced by the regime to accept a low administrative job at a large Prague factory. Even if he was not allowed by the

translated into English and Hungarian. Goldmann was personally less involved in the reform activities of the 1960s. In the second period, from the 1970s until his death, Goldmann continued in scientific research and published valuable works in the atmosphere very different from the 1960s. He also built and guided a group of a newer generation of economists, whose contributions, together with his, represented possibly the best economic research in socialist Czechoslovakia.

In Goldmann and Kouba (1967), the authors discussed the differences between supply-side determined growth models of socialist economies and demand determined models of capitalist economies. This book analyzed the barriers to growth and the relationship between different growth factors and their efficiency impact. They discuss the history of economic growth theories, with particular emphasis on the work of Kalecki, whose model they apply to Czechoslovakia. They explain the socialist economy's cyclical pattern by the in-built mechanism of the socialist planning process, making the final product depend on the growth of inputs, which the primary sectors cannot deliver. This mechanism creates a barrier that slows down growth. In other words, Goldmann and Kouba argued that central planning, which brought high rates of growth in the 1950s, led, in essence, to reverse outcomes in the 1960s. Adam (1995, p. 37) writes that initially, due to their industrialization drive, the socialist countries set ambitious economic growth targets and disregarded their future adverse effects.

Čihák (1997, p. 13) calls the work of Goldmann and Kouba a lightening example of the work in the field of macroeconomics in socialist Czechoslovakia. In the 1960s, Goldmann also used the term quasi-cycle to protect from the ideological critique, which stated that cycle in capitalism was necessary, while in socialism, it only reflected the lack of knowledge of the laws of socialist economies. Klacek and Kupka (2018).

Benáček (2013) and Turnovec (2002) mention that during the normalization, the only place where a student could achieve formal economic training alongside the political economy of socialism was the Graduate School of the Institute of Economics of the Czechoslovak Academy of

authorities to participate in the education and research, he remained a research economist working after the working hours. He participated in seminars at private apartments. However, with Josef Goldmann, he has published in Hungary in *Acta Oeconomica* and a Czechoslovak mathematical economic journal, *Matematicko-ekonomický obzor*. From 1988 he was re-admitted back to the Academy of Sciences. He became a professor in 1990, and from 1991 till 1993 was a Director of the Institute of Economic Studies at Charles University in Prague. Bauer (2005) provides a review of his life and research.

Sciences. The group of younger economists related mostly to the Institute of Economics, especially Miroslav Toms (1944–1988), Mojmír Hájek, Antonín Kotulan, Václav Kupka, Karel Dyba, Jan Klacek, contributed to the enriching of economic knowledge by applying analytical apparatus from the neoclassical theoretical background.

During normalization years, Josef Goldmann himself published and edited a trilogy dealing with the socialist economy's performance. In Goldmann (1975) he published *Makroekonomická analýza a prognóza* (Macroeconomic Analysis and Prognosis), in 1978 *Úvod do makroekonomické analýzy* (Introduction into Macroeconomic Analysis), and in 1985 *Strategie hospodářského růstu* (Strategy of Economic Growth).[9]

Introduction into *Macroeconomic Analysis and Prognosis* was published together with Karel Dyba (1940–), Kamil Janáček (1943–), Jan Klacek (1942–), Václav Kupka, and Ružena Vintrová (1929–2013). The book structure reflects the state of macroeconomics in the 1970s and represents the highest quality Czechoslovak quantitative macroeconomic research produced during the socialist era. In the first part of the book, the individual chapters discuss material balance as a primary instrument of macroeconomic analysis, analysis of macroeconomy as a dynamic process, consumption, production, investment in a socialist economy, and questions of balance of payment and adjustment to payment disequilibria. In the second part of the book, these authors present macroeconomic adaptation issues, equilibrium, growth stability, and macroeconomic efficiency.

In *Strategy of Economic Growth*, Goldmann (1985) analyzed the process of forming goals of the planning process. He argued that goals should not be exogenous to the socialist economy, determined by a superior body, but should be formed in a project discussed at wide echelons of the society.

Goldmann was a prominent Czech economist who worked during the socialist period due to his insistence on keeping the professional level of domestic economic output, not depending on the political context. Čihák (1997, p. 21)

[9] In this time period also other valuable work emerged, some with ideological undertones but still within the professional knowledge of the discipline. Among them we mention Nachtigal (1973), Toms (1976), Klacek and Nešporová (1980), Kotulan (1981, 1982), Dyba and Kupka (1983, 1984), Toms and Mejstřík (1986), Janáček, Klacek and Vintrová (1983), Tříska and Klaus (1988), Klusoň (1988), Dědek (1989), Janáček et al. (1990). In that period in Slovakia Laščiak et al. (1985), Laščiak et al. (1990), among others.

György Péter (1903–1969)[10]

He was born in 1903 in Budapest. His father, J. Gyula Pikler, worked as Deputy Head of the Statistical Office. György Péter studied in Vienna, Berlin, and Trieste, and worked in insurance mathematics till 1936. From the early 1930s, he sympathizes with the communist movement, and from 1935 he became a member of the illegal Communist Party. In 1936, Hungarian authorities imprisoned him and sentenced for fifteen years of prison.[11] In 1944 he escaped from prison.

After World War II, he took the position of the Head of the Statistical Office, from 1948 till 1968. He also held the position of a professor at Economics University in Budapest. In the early 1950s, he re-organized the Statistical Office, which in the spirit of the times meant that he got rid of highly knowledgeable personalities as was Ede Theiss (1900–1979), Dezső Elekes (1889–1965), Dezső Laky (1887–1962), and others. Hegedűs (1994, p. 19). He was active in the organization of demographic studies. Under his leadership, the Statistical Office organized the census of 1949 and 1960. In 1957 study was published *titled Adatok és adalékok a népgazdaság fejlődésének tanulmányozásához* 1949–1955 (Data and Supplements to the Study of Development of the Economy, 1949–1955) in which the Statistical Office published previous more than a hundred confidential reports. Already in 1952, he supported the publication of calculations concerning real wages and real income of households, results of which were in contrast to propaganda views of increasing socialist living standards. Mód (1994, p. 56). He also supported the development of modern sociology by providing data for researchers. Hegedűs (1994, p. 30).

It seems he remained devoted to the socialist movement until his death but slowly changed his way of thinking and became independent compared to other party members. Hegedűs (1994, p. 20) mentions that already in 1952, he went into the clash with political leadership, notably with Ernő Gerő (1898–1980), who did not want to accept information coming out from the Statistical Office concerning decreasing living standards. The fact that during the rule of Horthy, only Mátyás Rákosi and

[10] Kornai (1993), Árvay and Hegedűs (1994), Nyers (1984), Nyitrai (1983), Maltsik (2002), Friss (1995).

[11] Why a son of the upper social class joined the illegal Communist Party remains a mystery to which, in the case of Péter, Borsányi (1994, p. 42) provides some explanation. He also adds that fortunately, the system was corrupt, and wives of prisoners from better-off families visited the family of the officer in charge, and gifts improved the prison conditions.

Zoltán Vas spent more years in prison cemented his position in the after-war communist hierarchy. Hegedűs (1994, p. 17).

His and Kornai's research studies are considered the foundations of the Hungarian reform movement. His earliest reform-spirit writings in the first half of the 1950s preceded the actual reform leaning documents stemming out from the center of the political power. In 1956 he participated in the reform activities, but during the actual revolutionary days, he was not in Hungary. In 1957 he was under political critique inside the Communist Party for holding revisionist views, but as an old party member got a chance for self-critique. He responded to this critique but only reacted to the economic part of it, and did not get involved in self-critical political comments so common for those criticized for contradicting the orthodoxy. Gelegonya (1994, p. 103) argues that in the second half of the 1950s, the ruling apparatus considered him as 'standing close to revisionism.' In the late 1950s, he survived these critiques, partially due to his pre-war party connections. Hegedűs (1994, p. 27) and Gelegonya (1996).

In 1957 the political power established an Economic Committee with the leadership of non-Marxist István Varga (1897–1962), and György Péter was a member of this committee. In 1957, he wrote a supportive article about Kornai' (1959) book on *Over-Centralization* and supported Kornai in his endeavors. Kornai (1994, p. 84) writes that after publishing his book, the socialist orthodoxy criticized him and called his work 'the ideological preparation for the counter-revolution.' In this atmosphere, Péter wrote a positive review of Kornai's work and published it in a pro-party journal. Gelegonya (1994, p. 95) writes that this work was defended as a doctoral dissertation in September 1956 with György Péter acting as the doctoral committee chair. In 1963 he joined the reform teams under the leadership of Rezső Nyers.

The authorities perceived Péter's activity as challenging the political system and led to his isolation. The Politburo of the Communist Party blamed the Statistical Office for not representing the Party leadership's intentions credibly. Also, the Party's leadership criticized that the Statistical Office tended to publish data, which helped anti-communist propaganda. Hegedűs (1994, p. 28).

His first reform ideas appeared in 1954 and 1956 in the journal *Közgazdasági Szemle*. According to Kornai (1994, p. 76), György Péter was the first economist in the socialist camp who presented consistent ideas about the reforms of the central planning economies and preceded writings of Soviet reformers as Evsei Liberman as well as the writings of the Czech and Polish reformers. These were especially publications as Péter (1954) and Péter (1956). Kornai (1992b). Also, thanks to his works, already in the middle of the 1950s, "government experts and other economists were engaged in pioneering discussions of the Hungarian economic mechanism and its problems" earlier than reformers in other Central European countries. Seleny (2006, p. 55).

Hungarian Communist Party approved for the period 1964–1968 preparations for the economic reform. Kornai (1994, p. 77) argues that, in substance, rhetorics, and style, the official reform plan was close to the ideas of György Péter. The official reform documents and ideas of György Péter suggested weakening compulsory plan targets, increasing socialist enterprises' independence, and maintaining societal planning, especially in the sector of investment and foreign trade. Both fully supported public ownership of the means of production and did not mention privatization. Both the official documents and Péter's ideas rejected an increased role for workers' self-management (Kornai 1994). Kornai (1993, p. 92) writes that the ideas of Péter not mentioned in the official reform documents were market-clearing prices and the competition of the supply side for the customers.

The importance of people like Péter can be understood by trying to comprehend the intellectual atmosphere in the 1950s, increasingly determined by simplified Marxist doctrines taught to young apparatchiks. In such a dark intellectual environment, heretics, and Kornai (1994, p. 85) calls Péter a heretic, might play a role as they stand up against prevailing simplified dogmas. Protectors of the socialist order believed that once one part of the dogma weakened, other dogma parts could weaken, too, and thus, the system may collapse. Kornai adds that what matters is not only what is said and how much truth is in it, but also who says it. "Mises and Hayek clearly knew much more about what is the problem with the planned socialist economy than György Péter—but who listened to them in Hungary in the 1950s? Mises and Hayek were open enemies of socialism, clearly biased against the basic institutions of the system." As compared to them, Péter had high credibility in the party apparatus and spoke their jargon; so clearly—they thought—he did not criticize the system because he was against it. Kornai (1994, p. 86). He influenced the mindset of policymakers, that is, influenced their notions of the possible. György Péter played an inspirational role in this respect, and some reform economists considered him the grand seignior of socialist reform. They appreciated him as an economist in a high position who represented the spirit of professionalism in an atmosphere of hierarchy and apologetic writings. His tragic life, most likely he was hard-pressed to suicide, his personality, and impact on a generation of reform economists placed him in an iconic position, probably similar to Ota Šik in Prague.

János Kornai (1928–)[12]

János Kornai, born as Kornhauser, is the son of a prominent business attorney killed by the Nazis. From 1947 till 1955, at the beginning of his career, Kornai worked at the Communist Party daily, *Szabad Nép* (Free People). As a journalist, Kornai writes, became aware of issues of inefficiency in the socialist planning process. Initially, as so many other young devotees of the socialist idea, he did not think about abandoning the concept of a planned economy just improving it. According to Kornai, "Never for a moment did I think that the troubles (with socialism) were systemic, originating in the system itself. On the contrary, while perceiving many problems and faults in it, I was still convinced that socialism was superior to the capitalist system" (2006, p. 51). In 1955 he joined the Institute of Economics of the Hungarian Academy of Sciences.

Gradually, Kornai turned out to be a worldwide intellectual leader in research concerning the socialist economies' actual functioning.[13] Kornai's best-known books include *Overcentralization in Economic Administration*; *Anti-Equilibrium*; *Rush versus Harmonic Growth*; *Economics of Shortage*; *The Road to a Free Economy. Shifting from a Socialist System: The Example of Hungary*; and *The Socialist System. The Political Economy of Communism*. These books were translated into many languages. From 1986 he was a professor at Harvard University. He also had visiting positions at leading American and West European universities.

Kornai has been somewhat skeptical of those parts of the mainstream thought built on deductive principles. His book titled *Anti-Equilibrium, Kornai (1971),* nicely documents his skepticism. "That book was cited by

[12] Lindbeck (2007), Roland (2008), Chikán (2006), Hámori (2012).

[13] Chikán (2006, p. 203) quotes the study of István János Tóth from 2004 who showed that in the 1980s, based on the data in the Social Science Citation Index, Kornai was the most cited economist from socialist countries followed—in a certain distance—by Brus, Šik, and others. Besides, Baron and Hannan (1994) show that in the sociology journals in the early 1990s, Kornai was the most cited economist. Even Yang (2010) heavily cited Kornai in discussion on religious awakening in China under Communist rule, which appeared in a *Companion to the Sociology of Religion*.

Kenneth Arrow as an alternative approach to general equilibrium theory in his Nobel lecture (Arrow 1974), and was regarded as "a very influential book" that in France "was one of the books we all read" and "became part of the common knowledge" (Blanchard 1999); and was considered "the most ambitious enterprise of my entire research career" by the author (Kornai 2007)." Xu (2017, p. 193). However, for some researchers in the socialist world who faced the chaos of central planning and ideological terror of socialist scientific pretensions, the concept of equilibrium provided certainty and made Kornai's work difficult to understand. The concept of equilibrium was in the core of the economic analyses representing the belief that one could understand the world through some permanent balanced structures, which human understanding can reflect. Non-temporary disequilibria seemed outside of the structured analysis.

Kornai seems to start always from an inductive side, analyzing the reality of socialist economies. He based his work on empirical and intuitive observations, which he developed into theories. His approach contrasted with the mainstream economic theory, where after World War II, the importance of deductive principles was emphasized. The mainstream approach made it difficult to understand the socialist economy's actual workings as it built on the institutional framework of Western societies. Besides, mainstream models provided an illusion that actual socialist reforms can succeed, and as Stiglitz (1995) pointed out, the failure of socialist reforms is as much a failure of the mainstream theory as well as of the socialist reform ideas. However, we recognize that mainstream models played an important ideological role in suppressing the influence of communist ideas across the world. In other words, mainstream economic theory as an ideology played a vital role in halting communism's expansion. A large part of the mainstream developed after World War II turned out not entirely useful for understanding differences between capitalist and socialist economies. The mainstream did not deal extensively with the importance of different motivations under diverse property rights systems, and Kornai pointed to these weaknesses.

In his book on *Overcentralization*, Kornai provided evidence of severe efficiency problems in highly centralized command economies with the domination of public ownership and the priority of quantity planning indicators. A famous paper followed, written together with Tamás Lipták (1930–1998)—published in 1965 in *Econometrica, Kornai and Lipták (1965)*—concerning economic planning with quantity indicators, the exchange of information between the higher and lower level of planning institutions, state ownership of the means of production, and a market for consumer goods. Central planners set quantities for the producers, who would report back to central planners the shadow prices for production targets and used resources. This model would require information flow about the real processes happening in the socialist firm. However, as Kornai (2006, p. 146) later wrote: "the reality of the socialist economy is that all items of information are uncertain."

Gradually, Kornai abandoned the research on planning methods as he began to understand that the socialist economy's problems are more profound than central planning problems. He begins to realize that different reform proposals for improvement of socialist economies cannot change the overall excess demand derived from the non-strict financial checks of socialist enterprises.

In 1980 he published *Economics of Shortage*, Kornai (1980), which brought worldwide fame to him. He apprehended that at some markets, shortages prevailed while over-supply characterized some other markets. The reason seemed in the suppressed equilibrating role of market prices. "Excess supply for some goods does not fully "compensate" for excess demand for other goods—because of limited substitutability, or even strong complementarities between goods in excess demand and excess supply. ... It is, therefore, quite reasonable to emphasize shortages as a characteristic feature of real-world socialist economies." Lindbeck (2007, p. 5). For Kornai, shortages in the socialist economy are systematic. Shortages do not appear randomly, and even if prices were the equilibrium prices, shortages would emerge due to the socialist economies' institutional characteristics. This approach is quite close to an Austrian view, as highlighted by Leeson (2008).

Chikán (2006, p. 198) writes about the important political message of the *Economics of Shortage*: "Had Kornai explicitly stated the increase in economic effectiveness required for survival was unattainable without basic changes in property relations (i.e., prevalent private ownership), the book would have never appeared (or at most at samizdat with a concomitant radical reduction in effect). However, hardly anyone reading it failed to grasp that implicit conclusion." Chikán (2006, p. 201) makes a compelling argument that phenomena analyzed by Kornai's *Economics of Shortage* had a character of law and were "necessarily overruling any efforts by economic policymakers." In socialist reality, the state seemed an overwhelming power that seemingly can do anything. Kornai's thoughts helped build a specific skeptical view toward the socialist state's power to change economic subjects' behavior by will. It was an art how to avoid "open ideological confrontations while putting forth unorthodox proposals." Seleny (2006, p. 56).

Some Central European economists raised objections to Kornai's concepts. Soós (1984) pointed out that one should explain the phenomenon of shortage from the supply side of the economy using the inelasticity of the supply side instead of excessive demand leading to shortages. Klaus (1984), Ježek and Klaus (1987), and Klaus and Tříska (1995) consider Kornai's approach as an unnecessary new methodology when the mainstream economic weaponry was sufficient. Hámori (2012) provides a detailed review of different authors concerning the work of Kornai. He reviews the impact of Kornai on Russian policymakers as well as an impact on Chinese economic thought. Gewirtz (2016) describes the influence of Kornai on the beginning of the Chinese economic reforms.

Kornai is an original thinker who analyzed real-world problems faced by the socialist societies. During this process, he was able to shed light on different concepts, some of them, as the soft-budget constraint, became later part of the general knowledge in economic theory. Kornai (1986). Budget constraint is a constraint on the behavior of the economic unit. In principle, in a market economy, expenditures should equal income. However, it is not clear in which period the budget constraint should be hard. In contrast, in socialist planned economies, the budget constraint can be influenced by non-economic considerations, and thus, there could be a spectrum of different degrees of hardness and softness. The softening of the budget constraint is the ability of outside forces to enter the market and relax the relationship between expenditures and income. Van Brabant (1990, p. 164).

The fundamental idea of the soft-budget constraint is that the insolvent capitalist firm will sooner or later go bankrupt, while this is not a consideration for the socialist firm. In other words, the capitalist firm faces hard budget constraint, while the socialist one faces soft budget constraint.[14] The soft budget constraint has a clear implication for the socialist managers' motivation who need to develop good political relations with different hierarchies of power to guarantee protection against bankruptcy. "Since

[14] However, further research has shown that soft budget constraint also appears under the capitalist economic system. Dewatripont and Maskin (1995) formalized the soft budget constraint as a commitment problem within contract theory. A principal will not favor refinancing the project if the project's return is lower than expected. Nevertheless, a principal still might end up refinancing it as he/she considers the initial costs as sunk costs, and only the project's return is considered in the final decision whether to bail out the firm or not.

the budget constraints of firms under socialism are not binding, one understands that they must necessarily meet a resource constraint, that is, experience shortage." Roland (2008, p. 2). In other words: "As a result of the soft budget constraint, firms tend to expand investment and production until they encounter nonfinancial resource constraints (hence shortages)." Lindbeck (2007, p. 6). In a way, this concept has some resemblance to the idea of time inconsistency as the principal might want to re-finance the firm ex-post even if ex-ante there was an intention to avoid such a situation. Interestingly, van Brabant argues that while Kornai is critical of the concept of equilibrium, his interpretation of the concept of shortage can be understood in such a way that the state of shortage reproduces itself or returns into its "normal" shortage state. "This shortage equilibrium, though inefficient, is a state where effective demands and supplies are equalized in every market, and where no agent can achieve a better allocation through his own actions, owing to prevailing institutional and policy constraints." van Brabant (1990, p. 165).

After 1989 Kornai focused on issues of the transition of socialist countries into a market economy. Kornai wrote in 1990 a book entitled *The Road to a Free Economy*, supporting the privatization process with advice toward a gradual path of privatization. Kornai (1990). In 1992, Kornai published *The Socialist System*, where he argued that the centralized political control of the communist party leads to state ownership, control of the property, and influences the process of allocation of resources. Once the communist regime's total power collapses, the centralized economic system also weakens and finally is replaced by private property arrangements. Kornai (1992a).

Kornai played an essential role in efforts to weaken and finally destroy the socialist economic and political order. His work was especially important for economists, intellectuals, and the general public as he provided quality critical arguments toward the everyday reality of the socialist order and even more toward its impossibility for reform and rejuvenation. Importantly, Kornai was able to do it without explicitly calling for the abandoning of the socialist order.

Oskar Lange (1904–1965)[15]

Lange studied law and economics in Poznan and Cracow under the influence of Adam Krzyzanowski (1873–1963). Later he studied in London and in 1934–35 in the United States on a Rockefeller Foundation Grant scheme; he also stayed at Harvard University and worked under Schumpeter's tutorship. He lectured in statistics and economics in Cracow (1927–37), Chicago (1938–45), and Warsaw (1948–65).

Lange's political views were socialist. During World War II, he was involved in the Soviet dealings with the Americans and played a negative political role, as seen by the eyes of American Polonia and the Polish Government in London. Szymczak (1995a, 1995b) documents as Lange became a pro-Stalinist figure in Polish politics, or rather as Soviet political apparatchiks manipulated him into believing that the Soviet Union wants an independent and free Poland. After World War II, he served as ambassador of Poland in the United States (1945–1946) and was a Polish delegate in the United Nations Security Council. Later in Poland, he was a member of the Polish Parliament and a member of the State Council.

Lange's early interest, including his doctoral work, was in the study of business cycles. During his stay in the United States, he lectured about these issues and worked on the business cycle's empirics. He was interested in econometric studies and worked as acting editor of *Econometrica* from 1942 till 1946 after the arrest of Ragnar Frisch and until Frisch resumed his duties. Bjerkholt (1995, p. 763). At this time, his publications included, among others, Lange (1935), Lange (1936), Lange (1937), and Lange (1942).

Lange was profoundly educated both in the mainstream theory as well as in socialist thought. According to Kowalik (2008, p. 2), this knowledge "induced him to make several attempts at a 'major synthesis' and to undertake political actions for a rapprochement between the West and the Communist world, for peaceful coexistence and economic cooperation." Lange studied capitalist economies not only because of scientific interest but also because of his interest as a socialist writer. According to Kowalik (2008, p. 2), Lange initially believed that large corporations represent a movement from the chaos of free markets to a planned economy, that is, to organized capitalism. However, the Great Depression changed his

[15] Dobb (1966), Roberts (1971), Kowalik (2008), Neuberger (1973), Sadler (1977), Szymczak (1995a), Szymczak (1995b).

views as large corporations caused chaos in the economy. Lange was critical of monopolies, saw them as threats to political democracy, and blamed them for generating unemployment. Also, Lange believed that large corporations constrain technological development as innovations bring losses due to capital depreciation. This tendency could not be stopped by laissez-faire and neither by government regulation. "The only effective solution, then, is the socialization of big capital, the introduction of socialism." Kowalik (2008, p. 9).

Lange began to study socialist economics relatively early in his career. One of his first attempts was a joint work with a young economist murdered by Nazis, Marek Breit (1907–1942). The Lange-Breit model from the middle of the 1930s, published in the English language as Lange and Breit (2003), was one of the first reform socialist models. It was close to Soviet models, which emerged after the Bolshevik revolution. Lange and Breit model an economy in which companies are organized by industry into trusts transferred into public ownership. Worker's councils run the trusts, but still, the trusts have lots of autonomy. The Public Bank also limits trusts' autonomy as it supervises the trusts, and closes those who operate at a loss. As trusts work as monopolies, their policies need to be under society's control. The Public Bank also controls foreign trade and allocates capital to trusts. The private sector would still be functioning, especially in agriculture, crafts, and small enterprises. Kowalik (2008, p. 6).

Lange-Breit's approach and later, the more known Lange-Lerner approach reflect Lange's conviction that neoclassical theory is the groundwork of the theory of a socialist economy. For Lange, this was a pillar of his thought. While a large number of socialist thinkers and especially the revolutionaries, ignored arguments of Mises and Hayek about the practical infeasibility of socialism due to the absence of a market for capital, Lange—as a scientist—imagined the socialist economy as functioning rationally.

Lange based his thought on the neo-classical theory despite his socialist convictions. In his world, there is a market in consumer goods and labor, but the government owns the means of production. The planning board sets non-equilibrium prices for producer goods and firms. At these non-equilibrium prices, there will be shortages for one group of products and over-supply for another sending a signal to the central planners to change the prices into equilibrium ones, which they will achieve through trial and error. There was a widespread belief that these equilibria will have similar properties as competitive equilibria in the Walrasian economy in which there is no state ownership of production assets. In Lange's world, consumer preferences are decisive as they are behind the allocation of resources, and there is a market for consumer goods and labor. The Central Planning Board sets the price for the capital goods, and managers of enterprises make production decisions based on these prices. Managers then combine production factors to minimize the average costs, at the industry's level. The efficiency of these steps would lead to equilibrium, similar to the market economy. In Lange's world, then socialist and capitalist resource allocation was corresponding to each other, and the socialist one would have an advantage of the lower social inequality.

Lange's attempts to create a synthesis between Marxist and mainstream theory was an attempt to which he had an intellectual background and capacity. He had an in-depth knowledge of quantitative disciplines and was well versed in the mainstream theory and theoretical socialist economics. Lange argued that the equilibrium economic theory is universal, and "after some adaptation, it could be used for the day-to-day management of a socialist economy, a job Marxist economics was ill-suited to do." Kowalik (2008, p. 12). As if Lange wanted to synchronize the rationality of the economic theory and the Marxist historical materialism.

Once Lange returned to Poland, he faced reality run by Stalinists, who believed in the central command over the economy and did not care about the subtleties of its working. For them, economics was a servant to the revolution. Lange played a negative role during the Stalinization of Polish intellectual life in the late 1940s and the early 1950s. Czarny (2014, p. 96) quotes Lange's talk at the Economist Congress in December 1950: "To live up to the challenges ahead, Polish economics must become a Marxist-Leninist science. To this aim, it must completely overcome the remains of bourgeois thought… which stand in the way rather than contributing to the achievement of the tasks faced by the Polish economy."

Late in his life, he became captivated by the cybernetics and mathematical programming. He has begun to believe that computers could improve the performance of central planning. Lange (1967, p. 158) commented on his discussion with Hayek and Robbins concerning the functioning of the socialist economies. He writes: "My answer to Hayek and Robbins would be: so what is the trouble? Let us put the simultaneous equations on an electronic computer, and we shall obtain the solution in less than a second. The market process, with its cumbersome tatonnements, appears old-fashioned." However, at this time, he also continued with different publications as Lange (1959), Lange (1963), and Lange (1965).

In 1974, Wyzsza Szkoła Ekonomiczna (High School of Economics) was renamed Akademia Ekonomiczna im. Oskara Langego we Wrocławiu (Oskar Lange's Economic Academy in Wroclaw). In 2008, it was again renamed Uniwersytet Ekonomiczny (Economic University), the name of Oskar Lange was left out. Czarny (2014, p. 108).

Michal Kalecki (1899–1970)[16]

Kalecki was born in Lodz, Poland. He was a student at technical universities in Warsaw and Gdansk but never obtained a university degree. From 1929 he joined Lipinski's institute, and after short research work, he received a Rockefeller Fellowship and moved to the West. He stayed first in Sweden and then in England, where he worked at the Oxford Institute of Statistics. After War, he worked at United Nations, and in 1955 he returned to Poland. Kalecki was not involved in the Stalinization of Polish intellectual life.

In Poland, he was involved in the debates over industrialization speed and the relative size of consumption and investment. He undertook research and teaching at the Polish Academy of Sciences and the Central School of Planning and Statistics. He was also in favor of increasing the role to be played by workers' self-management. Kalecki criticized the over-industrialization and the sacrifice of consumption in the first decades after the socialist overturn. While he realized central planning's weaknesses, he was skeptical about the increased role of market mechanism and reforms in the socialist economy. Marxism is somehow his way of thought, not based on the Soviet political interpretation. He observed that the production relationships condition people's behavior and thinking, but it was not the labor theory of value or the theory of exploitation, which guided his thought. Sebastiani (1994, p. 14).

Similarly to Kornai, Kalecki self-taught economics and did not have a traditional training as he self-entered the discipline through the works of Marx, Rosa Luxemburg, and Mikhail Tugan-Baranovsky.[17] To an extent,

[16]Sebastiani (1994), Vaggi and Groenewegen (2003), Czarny (2014), and Sawyer (2008).

[17]Tugan-Baranovsky (1865–1919) graduated from Kharkiv University in 1888. His master thesis for Moscow University was on industrial cycles in Great Britain, and his doctoral dissertation on The Russian Factory, Past and Present (Russkaya fabrika v proshlom i nastoyashchem). His major contribution was Osnovy politicheskoi ekonomii (Foundations of Political Economy) (1917), which went through many editions and attempted to synthesize

this isolated him from the mainstream but helped him to avoid some prevailing preconceptions. In Poland, at a younger age, he worked on the business cycle oriented research, and in 1933, he published a book *Próba teorii konjunktury* (An Attempt for the Theory of Business Cycles), which the literature considers as one of the most influential forerunners of the work of Keynes. Kalecki was maybe the first who detected the idea of the importance of effective demand and the role of investment in it, which later became a basic Keynesian idea.

"Michal Kalecki in Poland developed a theory very close to Keynes's income–expenditure analysis, and in 1934 published in Polish a three-equation model of goods market equilibrium, money market equilibrium and aggregate supply." Dimand (2018, p. 8104). His theory of demand preceded the work of Keynes, but Keynes' dominance manifested in his upbringing, writing in English, and presenting a complete work. Vaggi and Groenewegen (2003, pp. 312–313) also argue that Kalecki could not have made the revolution in economic theory as his work "was too easy to ignore, as it still today to a large extent." It required a person of Keynes' intellectual prominence to achieve a worldwide audience.

There were also other substantial differences. "Keynes adhering to the liberal view, Kalecki to the Marxist—although neither of them rigidly adhered to ideological schemes." Sebastiani (1994, p. 14). Keynes believes that macroeconomic problems can be resolved to the benefit of all classes, while for Kalecki, there is class antagonism, which excludes a satisfactory solution, that is, a solution matched by stable full employment. Sebastiani (1994, p. 18). "The class distinction between capitalists and workers, which is only implicit in the General Theory, occupies centre stage in Kalecki's analysis. In place of a single consumption function, there are two. Workers save nothing from their wages, while capitalists save a constant proportion of their profit income." King (2018, p. 10525).[18]

the Marxist labor theory of value and subjective value theory. His academic career was mainly in the University of St. Petersburg. The Minister of Education vetoed his election to the chair of political economy in 1913, he was re-elected in 1917. However, he did not accept this appointment, returned to Ukraine, where he became dean of the Faculty of Law of Kyiv, and for a short period Minister of Finance. Nove (1987). For a review of his work in Central Europe, in the interwar period, see Heller (1945).

[18] In Kalecki the idea of the insufficiency of investments had its origin in underconsumption due to the poverty of the masses. New investments would affect the productive capacity more than the demand, which made the investments useless in an effort to create full-employment demand. Sebastiani (1994, pp. 15–16).

In the last decades, there is still an interest, or rather an increasing interest in the work of Kalecki. His opus in seven volumes was published in 1990–1997 as Collected Works of Michal Kalecki by Oxford Clarendon, edited by Jerzy Osiatynski (1941–). In Palgrave studies in the history of economic thought series, Jan Toporowski (1950–) published his intellectual biography.

References

Adam, Jan. 1995. *Why did the Socialist System Collapse in Central and Eastern Europe?* The Case of Poland, the former Czechoslovakia and Hungary. Houndmills, Basingstoke, London: Palgrave Macmillan.

Adibekov, Grant Mkrtychevich. 1994. *Kominform i poslevoennaia Evropa, 1947–1956.* Moskva: Izdatelskii tsentr Rossiia molodaia.

Aligica, Paul Dragos, and Anthony J. Evans. 2009. *The Neoliberal Revolution in Eastern Europe. Economic Ideas in the Transition from Communism.* Cheltenham, UK; Northampton, MA: Edward Elgar Publishing.

Arrow, Kenneth. 1974. General Economic Equilibrium: Purpose, Analytic Techniques, Collective Choice. *American Economic Review* 64 (3): 253–272.

Árvay, János, and András B. Hegedűs. 1994. *Egy reformközgazdász emlékére—Péter György (1903–1969) (To Remember One Reform Economist—Péter György (1903–1969)).* Budapest: Cserépfalvi Könyvkiadó T-Twins Kiadó.

Baron, James N., and Michael T. Hannan. 1994. The Impact of Economics on Contemporary Sociology. *Journal of Economic Literature* 32 (3): 1111–1146.

Bauer, Michal. 2005. Karel Kouba a jeho místo v českém ekonomickém myšlení (Karel Kouba and His Place in the Czech Economic Thought). *Politická ekonomie* 4: 527–543.

Benáček, Vladimír. 2013. Zdroje identity a české tradice teoretické ekonomie (Sources of Identity and Czech Tradition in Theoretical Economics). In *Soudobá ekonomie očima tří generací: Dvacet let ekonomie na Univerzitě Karlově (Contemporary Economics through the Eyes of Three Generations: Twenty Years of Economics at Charles University)*, ed. Lubomír Mlčoch et al., 45–56. Prague: Karolinum.

Bjerkholt, Olav. 1995. Ragnar Frisch, Editor of Econometrica 1933–1954. *Econometrica* 63 (4): 755–765.

Blanchard, Olivier. 1999. An Interview with Janos Kornai. *Macroeconomic Dynamics* 3 (3): 427–450.

Borsányi, András. 1994. Péter György az illegális komunista mozgalomban (Péter György in Illegal Communist Movement). In *Egy reformközgazdász emlékére—Péter György (1903–1969)*, ed. János Árvay and András B. Hegedűs, 35–43. Budapest: Cserépfalvi Könyvkiadó T-Twins Kiadó.

Bouška, Jiří, Jiří Skolka, and Zdeněk Tlustý. 1965. *Meziodvětvová analýza (Inter-Sectoral Analyses)*. Prague: Státní nakladatelství technické literatury.

Brus, Wlodzimierz. 1961. *Ogólne problemy funkcjonowania gospodarki socjalistycznej* (General Problems of Functioning of a Socialist Economy). translated as The Market in a Socialist Economy. London: Routledge & Kegan Paul, 1972.

Chikán, Attila. 2006. The Role of 'Economics of Shortage' in the Intellectual Preparations for Transition in Hungary. *Acta Oeconomica* 56 (2): 195–207.

Chytil, Zdeněk, and Milan Sojka. 2003. České ekonomické myšlení v letech 1948–1969 (Czech Economic Thought in Years 1948–1969). *Politická ekonomie* 4: 565–590.

Čihák, Martin. 1997. Josef Goldmann: legenda české poválečné makroekonomie (Josef Goldmann: The Legend of Czech Post-war Macroeconomics). *Politická ekonomie*: 3–24.

Connelly, John. 2000. *Captive University, the Sovietization of East German, Czech and Polish Higher Education 1945–1956*. Chapel Hill and London: The University of North Carolina Press.

Czarny, Bogusław. 2014. On Economics in Poland in 1949–1989: Introduction. *International Journal of Management and Economics* 41 (January–March): 92–112.

Dědek, Oldřich. 1989. Teorie všeobecné ekonomické rovnováhy a optimálního plánování (General Equilibrium Theory and Optimal Planning). *Politická ekonomie* 11: 1281–1294.

Dewatripont, Mathias, and Eric Maskin. 1995. Credit and Efficiency in Centralized and Decentralized Economies. *Review of Economic Studies* 62: 541–555.

Dimand, Robert. 2018. *Macroeconomics, Origins and History of. The New Palgrave Dictionary of Economics*. 3rd ed. London: Palgrave Macmillan.

Dobb, Maurice. 1966. Oskar Lange. *Journal of the Royal Statistical Society. Series A (General)* 129 (4): 616–617.

Doležalová, Antonie. 2018. *A History of Czech Economic Thought*. Abingdon and New York: Routledge.

Dyba, Karel, and Václav Kupka. 1983. *Vnější nárazy a odezva hospodářské politiky: ˇceskoslovenská ekonomika v letech 1974–1981 (External Shocks and Adjustment of Economic Policy: Czechoslovak Economy in 1974–1981)*. Praha: Útvar vědeckých informací Ekonomického ústavu Československé akademie věd.

———. 1984. Přizpusobení československé ekonomiky vnějším nárazům (The Adaptation of the Czechoslovak Economy to External Shocks). *Politická ekonomie* 1: 43–56.

Friss, Péter. 1995. *Egy reformközgazdász emlékére (To Remember One Reform Economist)*. Statisztikai Szemle.

Gelegonya, Judit. 1994. A Tervgazdaság megjavítása vagy revíziója? (Improvement or Revision of the Planned Economy). In *Egy reformközgazdász emlékére—Péter György (1903–1969) (Remembering One Reform Economist—Péter György*

(1903–1969)), ed. János Árvay and András B. Hegedűs, 95–104. Budapest: Cserépfalvi Könyvkiadó T-Twins Kiadó.

———. 1996. Péter György szerepe a magyar közgazdasági reformgondolkodás fejlődésében (Role of Péter György in Development of Hungarian Economic Reform Thought). In *Ünnepi dolgozatok Mátyás Antal tanszékvezetői kinevezésének 40. évfordulójára*, ed. Halász Géza and Mihalik István. Budapest: Aula Kiadó.

Gewirtz, Julian. 2016. *Unlikely Partners: Chinese Reformers, Western Economists and the Making of Global China*. Cambridge and London: Harvard University Press.

Goldmann, Josef. 1947. *Czechoslovakia, Test Case of Nationalization; A Survey of Post-War Industrial Development and the Two-Year Plan*. Prague: Orbis.

———. 1973. *Od nestability ke stabilitě ekonomického růstu v ČSSR (From Non-Stability to Stability of Economic Growth in Czechoslovak Socialist Republic)*. Praha: Ekonomický ústav ČSAV.

———. 1975. *Makroekonomická analýza a prognóza (Macroeconomic Analysis and Forecast)*. Praha: Academia.

———. 1985. *Strategie ekonomického růstu (Strategy of Economic Growth)*. Prague: Academia.

Goldmann, Josef, and Karel Kouba. 1967. *Hospodářský růst v ČSSR*. Prague: Academia. English version: *Economic Growth in Czechoslovakia*. Prague: Academia. English edition Economic Growth in Czechoslovakia. 1969. White Plains, New York: International Arts and Sciences Press/Prague: Akademia.

———. 1982. Nad deficitní ekonomií Jánose Kornaie (On Deficit Economics of János Kornai). *Ekonomicko-matematický obzor* 1: 96–105.

———. 1984. Terms of Trade, Adjustment Processes and the Economic Mechanisms (A Quantitative Approach). *Acta Oeconomica*: 1–2.

Goldmann, Josef, et al. 1978. *Úvod do makroekonomické analýzy (Introduction to Macroeconomic Analysis)*. Prague: Svoboda.

Habr, Jaroslav. 1959. *Lineární programování (Linear Programming)*. Praha: Státní nakladatelství technické literatury.

———. 1981. Počátky formalizovaného myšlení v ekonomii u nás (Beginning of Formalized Economic Thinking at Our Country). Státní banka československá, *Ekonomické modelování, Sborník referátu*, 1.

Habr, Jaroslav, and Bedřich Korda. 1960. *Rozbor meziodvětvových vztahů (Analysis of Inter-Sectoral Relationships)*. Praha: Státní nakladatelství technické literatury.

Habr, Jaroslav, and Jaromír Vepřek. 1972. *Systémová analýza a syntéza (System Analysis and Synthesis) Praha*. Praha: Státní nakladatelství technické literatury.

Hámori, Balázs. 2012. The Resonance and Impact of Economics of Shortage. *Acta Oeconomica* 62 (3): 385–395.

Havel, Jiří, Jan Klacek, Jiří Kosta, and Zdislav Šulc. 1998. Economics and System Change in Czechoslovakia, 1948–1992. In *Economic Thought in Communist and Post-communist Europe*, ed. Hans-Jürgen Wagener, 213–263. London and New York: Routledge.

Hegedűs, András B. 1994. Péter György pályafutása (Career of Péter György). In *Egy reformközgazdász emlékére—Péter György (1903–1969)*, ed. János Árvay and András B. Hegedűs, 14–34. Budapest: Cserépfalvi Könyvkiadó T-Twins Kiadó.

Heller, Farkas. 1945. *A közgazdasági elmélet története (History of Economic Theory)*. Budapest: Gergely R. Könyvkereskedése.

Horváth, Julius, and Vitězoslav Sommer. 2018. From Nationalization to Privatization: Understanding Concept of Ownership in Czechoslovakia: 1948–1992. In *Populating No Man's Land: Concepts of Ownership in Economic Thought under Communism*, ed. János M. Kovács, 87–112. Lanham, Boulder, New York and London: Lexington Books.

Janáček, Kamil, Jan Klacek, and Růžena Vintrová. 1983. Naléhavost obratu k intenzifikaci reprodukčního procesu v ČSSR v osmdesátých letech (The Necessity of Intensification of the Czechoslovak Economy in the Eighties). *Politická ekonomie* 12: 1311–1314.

Janáček, Kamil, et al. 1990. *Československá ekonomika na prahu devadesátých let (Czechoslovak Economy in the Beginning of 1990s)*. Prague: Ekonomický ústav ČSAV.

Ježek, Tomáš, and Václav Klaus. 1987. Rozpory a dilemata Jánose Kornaie (contradictions and dilemmas of János Kornai). *Finance a úvěr* 2: 134–139.

Kaplan, Karel. 1966. *Utváření generální linie výstavby socialismu v Československu (od Února do IX. sjezdu KSČ) (Making of the General Course of Formation of Socialism in Czechoslovakia: From February 1948 to the Ninth Party Congress)*. Prague: Academia.

Katsenelinboigen, Aron. 1980. *Soviet Economic Thought and Political Power in the USSR*. New York: Pergamon Press.

Kennan, George. 1979. *The Decline of Bismarck's European Order: Franco-Russian Relations, 1875–1890*. Princeton: Princeton University Press.

King, J.E. 2018. Post Keynesian Economics. In *In The New Palgrave Dictionary of Economics*, 3rd ed. London: Palgrave Macmillan.

Klacek, Jan, and Václav Kupka. 2018. Když tály ledy v české ekonomii : připomínka 50. výročí Pražského jara 68 (Thaw in the Czech Economy: Remembering the 50th Anniversary of Prague Spring). *Regionální rozvoj mezi teorií a praxí* 3: 1–25.

Klacek, Jan, and Alena Nešporová. 1980. Ekonomický růst v ČSSR—aplikace produkční funkce CES (Economic Growth in Czechoslovakia—Application of the CES Production Function). *Politická ekonomie* 6: 603–616.

Klaus, Václav. 1984. Dr. Goldmann, ekonomická strategie a makroanalýza (Dr. Goldmann—Economic Strategy and Macro-analysis). *Ekonomické modelováni, Státní banka ˇceskoslovenská* 1: 1–32.

Klaus, Václav, and Dušan Tříska. 1995. Recenzní zamyšlení nad knihou Jánose Kornaie "Socialistický systém: Politická ekonomie komunizmu" (Review Thoughts on the Book of Janos Kornai 'Socialist System: Political Economy of Communism'). *Finance and úvěr* 45 (3): 137–142.

Klusoň, Václav. 1988. K prognóze vývoje hospodářského mechanismu (On the Prognosis of Development of Economic Mechanism). *Politická ekonomie* 36 (11): 1123–1138.

Komenda, Bohumil. 1964. *Ekonomická funkce velkoobchodních cen (The Economic Function of Wholesale Prices)*. Prague: Academia.

———. 1969. Společenské vlastnictví v tržním systému (Social Ownership in a Market System). *Nová mysl* 23 (7): 871–882.

Komenda, Bohumil, and Čestmír Kožušník. 1964. Některé základní otázky zdokonalení soustavy řízení socialistického národního hospodářství (Some Basic Issues of Perfecting of the System of Management of a Socialist Economy). *Politická ekonomie* 3: 219–272.

Komenda, Bohumil, et al. 1963. *Návrh tezí o zdokonalení soustavy plánovitého řízení národního hospodářství* (Proposal of Theses on Improving the System of Planned Management of the National Economy). Working Paper, Prague: Ekonomický ústav ČSAV.

Korda, Benedikt. 1960. *Ekonomická statistika (Economic Statistics)*. Praha: Státní nakladatelství technické literatury.

Korda, Benedikt, et al. 1967. *Matematické metódy v ekonomii (Mathematical Methods in Economics)*. Prague: Státní nakladatelství technické literatury.

Kornai, János. 1959. *Overcentralization in Economic Systems*. Oxford: Oxford University Press.

———. 1971. *Anti-Equilibrium*. Amsterdam: North Holland.

———. 1980. *Economics of Shortage*. Amsterdam: North Holland.

———. 1986. The Soft Budget Constraint. *Kyklos* 39 (1): 3–30.

———. 1990. *The Road to a Free Economy: Shifting from a Socialist System. The Example of Hungary*. New York: W. W. Norton. (Originally in Hungarian in 1989).

———. 1992a. *The Socialist System, The Political Economy of Communism*. Princeton: Princeton University Press.

———. 1992b. Az eretnekség történelmi hivatása. Péter György, a reformközgazdász (The Historical Mission of Heresy. György Péter, the Reform Economist). *Mozgó Világ* 18 (9): 43–49.

———. 1993. The Historical Mission of Heresy: György Péter, the Reform Economist. *Acta Oeconomica 45* (1/2): 89–100.

———. 1994. Péter György, a reformközgazdász (Péter György, a Reform Economist). In *Egy reformközgazdász emlékére—Péter György (1903–1969)*, ed. János Árvay and András B. Hegedűs, 75–89. Budapest: Cserépfalvi Könyvkiadó T-Twins Kiadó.

———. 2006. *By Force of Thought: Irregular Memoirs of an Intellectual Journey*. Cambridge: MIT Press.

Kornai, János, and Tamás Lipták. 1965. Two-Level Planning. *Econometrica* 33: 141–169.

Kosta, Jiří. 2005. K historii a koncepci československé ekonomické reformy v letech 1965–1969 (On history and concept of Czechoslovak economic reform in 1965–1969). *Acta Oeconomica Pragensia* 13 (3): 27–47.

Kotulan, Antonín. 1981. Agregátní produkční a nákladové funkce, teorie indexu a měření syntetické efektivnosti (Aggregate Production and Cost Functions, Index Theory and Measuring Synthetic Efficiency). *Politická ekonomie* 12.

———. 1982. Agregátní produkční a nákladové funkce, teorie indexu a měření syntetické efektivnosti (Aggregate Production and Cost Functions, Index Theory and Measuring Synthetic Efficiency). *Politická ekonomie* 3.

Kouba, Karel. 1964. *Politická ekonomie socialismu (Political Economy of Socialism)*. Prague: Nakladatelství politické literatury.

———. 1966. The Plan and Economic Growth. *Czechoslovak Economic Papers* 6: 7–21.

Kouba, Karel, et al. 1968. *Úvahy o socialistické ekonomice (Reflections on a Socialist Economy)*. Prague: Svoboda.

Kowalik, Tadeusz. 2008. Oskar Ryszard Lange (1904–1965). In *The new Palgrave dictionary of economics*, ed. John Eatwell, Murray Milgate, and Peter Newman. London: Palgrave Macmillan.

Kožušník, Čestmír. 1964. *Problémy teorie hodnoty a ceny za socialismu (Problems of Value and Price Theory under Socialism)*. Prague: Nakladateství Československé akademie věd.

Kýn, Oldřich. 1970. The Rise and Fall of Economic Reform in Czechoslovakia. *American Economic Review* 60: 300–306.

Kýn, Oldřich, and Pavel Pelikán. 1965. *Kybernetika v ekonomii (Cybernetics in Economics)*. Prague: Nakladatelství politické literatury.

Kýn, Oldřich, Bohuslav Sekerka, and Lubomír Hejl. 1969. A Model for the Planning of Prices. In *Socialism, Capitalism and Growth Essays Presented to Maurice Dobb*, ed. C.H. Feinstein, 101–124. Cambridge: Cambridge University Press.

Lange, Oskar. 1935. Marxian Economics and Modern Economic Theory. *Review of Economic Studies* 2 (3): 189–201.

———. 1936. On the Economic Theory of Socialism, Part I. *Review of Economic Studies* 4 (1): 53–71.

———. 1937. On the Economic Theory of Socialism, Part II. *Review of Economic Studies* 4 (2): 123–142.

———. 1942. The Foundations of Welfare Economics. *Econometrica* 10: 215–228.

———. 1959. *Introduction to Econometrics*. Oxford/London: Pergamon Press.

———. 1963. *Political Economy, Vol. 1: General Problems.* Oxford/London: Pergamon Press.

———. 1965. *Wholes and Parts: A General Theory of System Behaviour.* Oxford/ London: Pergamon Press.

———. 1967. The Computer and the Market. In *Socialism, Capitalism and Economic Growth: Essays Presented to Maurice Dobb*, ed. C.H. Feinstein, 158–161. Cambridge: Cambridge University Press.

Lange, Oskar, and Marek Breit. 2003. The Way to the Socialist Planned Economy. *History of Economics Review* 37: 51–70.

Laščiak, Adam, et al. 1985. *Dynamické Modely* (Dynamic Models). Joint publication of Bratislava: Alfa Publishing House and Prague: Státní nakladatelství technické literatury.

———. 1990. *Optimálne Programovanie (Optimal Programming).* Bratislava: Alfa.

Leeson, Peter T. 2008. We're All Austrians Now: Janos Kornai and the Austrian School of Economics. *Research in The History of Economic Thought and Methodology* 26: 209–219.

Lindbeck, Assar. 2007. *János Kornai's Contributions to Economic Analysis.* IFN Working Paper No. 724.

Maltsik, Balázs. 2002. Péter György közgazdasági reformelképzelései 1953–1956 (Economic Reform Ideas of Péter György in 1953–1956). *Kutatási füzetek* 9: 33–52.

Mód, Aladárné. 1994. Péter György—egy ember mint vezető (Péter György—a Human as a Leader). In *Egy reformközgazdász emlékére—Péter György (1903–1969)*, ed. János Árvay and András B. Hegedűs, 51–59. Budapest: Cserépfalvi Könyvkiadó T-Twins Kiadó.

Nachtigal, Vladimír. 1973. *Časové řady makroekonomických agregátu ČSSR za šedesátá léta a jejich metodologické problémy (Time Series of the Macroeconomic Aggregates of Czechoslovakia for the 1960s and their Methodological Problems).* Prague: Ekonomický ústav ČSAV.

Nekipelov, Aleksandr Dmitrievich. 2000. *Tsentralno-Vostochnaia Evropa vo vtoroi polovine XX veka.* Moskva: Nauka.

Neuberger, Egon. 1973. The Plan and the Market: The Models of Oskar Lange. *The American Economist* 17 (2): 148–153.

Nikl, Miroslav. 1961. O šíření marxistické politické ekonomie v buržoazním Československu (About Spreading of Marxist Political Economy in the Capitalist Czechoslovakia). *Politická ekonomie*: 744–761.

Nove, Alec. 1987. Tugan-Baranovsky, Mikhail Ivanovich (1865–1919). In *The New Palgrave Dictionary of Economics*, ed. John Eatwell, Murray Milgate, and Peter Newman. London: Palgrave Macmillan.

Nyers, Rezső. 1984. Péter György a kommunista és a reformer (Péter György a Communist and a Reformer). *Medvetánc* 4 (2–3): 247–251.

Nyitrai, Ferencné. 1983. Péter György a szocialista statisztikáért (Péter György and Socialist Statistics). *Statisztikai Szemle* 12: 1205–1215.
Orlik, I.I., ed. 2015. *Osnovnye tendentsii vo vzaimootnosheniiakh Rossii i stran Tsentral'no-Vostochnoi Evropy*. Institut Ekonomiki, Rossiiskaia Akademiia Nauk: Moskva.
Péter, György. 1954. A gazdaságosság jelentőségéről és szerepéről a népgazdaság tervszerű irányításában (On the Importance and Role of Efficiency in Managing Planned Economy). *Közgazdasági Szemle* 1 (3): 300–324.
———. 1956. A gazdaságosság és a jövedelmezőség jelentősége a tervgazdaságban, I-II (On the Role of Efficiency in Planned Economy) *Közgazdazdasági Szemle* 6 (7–8): 695–711 and 851–869.
Richterková, Zuzana. 2013. *Přínos Čestmíra Kožušníka ˇceskému ekonomickému myšlení (The Contribution of Čestmír Kožušník to Czech Economic Thought)*. Prague: Národohospodářský ústav Josefa Hlávky.
Roberts, Paul Craig. 1971. Oskar Lange's Theory of Socialist Planning. *Journal of Political Economy* 79 (3): 562–577.
Roland, Gerard. 2008. Soft Budget Constraint. In *The New Palgrave Dictionary of Economics*, ed. Steven Durlauf and E. Lawrence. Blume, London: Palgrave Macmillan.
Rumler, Miroslav. 1965. *Keynes a soudobý kapitalismus (Keynes and Contemporary Capitalism)*. Prague: NPL.
Rychetník, Luděk. 1968. *Úvod do matematické ekonomie (Introduction into Mathematical Economics)*. Prague: Vysoká škola ekonomická, fakulta politické ekonomie.
Rychetník, Luděk, and Oldřich Kýn. 1968. Optimal Central Planning in a Competitive Solution. *Czechoslovak Economic Papers* 10: 29–44.
Sadler, Charles. 1977. Pro-Soviet Polish-Americans: Oskar Lange and Russian's Friends in the Polonia, 1941–1945. *The Polish Review* 22 (4): 25–39.
Sawyer, Malcolm. 2008. Kalecki, Michal (1899–1970). In *The new Palgrave dictionary of economics*, 1899–1970. London: Palgrave Macmillan.
Sebastiani, Mario. 1994. *Kalecki and Unemployment Equilibrium*. New York: St. Martin's Press.
Seleny, Anna. 2006. *The Political Economy of State-Society Relations in Hungary and Poland. From Communism to the European Union*. Cambridge: Cambridge University Press.
Šik, Ota. 1953a. Socialistická hospodářská soustava a charakter ekonomických zákonů této soustavy (Socialist Economic System and Character of Economic Laws of This System). Prague: Záznam přednášky z kurzu politické ekonomie. Vysoká škola politická ústředního výboru Komunistické strany Československa.
———. 1953b. Zákon plánovitého proporcionálního rozvoje národního hospodářství: Záznam přednášky ze semináře ke statím J. V. Stalina (Law of the Proportional Development of National Economy: Transcript of Lecture at the

Seminar on J. V. Stalin's Papers). Prague: *Vysoká škola politická ústředního výboru Komunistické strany Československa*, 25 April.

———. 1962. *Ekonomika, zájmy, politika: jejich vzájemné vztahy do socialismu (Economy, Interests, Politics: Their Mutual Relations under Socialism)*. Prague: Nakladatelství politické literatury.

———. 1965a. Czechoslovakia's New System of Economic Planning and Management. *Eastern European Economics* 4 (1): 3–12.

———. 1965b. *K problematice socialistických zbožních vztahů (On the Issue of Socialist Commodity Relations)*. Prague: Nakladatelství Československé akademie věd.

———. 1967. *Plan and Market under Socialism*. White Plains, NY: International Arts and Sciences Press.

———. 1968. *Plán a trh za socialismu (Plan and Market under Socialism)*. Prague: Academia.

———. 1972. *Czechoslovakia: The Bureaucratic Economy*. White Plains, NY: International Arts and Sciences Press.

———. *1990. Jarní probuzení—iluze a skutečnost (Awakening in Spring—Illusion and Reality)*. Praha: Mladá fronta.

Soós, Károly Attila. 1984. Apropos the Explanation of Shortage Phenomena: Volume of Demand and Structural Elasticity. *Acta Oeconomica* 33 (3–4): 305–320.

Stiglitz, Joseph. 1995. *Whither Socialism?* Boston: MIT Press.

Šulc, Zdislav. 1998. Stručné dějiny ekonomických reforem v Československu (České republice) 1945–1995 (Short History of Economic Reform in Czechoslovakia (Czech Republic) 1945–1995). Brno: Doplněk.

———. 2007. Jak se rodila, kam smerovala, a proč byla potlačena tzv. Šikova reforma (The Birth, Direction, and Reason for Suppressing of the so Called Šik' Reform). *Acta Oeconomica Pragensia* 15, 7.

Szymczak, Robert. 1995a. Oskar Lange, American Polonia, and The Polish-Soviet Dilemma During World War II: The Public Partisan as Private Emissary. *The Polish Review* 40 (1): 3–27.

———. 1995b. Oskar Lange, American Polonia, and The Polish-Soviet Dilemma During Worldwar II: Making The Case For a "People's Poland" Part two. *The Polish Review* 40 (2): 131–157.

Ježek, Tomáš and Václav Klaus. 1987. Rozpory a dilemata Jánose Kornaie (Contradictions and Dilemmas of János Kornai). *Finance a úvěr* 2: 134–139.

Toms, Miroslav. 1968. Investice, inovace a Cobb-Douglasova produkční funkce (Investment, Innovation and the Cobb-Douglas Function). *Politická ekonomie* 3: 260–275.

———. 1976. Towards a Marxian Model of Capital Accumulation, Unemployment and Distribution. *Czechoslovak Economic Papers* 16.

Toms, Miroslav, and Mojmír Hájek. 1965. *Dva modely ekonomického růstu (Two Models of Economic Growth)*. Prague: Ekonomický ústav CSAV.

———. 1967. Produkční funkce a hospodářský růst Československa v letech 1950–1964 (Production Function and Economic Growth in Czechoslovakia in 1950–1964). *Politická ekonomie* 1: 15–28.

Toms, Miroslav, and Michal Mejstřík. 1986. *Nerovnováha, kvalita výrobku a ceny plánované vybilancovanosti (Disequilibrium, Quality of Goods and Balanced Prices)*. Prague: Ekonomický ústav ČSAV.

Toporowski, Jan. 2018. *Michał Kalecki: An Intellectual Biography Volume II: By Intellect Alone 1939–1970*. Palgrave Macmillan.

Tříska, Dušan, and Václav Klaus. 1988. Ekonomické centrum, přestavba a rovnováha (Economic Center, Perestroika and Economic Equilibrium). *Politická ekonomie* 8: 817–830.

Turnovec, Frantisek. 2002. Economics—Czech Republic. In *Three Social Science Disciplines in Central and Eastern Europe: Handbook on Economics, Political Science and Sociology (1989–2001)*, ed. Max Kaase, Vera Sparschuh, and Agnieszka Wenninger. Berlin: GESIS/ Social Science Information Centre (IZ) and Budapest: Collegium Budapest Institute for Advanced Study.

Vaggi, Gianni, and Peter Groenewegen. 2003. *A Concise History of Economic Thought, from Mercantilism to Monetarism*. New York, Basingstoke, Hampshire: Palgrave Macmillan.

van Brabant, Jozef M. 1990. Socialist Economics: The Disequilibrium School and the Shortage Economy. *Journal of Economic Perspectives* 4 (2): 157–175.

Vančura, Filip. 2014. *A Critical Overview on the Work of Prof. Ota Šik*. Presentation at the 18th European Society of History of Economic Thought Conference.

Verdery, Katherine. 1996. *What Was Socialism, and What Comes Next?* Princeton Studies in Culture, Power, History. Princeton: Princeton University Press.

Volokitina, T.V., G.P. Murashko, A.F. Noskova, and T.A. Pokivailova. 2002. *Moskva i Vostochnaia Evropa: Stanovlenie Politicheskikh Rezhimov Sovetskogo Tipa: 1949–1953: Ocherki Istorii*. Moskva: ROSSPĖN.

Wagener, Hans Jürgen. 1998a. *Economic Thought in Communist and Post-Communist Europe*. London and New York: Routledge.

———. 1998b. Between Conformity and Reform, Economics under State Socialism and Its Transformation. In *Economic Thought in Communist and Post-communist Europe*, ed. Hans-Jürgen Wagener, 1–32. London and New York: Routledge.

Walter, Jaromír. 1981. Počátky ekonomického modelováni v oblasti aplikované matematiky v letech 1930–1950 (Beginning of Economic Modelling in the Field of Applied Mathematics in the Period of 1930–1950) ČSVTS—Státní banka československá, *Ekonomické modelování*, Sborník referátu, no. 1.

Walter, Jaromír, and Jozef Lauber. 1975. *Simulační modely ekonomických procesů (Simulation Models of Economic Processes)*. Praha: Alfa, Státní nakladatelství technické literatury.

Webb, Adrian. 2008. *The Routledge Companion to Central and Eastern Europe since 1919.* Abingdon and New York: Routledge.

Wilke, Manfred. 2010. Ulbricht, East Germany, and the Prague Spring. In *The Prague Spring and the Warsaw Pact Invasion of Czechoslovakia in 1968*, ed. Günter Bischof, Stefan Karner, and Peter Ruggenthaler, 341–370. Plymouth, UK: Lexington Books.

Xu, Chenggang. 2017. Capitalism and Socialism: A Review of Kornai's Dynamism, Rivalry, and the Surplus Economy. *Journal of Economic Literature* 55 (1): 191–208.

Yang, Fenggang. 2010. Religious Awakening in China under Communist Rule, A Political Economy Approach. In *The New Blackwell Companion to the Sociology of Religion*, ed. Bryan S. Turner, 431–455. Chichester: Wiley-Blackwell.

CHAPTER 5

Early Years After the Break-up of Socialism

The quick disintegration of the Communist Parties in Central Europe in 1989, together with the weakening of control by the Soviet Union, was another exogenous event affecting the region fundamentally. These events were neither expected by policymakers nor by the scholars specialized in socialism.

During socialism, the West acknowledged that Central Europe belonged to the sphere of Soviet interests, and the governments of the NATO-members were not ready to intervene. Since 1988/1989, Western political elites had realized that under the condition of deepening economic dependence of the Soviet Union on the West, the Soviets were not going to use force to keep their interest in Central Europe. As a result, the Central European socialism collapsed (Gaidar 2018).

After the socialist system's fall, the Central European countries searched for closer collaboration with the West. The economic effects of the break-up of socialism were in certain aspects similar to previous massive societal changes as these countries began to re-orient to Western markets. In some countries, inflation rose to significant levels, unemployment increased, and different sub-sectors of the economy weakened as activity was re-oriented to sectors potentially more viable in the new environment. Furthermore, the change in ownership patterns influenced the societal atmosphere profoundly. Central European countries—together with the newly independent Slovakia—became members of the European Union, and their

J. Horvath, *An Introduction to the History of Economic Thought in Central Europe*, Palgrave Studies in the History of Economic Thought, https://doi.org/10.1007/978-3-030-58926-4_5

economies began to resemble the Western model to no small extent (Ther 2016).

Economic thought in these countries began to follow, for the most part, the mainstream path. Again, a large number of talented economists found employment at top Western European and American universities. The level of education of economics significantly increased. However, only a small number of educational institutions provided high-quality training for their graduates. We can mention Center of Economic Research and Graduate Education in Prague, the Institute of Economic Studies at Charles University in Prague, and Central European University in Budapest.

Names of some economists persecuted during socialism retained symbolic value, and squares and schools became named after them. Slovak Central Bank locates at the square named after Imrich Karvaš. In Prague, the authorities named a prestigious street after Alois Rašín, and in Brno, a new university after Karel Engliš. In Hungary, in Miskolc, a secondary school was named after Elemér Hantos. The former members of the Hungarian Academy of Sciences Heller Farkas and Navratil Ákos were readmitted as full members of the Hungarian Academy of Sciences.

An essential role in transforming societies after the socialist regimes' break-up was accomplished by economists who rose to prominence during the post-socialist period. These policy leaders influenced the creation of new economic policies and shaped the transformation into the market economies. One should mention, among others, Václav Klaus, Tomáš Ježek in the Czech Republic, Leszek Balcerowicz, (1947–), Grzegorz Kolodko (1949–), and Jacek Rostowski (1951–) in Poland, Ivan Mikloš (1960–) and Ludovít Odor (1976–) in Slovakia, and Péter Ákos Bod (1951–) and Lajos Bokros (1954–) in Hungary.

A crucial part of the new economic system was the privatization, that is, the break-up of the former state ownership of the means of production. Privatization became a symbol of new economic reality, generating support from different sources as it was the tangible symbol of the end of socialism. The transformation of state property into the private hands determined these societies' future for an extended period. Naturally, it was criticized by a large portion of the population as unjust as in the number of cases owners became the captains of the socialist industry and people from former socialist power institutions. However, the real injustice happened during the socialist nationalization when the former owners were humiliated, often imprisoned, and their property was taken away without compensation. Even worse injustices happened during World War II.

Changes brought from around 1989 till the early 1990s were immense. Initially, the capitalist market ideology found weak opponents. Media and generally younger strata of the population were pro-market oriented to build an individualist consumer society and replace socialist collectivism. However, later, this market-oriented ideology runs against traditional societal currents. Collectivists and nationalists of Central Europe re-emerged. Gradually, populist and nationalist forces got more influential in all four countries. One of the reasons was that those representing liberal democracy were not firm in defending their movement. Constitutional courts were weak vis-à-vis populist agenda, so different rights were taken away simply by a vote of the majority party (or coalition) in the Parliaments. The law's Western formalism was not fully implemented as judges and prosecutors were not protected sufficiently from clientelism and corruption.

The spirit of the time favored the "shock therapy" measures, to cope with regime change problems and enter the Western Club as early as possible. This was the time for policies that would be difficult to pass later. Economic policies were opening countries and providing opportunities for ownership to Western entities.

In August 1989, a government led by Solidarity activists came to power with Leszek Balcerowicz as finance minister. Balcerowicz, in an inflationary environment, presented a plan for the transformation of the Polish economy with help from the International Monetary Fund. The Balcerowicz Plan, implemented in January 1990, called for immediate decontrol of most prices, introducing a competitive exchange rate, removal of exchange controls, and legalization of private enterprise.[1]

Balcerowicz—already in the 1980s a noted advisor to the Solidarity movement—became world-famous as the architect of the first radical pro-market reform program after the fall of socialism in January 1990.

[1]The transition process was complete when Jaruzelski resigned the presidency in 1991, and Lech Wałesa was elected President of Poland after he defeated Prime Minister Tadeusz Mazowiecki. Initial reaction to the transformation shock meant a decline of output, a rise in unemployment together with a sharp spike in prices and income inequalities. As a result, in the September 1993 election, the leftist coalition won and continued in transition efforts within a more gradual approach. The finance minister from 1994 to 1997 was Grzegorz Kolodko, who continued privatization and a strict monetary policy to combat inflation and kept the country fairly generous social safety net.

Later, he was a Minister of Finance and also Governor of the National Bank of Poland. Balcerowicz shared with Klaus and Ježek in Prague doubts about the validity of the mainstream economics concerning its usefulness in understanding the socialist economic reality as well as being helpful in the early stages of the transformation process. Moreover, they all shared respect for the opinions of Hayek and Friedman.[2] Indeed, they preferred standard economic growth to an imaginary inclusive and more egalitarian growth.

Hungary has engaged in gradual transformation. It was a natural choice as the country began a gradual movement toward a market economy after introducing its New Economic Mechanism in 1968. Already in the 1960s, the power relaxed the repression, issuing a political amnesty followed by less control of the everyday life of the citizens. This led to a government policy of reconciliation between the power and the society, which provided more space to economists and reformers to engage in political dialogue. Hungarian reform economists were the leaders of reformism in Central Europe. Seleny (2006, p. 41) writes: "Specifically, reform-minded technocrats and economists networked back and forth between ministerial and research positions, forming in the process dense personal and professional links that enabled them over a period of almost three decades to seize reform opportunities, survive political reversals, and continue to shape new generations of reformers." This was a specific situation much different from Czechoslovakia and Poland.

In the second half of 1989, the socialist government allowed East Germans to emigrate through Austria to West Germany, which led to processes culminating in the Berlin Wall fall. Thus, in May 1990, new political parties came into power, led by a government of József Antall (1932–1993). Most of the framework for the economic transition policies were already in place. The Antall government introduced a gradual policy of continuation in reforms. However, in 1994 the Socialists under Gyula Horn won

[2] For example, Balcerowicz stated concerning the mainstream economic theory: "I was struck by the level of absurdities as propagated by top-level Western economists … since I studied the socialist economic system and knew that it was basically flawed because it deprived people of economic freedom, which is one of the other fundamental freedoms, private property, and the right to set up enterprise. I was really very, very surprised that in the West, most of the economists, who were technically very good, could propagate such absurdities for such a long time. And against this background, people like Hayek or von Mises or then Friedman … came to me as people who were not mistaken, who could recognize problems early on before they really emerged" (Aligica and Evans 2009, pp. 149–150).

the election and formed a coalition government. The government's economic policymaker, Lajos Bokros, introduced a fiscal austerity program in March 1995 as Hungary's current account deficit and budget deficit had both surged in a previous year with fear that a debt crisis might spread into the country. This fiscal austerity program devaluated the currency, introduced an import surcharge, reduced real wages, and heavily cut public expenditures, substantially reducing the previously generous social safety net.

Ideas in the Early Czech Transformation

In the late 1980s, the atmosphere in international economic policy circles favored the neo-classical, liberal approach expressed in short by the Washington Consensus. In the 1980s, in France, the socialist government's privatization efforts helped to weaken beliefs in the state's ability to successfully run the economy. A similar situation was in Greece, where the socialists also began to de-nationalize. In the 1980s, one observes an increasing number of intellectuals and economists who shared credos in the efficiency of the democratic market capitalism. Compared to the previous decades, people forgot the Great Depression's trauma, and optimistic beliefs in the totalitarian ideologies substantially weakened (Amadae 2003).

In this international atmosphere, in the former socialist economies of Poland, Czechoslovakia, and even Russia, the liberal ideas achieved prominence. This section presents some exploratory thoughts about the birth of liberal ideas in Czechoslovakia during the socialist period and their transformation into policy proposals in the early 1990s.

In the 1970s and 1980s, Czechoslovakia differed much from the so-called reform-socialist countries as Yugoslavia, Hungary, and Poland. Compared to these economies, Czechoslovakia represented a communist orthodoxy. One might expect that this could create a disadvantage at the beginning of the transition period. However, even though it introduced some aspects of the market economy, the socialist reform process began to be a liability when the transition process began. The reform economies faced high foreign indebtedness, medium to high-level inflation, rising government debt, and powerful trade unions. Thus, in a certain sense, these reform economies started the transition under less favorable macroeconomic conditions than Czechoslovakia. Furthermore, the new economic policymakers could take advantage of the Czechoslovak state's inherited authority, which had been practically unchallenged by non-state interests during the socialist period. Besides, the relative weakness of labor unions, local and non-governmental organizations allowed to introduce market institutions at a relatively high speed. In a sense, this made the Czechoslovak transformation easier (Horváth and Jonáš 1998).

Except for the second half of the 1960s, Czechoslovakia looked as 'a model satellite.' In comparison, the citizens of Poland and Hungary were politically less in apathy. In Czechoslovakia, nationalism manifested itself in Slovak dissatisfaction with Praguese centralization efforts, which eventually—after the break-up of socialism—led to Czechoslovakia's break-up (Holbraad 2003).

In the 1980s, compared to the 1960s, the political atmosphere changed. Belief in the superiority of socialism evaporated among the general population. Even more, the inferiority of socialism began to be acknowledged. Liberal ideas in Prague did not appear in isolation. In the 1980s, there were active groups of economists discussing works of Milton Friedman, George Stigler, Friedrich von Hayek, Irving Kristol, James Buchanan, and others. What made these authors appealing for economists in socialist Prague was their intellectual depth and clear anti-socialist stance.

In the 1980s, the future liberal elite lived in a private world of ideas, at seminars discussing critical economic topics. From 1979 till 1986, economists around Václav Klaus[3] had participated at regular seminars at the Czechoslovak central bank (Státní banka československá).[4] Several participants of these seminars played a central role in the transformation of Czech politics and economics after the fall of the socialist system.[5]

[3] Václav Klaus (1941–) was born in Prague and graduated from the University of Economics in Prague in 1963. He was active intellectually during the second half of the 1960s and worked for the Czechoslovak Academy of Sciences Economic Institute. From that period, his notable publications included Klaus et al. (1969), and later Klaus (1979), and Klaus (1988). He was pushed to leave the Institute in 1970 and joined the staff at the Czechoslovak central bank. In 1987 Klaus joined back the Academy of Sciences, this time the Institute for Prognostics, led by Valtr Komárek. From December 1989, he was Minister of Finance in the Czechoslovak government, from 1992, the Czech Prime Minister. Later the Chairman of the Czech Parliament, and from 2003 till 2013, President of the Czech Republic.

[4] Different, politically less controlled, organizations often published proceedings of these discussions. *ČSVTS-ŠBČS Ekonomické modelování, Sborník Referátu* (Publication of Czechoslovak Scientific Society at the State Bank of Czechoslovakia, Economic Modelling, Collection of Presentations) published presentations of the Klaus's seminars.

[5] Besides Klaus, Karel Dyba was Minister of Economy (1992–1996). Tomáš Ježek became the first Czech Minister of Privatization (1990–1992), Chairman of the National Property Fund (1991–1994), and Chairman of the Prague Stock Exchange Chamber. Ivan Kočárník

In the discussions, still, during socialism, the enthusiasm for market economy stood in contrast to skepticism toward the socialist market reforms.[6] Market fundamentalism prevailed as markets' limitations as market failures, externalities, or imperfect information—while being realized—were considered second-order problems faced once the economy returns to its natural market state, which could happen only once the country abandons the socialist path.

The atmosphere in the seminars at the Czechoslovak central bank was professional with long discussions and views opposing each other, a somewhat unusual phenomenon in the politically controlled socialist country. These discussions reflected different strands of the Czech economic thought, which became apparent in the 1990s and beyond. At these seminars, one observed liberal thought, the institutional views, and reform socialist views. Symbolically, these were differences between views of

became Czech Minister of Finance, Václav Kupka was Vice-Minister at the Ministry of Economy (Havel, Klacek, Kosta, and Šulc 1998, p. 256). Besides, Josef Zieleniec (1946–) was Minister of Foreign Affairs of Czechoslovakia and the Czech Republic from 1992 till 1997, and Dušan Tříska (1946–) was the leading figure behind coupon privatization in the early 1990s. Vladimír Dlouhý (1953–) was Minister of Economy of the former Czechoslovakia, and in the period 1992–1997 he was a Minister of Industry and Trade in the government of Václav Klaus. Vladimír Rudlovčák, who died in 2002, was a Deputy Minister of Finance.

[6] Bockman and Eyal (2002) contend that radical reform representatives were to an extent 'pushed' into liberal positions as believed that reform-socialism attempts were a failure. Already in the second half of the 1980s, there was quite a widespread skeptical opinion in the liberal circles toward the Hungarian market reforms. This author recollects an episode in an apartment of Rita Klímová in Prague in the early 1980s. At this meeting, a noted Hungarian economist, Tamás Bauer, participated. While people in the room were fascinated by Budapest's changes, Klaus presented a passionate critique of the Hungarian socialist market-reform process. In Győr, in March 1988, on the conference *Alternatives of the Socialist Economic Reforms*, some Hungarian economists have already raised a critical voice toward the socialist market reforms. László Lengyel (1950–) argued that to mix the market system with the command economy was futile. Kálmán Pécsi (1930–2001) maintained that "we had enough of so-called semireforms" (Kusin 1988). However, there were still presentations in the socialist reform style. This author recollects Morris Bornstein (1927–2012) repeatedly pacifying Klaus to prevent his critical public remarks toward the reform-socialist presentations.

Klaus, Tomáš Ježek,[7] vis-à-vis the views of Lubomír Mlčoch,[8] Karel Kouba, and others. The most active presenters at these seminars were Václav Klaus, Karel Dyba, Václav Kupka, Lubomír Mlčoch, Vladimír Rudlovčák, Vladimír Dlouhý, Tomáš Ježek, and others. These discussion forums made liberals well prepared for public discussion once socialism collapsed.[9]

When in 1989, Klaus and other liberals entered the political forums established after the collapse of communism, they quickly began to rule the economic discourse. It was an advantage for the liberals that former dissidents around Havel had almost no interest in economic matters as they considered economics a field for specialists. On the contrary, Klaus considered economic reforms as a core of the transition, but also understood that to remain only on the position of a market reformer was too

[7]Tomáš Ježek (1940–2017) was born in Plzeň, graduated from the University of Economics in Prague, and worked for the Economic Institute of the Czechoslovak Academy of Sciences. He was a Minister responsible for privatization in the first years after the breakup of socialism. During the 1980s, Tomáš Ježek was translating Hayek's work into the Czech language. Ježek shared Hayek's belief that one should submit to arbitrary, sometimes poorly understood, market forces. For Ježek, it had, most likely, a profound religious connotation. Ježek had a deep mistrust of that part of the mainstream economic thought, which valued market-socialism on par with the capitalist market economy. His mistrust was even higher toward radicals and progressives of the Western and developing world who worshipped so much socialist economies he lived in. His recollections appeared in Ježek (2007).

[8]Despite his early publications as Mlčoch (1967), Mlčoch (1969), and Mlčoch (1970), Lubomír Mlčoch (1944–) has lost his academic job in the early 1970s, after the Prague Spring purges, and worked as a clerk in an enterprise. In the seminars, Mlčoch argued that the managers of socialist enterprises, together with the local party elite and branch ministries representatives, exercised property rights. Mlčoch considered central planning a reversed pyramid as managers of enterprises held an informational advantage, which substantially weakened a vertical character of the relationship between planners and enterprises. He rejected the view that a socialist enterprise is a passive unit that only fulfills the plan's targets (Mlčoch 2000b). Klacek and Kupka (2018) rightly summarize that these were revolutionary and risky thoughts in the 1970s and the 1980s, even if some researchers might consider it a common knowledge today. Most likely, the privatization in the early 1990s confirmed Mlčoch's view as managers of the former socialist enterprises used their informational advantage, and in several cases, became real owners. In other words, to an extent, socialist managers transformed informal property rights into formal legal rights in the first years of the transformation (Mlčoch 2000a). His views from the socialist period are summarized in Mlčoch (1990, 1992).

[9]The socialist authorities were aware of these seminars, and finally, the security police closed these seminars in 1986. Durčák (2018), based on archives investigation, provides a good description of the knowledge of security forces about these seminars. This knowledge stemmed from reports of some less known participants, economists, who reported to the security police.

technocratic without appeal to the general population. To gain political support and obtain popular backing, Klaus and his colleagues founded and led the Civic Democratic Party to election victory. This movement happened in times when in some other transition countries, already nationalists and other radicals gained support. After 1992 the new Czech Republic made an impression of an island of democracy and free-market ideals in a sea of nationalism, populism, and post-communism (Hanley 1999; Hanley 2008).

Klaus, with his colleagues, quickly moved toward rapid economic liberalization. The idea was that quick reforms should be introduced in the early 1990s when the potential opponents from the political left were still weak, and the public tolerates radical reform steps only in the initial period of transition. In the late spring of 1990, the State Planning Committee, together with the Federal Finance Ministry, prepared Strategy of Radical Economic Reform supported by the Federal Parliament in early fall 1990 (Dlouhý and Klaus 1990).

This Strategy combined radical macroeconomic steps with price liberalization. The radical reform representatives understood that during socialism, the consumption was under the threshold people would prefer. Thus, quickly transforming the supply side to levels as in Western societies was to help to achieve the early political support of masses of the Czechoslovak society. Their political intuition expected the move from socialism to consumerism, that is, from communists' pretension of the building of the future to consuming a variety of products in the present.

The liberal economic reform strategy was built on stable currency, anti-inflationary policies, and on keeping a balanced or low budget deficit. The slow variants of reforms were seen as prolonged co-existence of state planning and market, with decision making based on non-market clearing prices. Also, the support of Western countries was seen as proportional to the resoluteness of the reform efforts. In other words, liberal reformers have seen radicalism as providing a guarantee of the reform process's credibility. Klaus's slogan of "market economy without attributes" sent the signal that this reform differs from the socialist reform of the 1960s. The Prague liberals put a low emphasis on specifics of the Slovak economy. Partly, because at the beginning of the transition, the Slovak political elite was more left-leaning and nationalist. The country's break-up temporarily strengthened the Czech liberals as their domestic opponents lost potential allies from Slovakia.

Also, other transformation proposals appeared, which were close to the liberal proposal.[10] Some economists were in favor of more moderate steps and had emphasized the Czechoslovak context.[11] In early 1990, a group of economists gathered who were critical of Klaus policy reforms.[12] There were also proposals of people close to the former ruling elite. Finally, there were proposals from the Western economists of Czech origin as Ota Šik, Jan Švejnar, Jaroslav Vaněk, Milan Zelený, Jiří Kosta, and others.

Liberal policies, which emerged in the early 1990s, became foremost politics; they weakened the communist organization of the society and prepared the ground for the emergence of domestic proprietary class, which would utterly alter the societal, economic, and power relations. For Ježek and Klaus of the primary importance was to help to create this group of new owners (Aligica and Evans 2009, p. 23).

In the early 1990s, the new government preferred voucher privatization and limited restitution to public auctions or direct sales. The societal atmosphere did not support selling assets to foreigners or those who

[10] For example, a group of economists published a manifesto in *Lidové Noviny* on the last day of 1991 entitled *Economic Transformation: Strong and Weak Side, A Statement of Independent Czech and Slovak Economists.* Vladimír Benáček, Aleš Bulíř, Jiří Hlaváček, Milan Horniaček, Jiří Kosta, Karel Kouba, Josef Kučerák, Oldřich Kýn, Michal Mejstřík, Pavel Pelikán, Jiří Sláma, Zdeněk Tuma, Petr Zahradník, and Alena Zemplinerová signed this manifesto. These economists agreed with the basic principles of liberal reform but pointed to the importance of institutional aspects, and relationships of market and state. One should also mention Klacek et al. (1991).

[11] This group includes Miloš Zeman, Valtr Komárek, Lubomír Mlčoch, and also economists from the 1968 reform as Karel Kouba, Otakar Turek, Zdislav Šulc, and others. An independent vision of a slower path of reform is associated with Valtr Komárek (1930–2013), the former director of the reform-oriented Prognostic Institute of the Czech Academic of Science. Komárek envisaged a more substantial state involvement as an alternative to radical reform. Komárek had a voice in the new government and was initially popular, but later lost politically to liberals. His publications included Komárek (1985), Komárek et al. (1990) and Šulc (1998).

[12] This group included František Vlasák, Karel Kouba, Otakar Turek, Zdislav Šulc, Václav Klusoň, Lubomír Mlčoch, and others. This group believed in more gradual privatization after socialist enterprises became fully fledged market subjects. They opposed the voucher privatization based on the idea that it does not create clear ownership, and replaces inefficient state ownership with dispersed impersonal ownership. These economists seemed inspired by post-war German experience and considered Klaus' reform as an example of Latin American liberalization, which was non-applicable to the Czech reality. Their views appeared in *Alternativní přístupy ke scenáři přechodu k tržní ekonomice* (Alternative Approaches of Transformation Toward Market Economy) in 1990 (Sojka 2000; Rameš 2020).

obtained sufficient savings during the socialist system (Appel 1995). However, the state's non-sufficient legal framework and the effects of voucher privatization as tunneling created an atmosphere in which predatory behavior led to the fast redistribution of assets and the creation of the new wealthy class not supported by the general public (Sojka 2000; Mlčoch et al. 2010). Once the society knew the privatization results, agony spread in the Czech Republic. A non-sufficiently developed legal framework, laissez-faire attitude to the market regulation had an adverse societal effects. All these factors slowly weakened Klaus's dominance of the Czech political and economic scene (Appel 1995; Schwartz 2006).[13]

References

Aligica, Paul Dragos, and Anthony J. Evans. 2009. *The Neoliberal Revolution in Eastern Europe. Economic Ideas in the Transition from Communism*. Cheltenham, UK and Northampton, MA: Edward Elgar Publishing.

Amadae, S.M. 2003. *Rationalizing Capitalist Democracy: The Cold War Origins of Rational Choice Liberalism*. Chicago, IL and London: University of Chicago Press.

Appel, Hilary. 1995. Justice and the Reformulation of Property Rights in the Czech Republic. *East European Politics and Societies* 9 (1): 22–41.

Aven, Petr, and Alfred Kokh. 2015. *Gaidar's Revolution: The Inside Account of the Economic Transformation of Russia*. London: I. B. Tauris.

Bockman, Johanna, and Gil Eyal. 2002. Eastern Europe as a Laboratory for Economic Knowledge: The Transnational Roots of Liberalism. *American Journal of Sociology* 108 (2): 310–352.

Dlouhý, Vladimír, and Václav Klaus. 1990. *Strategie radikální ekonomické reformy* (Strategy of Radical Economic Reform). Státní plánovací komise a Federální

[13] Aven and Kokh (2015) discuss the success of Polish and Czech transformations at the beginning of the 1990s compared to Russia's failed transformation. They emphasize that the leading Russian reformists Gaidar and Yavlinsky—as compared to Klaus and Balcerowicz—were never able to receive substantial political power needed for the implementation of reforms. They quote Gaidar (p. 376), who said, "It was easier for Eastern Europe. They could always find a person from the alternative elite—for instance, from the Church—who had never been a member of the Communist Party." Aven says on page 384, "The quality of the elites is the main difference between Russia and East European countries. Over 70 years, our ruling class was fully replaced, and the intellectual elite mostly integrated with the state, while the other countries preserved a counter-elite throughout 40 years of the communist regime—clerics and a broad anti-communist intelligentsia."

ministerstvo financí (State Planning Committee and Federal Ministry of Finance).

Durčák, Michael. 2018. *Semináře Václava Klause jako součást myšlenkového světa pozdního socialismu* (Václav Klaus' Seminars as Part of the Late Socialist World of Thought). Praha: Charles University, Filozofická fakulta.

Gaidar, Egor. 2018. *Gibel imperii. Uroki dlia sovremennoi Rossii.* Moscow: ROSSPEN.

Hanley, Seán. 1999. The New Right in the New Europe? Unravelling the Ideology of 'Czech Thatcherism'. *Journal of Political Ideologies* 4 (2): 163–189.

———. 2008. *The New Right in the New Europe Czech Transformation and Right-Wing Politics, 1989–2006.* New York: Routledge.

Havel, Jiří, Jan Klacek, Jiří Kosta, and Zdislav Šulc. 1998. Economics and System Change in Czechoslovakia, 1948–1992. In *Economic Thought in Communist and Post-communist Europe*, ed. Hans-Jürgen Wagener, 213–263. London and New York: Routledge.

Holbraad, Carsten. 2003. *Internationalism and Nationalism in European Political Thought.* New York and Basingstoke Hampshire: Palgrave Macmillan.

Horváth, Julius, and Jiří Jonáš. 1998. Exchange Rate Regimes in the Transition Economies. Case Study of the Czech Republic: 1990–1997. *ZEI Bonn, Working Paper*, p. B11, September.

Ježek, Tomáš. 2007. *Zrození ze zkumavky: Svědectví o české privatizaci 1990–1997* (Birth from the Test-Tube: Testimony about Czech Privatization 1990–1997). Prague: Publishing House Prostor.

Klacek, Jan, and Václav Kupka. 2018. Když tály ledy v české ekonomii: připomínka 50. výročí Pražského jara 68 (Thaw in the Czech Economy: Remembering the 50th Anniversary of Prague Spring). *Regionální rozvoj mezi teorií a praxí* 3: 1–25.

Klacek, Jan, et al. 1991. Ekonomická reforma v ČSFR (Economie Reforms in ČSFR). *Politická ekonomie* 9–10: 721–742.

Klaus, Václav. 1979. Metodologické problémy makroekonomického modelování (Methodological Problems of Macroeconomic Modeling). *Politická ekonomie* 7: 697–706.

———. 1988. Příčiny zahraničně ekonomického problému (Causes of the Foreign Trade Problem). *Politická ekonomie* 12: 1283–1288.

Klaus, Václav, Kamil Janáček, and Václav Kupka. 1969. *Úvod do zkoumání inflace v československé ekonomice* (Introduction to an Investigation of Inflation in the Czechoslovak Economy). Prague: Ekonomický ústav ČSAV.

Komárek, Valtr. 1985. *Struktura československé ekonomiky* (Structure of the Czechoslovak Economy). Prague: Academia.

Komárek, Valtr et al. 1990. *Prognóza a program* (Prognosis and Program). Prague: Academia.

Kusin, Vladimir. 1988. *Free-Wheeling Reformist Debate in Gyor: Participant Interviewed*. Radio Free Europe Research, RAD Background Report/56, 29 March. Accessed 11 May 2020. http://www.osaarchivum.org/digital-repository/osa:f80cb1e2-fb79-4068-af0f-80c7a39465cb.

Mlčoch, Lubomír. 1967. Alternativní chování podniku v decentralizovaném modelu socialismu (Alternative Behavior of the Enterprise in a Decentralized Socialist Model). *Politická ekonomie* 11: 979–988.

———. 1969. Symposium o podniku (Symposium on Enterprise). *Politická ekonomie* 17 (3): 278–281.

———. 1970. *Teorie firmy* (Theory of the Firm). Prague: Ekonomický ústav ČSAV.

———. 1990. Chování československé podnikové sféry (Behavior of Czechoslovak Enterprise Sector), 348. Prague: Ekonomický ústav ČSAV.

———. 1992. A Synthesis of Descriptive Analyses of a Traditional Model. *Prague Economic Papers* 4: 311–332.

———. 2000a. *Úvahy o české ekonomické transformaci* (Reflections on Czech Economic Transformation). Prague: Vyšehrad.

———. 2000b. Restructuring of Property Rights: An Institutional View. In *Economic and Social Changes in Czech Society after 1989: An Alternative View*, ed. Milan Sojka, Pavel Machonin, and Lubomir Mlčoch, 7–47. Budapest: Open Society Support Foundation.

Mlčoch, Lubomír et al. 2010. *Soudobá ekonomie očima tří generací* (Modern Economics as Seen by Three Generations). Praha: Karolinum.

Rameš, Václav. 2020. *Spory o podobu vlastnické transformace v Československu v 90. letech* (The Conflicts over the Czechoslovak Ownership Transformation in the 1990's). Praha: Charles University, Filozofická fakulta.

Schwartz, Andrew Harrison. 2006. *The Politics of Greed: How Privatization Structured Politics in Central and Eastern Europe*. New York: Rowman and Littlefield Publishers.

Seleny, Anna. 2006. *The Political Economy of State-Society Relations in Hungary and Poland From Communism to the European Union*. Cambridge: Cambridge University Press.

Sojka, Milan. 2000. Ten Years of Transformation in the Czech Way: Transformation, Inequality, and Integration. In *Economic and Social Changes in Czech Society after 1989: and Alternative View*, ed. Milan Sojka, Pavel Machonin, and Lubomir Mlčoch. Budapest: Open Society Support Foundation.

Šulc, Zdislav. 1998. *Stručné dějiny ekonomických reforem v Československu (České republice) 1945–1995* (Short History of Economic Reform in Czechoslovakia (Czech Republic) 1945–1995). Brno: Doplněk.

Ther, Philipp. 2016. *Europe since 1989, a History*. Princeton and Oxford: Princeton University Press.

Conclusion

This book is a contribution to the project on regional European histories of economic thought. Notably, we attempt to show on an example of four Central European nations that it is possible to see their national history of economic thought as part of a regional—Central European—history.

We construct the argument based on both economic and non-economic considerations. We also introduce periodization of the history of economic thought based on historical events that had significantly influenced these lands.

Across a long historical time, we do not observe any independent national school of thought in this region. Re-emerging discontinuities, which are the results of wars and abrupt systemic political changes, are robust social evolution characteristics in the region.

The economic thinkers needed to reconcile the analytic principles of economics and political economy with policy and ideology-driven views, which stemmed from Central Europe's reality. We discern the strong influence of political and ideological matters on domestic economic thought. The crucial economic policy steps (abolition of serfdom, land reform after World War I, socialist nationalization, and privatization after the break-up of socialism) happened only partly because of efficiency and economic considerations. Political and ideological considerations had driven these policy steps. Under these constraints, economists of Central Europe also played roles as policymakers and intellectuals with influence on the general

J. Horvath, *An Introduction to the History of Economic Thought in Central Europe*, Palgrave Studies in the History of Economic Thought, https://doi.org/10.1007/978-3-030-58926-4

public. Consequently, a large number of economists held high public office in all four periods we analyzed. We tried to reflect this fact by including into this book passages dealing with economic policy episodes.

This book is just a preparatory work, and further work is needed. An additional effort needs to clarify these issues into a more coherent view and point to connections among Central European economists across national borders in different historical periods.

Appendix: Economists from Central Europe in West

The Appendix provides short information about those economists who were born or originated from lands that are today part of Central Europe.

The first group of economists includes those born before World War I. Most of them were active in the interwar period and after World War II. Excellent works provided valuable help: The New Palgrave Dictionary of Economics, the second and the third editions, published by Palgrave Macmillan, Encyclopedia of Bohemian and Czech-American Biography by Miloslav Rechcigl, and Dictionary of Political Economy.[1] We order the scientists mentioned below by the year of birth.

Michal Baludjansky (Balugyansky) (1769–1847), mentioned in the main text.

Louis Francois Michel Raymond Wolowski (1810–1876) was born in Warsaw, from 1834 became a naturalized French citizen, where he started the Revue de Legislation et de Jurisprudence. In the 1850s, he translated into French works of Copernicus, Wilhelm Georg Friedrich Roscher, and Luigi Cibrario. Wolowski stood on the position of the historical school. Among his books, we note *Etudes d'economie politique et de statistique* and *Les finances de la Russie*. Wolowski (1848, 1864). Source: Dictionary of Political Economy (1987), various.

[1] Note also Kosta (1991) and Simon (2012).

J. Horvath, *An Introduction to the History of Economic Thought in Central Europe*, Palgrave Studies in the History of Economic Thought, https://doi.org/10.1007/978-3-030-58926-4

Ede Horn (Ignác Einhorn, Edward Horn) (1825–1875) was born in Vágújhely (Neustadt an der Waag, Nové Mesto nad Váhom). After participating in the 1848 revolution, he was to leave the Monarchy. Horn went to Germany, where after publishing a politically oriented book needed again to leave, this time to Belgium, where he published *Statistisches Gemülde des Königreichs Belgien*. While living in Paris, from 1855, Horn contributed to *Journal des Economistes*, *Revue Contemporaine*, *Journal des Debats*, and published *Das Kreditwesen in Frankreich* and *John Law einfinanzgeschichtliche Versuch*. In 1866 he published *La Liberte des Banques*, and later *L'economie politique avant les physiocrates*. After being naturalized in France, he returned to Budapest, worked as an influential newspaper editor, became a member of Parliament, and unexpectedly died. Horn (1853, 1857, 1858, 1866, 1867). Source: Dictionary of Political Economy (1987), various.

Ladislaus von Bortkiewicz (1868–1931) was born in St. Petersburg into a family of Polish origin. He studied in St. Petersburg and the University of Strasbourg and taught most of his life at the University of Berlin. He worked in statistical methodology. He was highly considered for his critical, analytical mind and review articles. Source: Schumpeter (1932).

Richard Schüller (1870–1972) was born in Brno. He was a doctoral student of Carl Menger. He was an expert on international trade and trade treaties. He worked in Vienna in the public sector and taught at the University of Vienna till 1928. From 1930 till 1937, he was a co-editor of Zeitschrift für Nationalökonomie. In 1940 left for the United States, where he was a visiting professor at the New School of Social Research until 1952. His first book is *Die Klassische Nationalökonomie und ihre Gegner. Zur Geschichte der Nationalökonomie und Sozialpolitik seit A. Smith*. He also published *Schutzzoll und Freihandel. Die Voraussetzungen und Grenzen ihrer Berechtigung*. Schüller (1895, 1905). Source: Bös (1974), Rechcigl (2016), Dekker and Kolev (2016), and Schulak and Unterköfler (2011).

Karl Eman Přibram (1877–1973) was born in Prague and studied law at the University of Prague. From 1914 he was at the University of Vienna. Later worked in international labor institutions and from 1928 till 1933 at Frankfurt am Main University. In 1934 he immigrated to the United States. From 1939 till 1952 was Professor at the American University. His works include *Die Probleme der internationalen Sozialpolitik*, *Geschichte der österreichischen Gewerbepolitik von 1740 bis 1860*, *Conflicting Patterns of Thought*, and *A History of Economic Reasoning*. Přibram (1927, 1907, 1949, 1983). Source: Various.

Evgeny (Jenő) Varga (1879–1964) was born in Nagytétény in Hungary and died in Moscow. He was a People's Commissar of the Hungarian Soviet Republic in 1919, consequently forced to leave for Austria, worked for the Secretariat of the Communist International in Moscow, and the Soviet Trade Mission in Berlin. From 1927 to 1947, Varga was Director of the Institute of World Economy and World Politics in Moscow. From 1929 he was a full member of the Soviet Academy of Sciences. He was one of the chief architects of Hungary's successful currency stabilization after World War II. His works include *The Great Crisis and Its Political Consequences. Economics and Politics, 1928–1934*; *Izmeneniia v ekonomike kapitalizma v itoge vtoroi mirovoi voiny*, *Osnovnye voprosy ekonomiki i politiki imperializma—posle vtoroi mirovoi voiny*, and *Politico-economic Problems of Capitalism.* Varga (1935, 1946, 1953, 1964). Source: Nötel R., Varga, Evgeny (Jenö), in The New Palgrave Dictionary of Economics (2008).

Arthur Salz (1881–1963) was born in Staab (today Stod in the Czech Republic), completing secondary education in Pilsen and studying economics in Berlin, and attending Georg Simmel classes. He also studied in Munich and Heidelberg. Salz defended his doctoral thesis under Lujo Brentano in 1903. He taught at the Handelshochschule in Mannheim and the Akademie der Arbeit in Frankfurt. Salz completed his habilitation in 1909 and became a professor at the University of Heidelberg in 1916. In 1933, Salz was forced to leave his position at the University of Heidelberg and left for England, where he had a visiting position at the University of Cambridge. In 1934, he immigrated to the USA and became a professor at the Ohio State University. Among his books see *Geschichte der böhmischen Industrie in der Neuzeit*, *Macht und Wirtschaftsgesetz*, and *Das Wesen des Imperialismus.* Salz (1913, 1930, 1931). Source: various.

Henryk (Chaskel) Grossmann (1881–1950) was born in Cracow. He studied in Cracow and lived from 1908 to 1918 in Vienna, and 1918 to 1925 in Warsaw. From 1925 to 1933, he was a political refugee in Germany, where he stayed at the University of Frankfurt. Later he left for France, England, and the USA, and towards the end of his life, the German Democratic Republic. In his main work, *Das Akkumulations- und Zusammenbruchsgesetz des kapitalistischen Systems*, he deals with the inevitability of the breakdown of capitalism, and attempts to restore the orthodoxy of the real Marx. Grossmann (1929). Source: Josef Steindl, Grossmann, Henryk, The New Palgrave Dictionary 2008.

Emil Lederer (1882–1939) was born in Pilsen (Plzeň) in Bohemia and studied law and national economy at Vienna University. He was habilitated in 1912 at Heidelberg, where he became professor from 1920. Together with Alfred Weber, Lederer led the Institute for Social- and State Sciences. In 1931, he succeeded Werner Sombart at Humboldt University of Berlin. In 1933 Lederer was suspended by the Nazis and left to the United Kingdom and then to the United States, where he co-founded the *University in Exile* at The New School for Social Research in New York City, which would become the Graduate Faculty of Political and Social Science. His work included *Aufriss der ökonomischen Theorie*, and *The New Middle Class*. Lederer (1931, 1937). Source: Robert A. Dickler, Emil Lederer in The New Palgrave Dictionary of Economics (2008).

Joseph Alois Schumpeter (1883–1950) was born in Triesch (today Třešť in the Czech Republic). Excellent biographies document his work, as Swedberg (1991). His books include *The Theory of Economic Development*, published initially in German, which had multiple reprints and was translated into several languages. Similar fame met Schumpeter's *Capitalism, Socialism, and Democracy*. In 1954 E. Boody edited his masterwork *History of Economic Analysis*. Schumpeter (1912, 1942, 1954). Sources: Heertje, Arnold, Schumpeter, Joseph Alois. The New Palgrave Dictionary of Economics (2008), Heilbroner, Robert, The Worldly Philosophers, sixth edition, Penguin Books, 1986.

Karl Polanyi (Pollacsek, Polányi) (1886–1964) was born in Vienna and grew up in Budapest, where he studied law and philosophy. In 1933 he moved to England. After that, he is invited by John Maurice Clark to Columbia, where he remains till his retirement in 1954. Polanyi's *The Great Transformation* became an influential book arguing, for example, that during the Industrial Revolution, the West attempted to remove several government control mechanisms to create a 'self-regulating' market in which labor, land, money, and goods transact as market commodities. This created a productive system, however, with destructive features as unemployment and depressions. Polanyi (1944). Source: Dalton G., Polanyi, Karl. The New Palgrave Dictionary of Economics (2008).

Josef Macek (1887–1972) was born near Zábřeh, today the Czech Republic. Macek studied law at Charles University, received his doctorate in 1911, listened to lectures of Albín Bráf and Josef Gruber. Also, Macek studied at the University of Berlin. After the war, he taught the national economy at Vysoká škola obchodní in Prague, where from 1926, he was a full professor. Macek was involved in economic policy debates, especially with Karel Engliš. At the beginning of his career, he was close to the cooperative movement but later converged toward social democracy. In the 1925 election, he was elected to the Czechoslovak Parliament for the Social Democrats. In the election of 1929 and 1935, he was re-elected. During the German occupation, Macek was forced to renounce his university position. He fled the country in 1949 and settled in the United States. He lectured at Pittsburgh University, where he worked as a professor from 1953. His books include *An Essay on The Impact of Marxism* from 1955. Macek (1955). Sources: https://upclosed.com/people/josef-macek-1/, accessed 21 January 2019.

Selig Perlman (1888–1959) was born in 1888 at Bialystok, today Poland, then in Russia. Perlman grew up in an atmosphere shaped by the labor movement and socialism. He emigrated to the United States in 1908 and studied with John R. Commons at the University of Wisconsin, where he became a professor of economics in 1927. In his work, *A Theory of the Labor Movement*, after early sympathies for Marxism, Perlman came to regard socialism's ideas at odds with manual workers' aspirations and experience. He preferred the labor movement to free itself from the revolutionary intellectuals. He believed in a limited, practical job-consciousness, struggling toward collective control of employment opportunities, but he did not support challenging capitalists' entitlements. Perlman (1928). Source: Donnelly M., Perlman, Selig, The New Palgrave Dictionary of Economics (2008).

Karl Schlesinger (1889–1938) was born in Budapest. In 1919, after the communist revolution, he moved to Vienna, where he committed suicide when Nazis occupied the country. In 1914 he had published *Theorie der Geld- und Kreditwirtschaft*. Schlesinger was not a university teacher but a banker and influential member of the financial community. Nevertheless, he became a respected member of the Vienna Economic Society and, in the 1930s, one of the most active participants in Karl Menger's mathematical colloquium. He also contributed to the study of the general economic equilibrium. Schlesinger (1914). Source: Schwödiauer G., Schlesinger, Karl, The New Palgrave Dictionary of Economics (2008), Schulak and Unterköfler (2011).

Michael (Mihály) Polanyi (Pollacsek, Polányi) (1891–1976) was born in Budapest. He studied medical sciences, and in 1919 received a doctorate at the Budapest University from natural sciences. In 1920 he moved to Germany, where he worked in Berlin as a researcher in chemical science. In 1933 he came to England and became a professor of natural sciences at the University of Manchester. His son John Charles Polanyi (1929–) received a Nobel Prize in chemistry in 1986. As he was increasingly publishing in social sciences, he became a social sciences professor from 1948 to 1958. He was one of the founders of the Society for Freedom in Science. In his books *The Contempt of Freedom* and *The Logic of Liberty*, he argued that scientific co-operation evolves as a spontaneous order analogous to the unconstrained market. He was an opponent of the positivist movement as he believed that the value-neutral approach undermines freedom in society. Like Hayek, he disapproved of reductionistic attempts in science, which in social and human sciences create false beliefs, and disdained those who appeal logic in history and politics and disregard morality. His books on social science include *Science, Faith, and Society* and *The Study of Man*. On his economic views, see Bíró (2019). Polanyi (1940, 1946, 1951, 1966). Source: https://www.newworldencyclopedia.org/entry/Michael_Polanyi, accessed 11 May 2020, and various.

Erwin Paul Hexner (1893–1968) was born in Liptovský Mikuláš, today Slovakia. He studied political science at the University at Kolozsvár and law in Bratislava. He worked in the Slovak Federation of Industries and the Czechoslovak Chamber of Commerce. He lectured on public administration and administrative law at University in Bratislava in the period 1931–1939. He left Czechoslovakia and emigrated to the United States in 1939, where he participated at the Bretton Woods Conference and the International Trade Conference of the United Nations in Geneva. Hexner held positions at the University of North Carolina from 1939 till 1946, and at the International Monetary Fund, from 1946 till 1958. He was a professor of political science and economics at the University Pennsylvania, 1958–1964. His publications include *International Cartels*; *International Steel Cartel*. Hexner and Paul (1943, 1945). Source: Roman Holec, Ervin Hexner (Zabudnutý ekonóm) (Ervin Hexner, a Forgotten Economist), Biatec, 2015, 10, 28–30, and various.

Antonin Basch (1896–1971) was born in Německý Brod (Havlíčkův Brod), today in the Czech Republic. He studied at the Law Faculty of Charles University and later in Vienna and Berlin. From the early 1920s, he taught at the Law Faculty in Prague and then worked at the National Bank of Czechoslovakia. In the 1920s, he lectured at the Law Faculty of Comenius University in Bratislava. In the middle of the 1930s, he became involved in executive positions in a chemical factory. In 1939 he emigrated, lectured at the University of Chicago, and worked for the Czech government in exile. He participated as a member of the Czechoslovak delegation at Bretton-Woods meetings. After World War II, he had a career at World Bank and was teaching at the University of Michigan. His books include *The New Economic Warfare, Germany's Economic Conquest of Czechoslovakia*; *A Price for Peace: the New Europe and World Markets*; *The Danube Basin and the German Economic Sphere.* Basch (1941, 1944, 1945). Source: Figura (2018), Nikodym, Nikodym, and Brhelová (2016).

Tivadar (Theodor) Surányi-Unger (1898–1973) was born in Budapest. He studied economics and philosophy in Graz, Budapest, and Vienna. He was teaching at Budapest, Szeged, and Miskolc Law Academy. His habilitation was in 1925, from 1929 became professor, and from 1935 member of the Hungarian Academy of Sciences. From 1929 till 1940 was a professor at University in Szeged, where he was the Head of the Statistical and Economic Department. During the war, he was teaching at the University of Pecs and, in 1945, emigrated from Hungary to the West. He was visiting first at Innsbruck University and from 1946 till 1958 at Syracuse. In 1958 he returned to Europe to teach at Göttingen. His works include *Geschichte der Wirtschaftsphilosophie*; *Nationale und internationale preispolitik*; *Comparative Economic Systems*; *Economic Philosophy of the Twentieth Century.* Surányi-Unger (1931, 1938, 1952, 1972). Source: various.

Franz Pick (1898–1985) was born in Böhmisch-Leipa (today Česká Lípa, Czech Republic). He studied law and business administration at the University of Leipzig, where he received a doctorate in 1922. He further studied at the University of Hamburg and Sorbonne. In 1945 he began to publish a monthly entitled *Pick World Currency* and later also *Pick's Currency Yearbook.* He published more than 50 books on currency and gave seminars on currency theory. Source: https://www.nytimes.com/1985/12/03/nyregion/franz-pick.html, accessed 17 May 2020.

Michael Kalecki (1899–1970) lived a large portion of his life in the Western countries but eventually returned to Poland. We devote a section to his contributions in the text.

Emil Georg Spitzer (1900–1982) was born in Opava and studied law in Vienna. He has worked for the International Monetary Fund. He collaborated in works on the history of the International Monetary Fund. Source: Rechcigl (2016).

Paul Rosenstein-Rodan (1900–1985) was born in Cracow, Poland. Studied in Vienna and taught in University College London and London School of Economics. In 1943, he published a seminal paper *Problems of Industrialisation of Eastern and South-Eastern Europe*, in the Economic Journal. This paper warned the countries not to follow the Soviet-type modernization as it will lead to creating an isolated unit in the world economy. Rosenstein-Rodan (1943). His papers argued that in less developed economies, complementarities and externalities in demand created pressure for planning of investments. This argumentation led to a concept of 'big push' for an initiation of the modern development. He was involved in the World Bank policymaking. In 1954 he obtained a position at the Massachusetts Institute of Technology. After retirement from MIT in 1968, he worked at Latin American development policies. Source: Richard S. Eckaus, Rosenstein-Rodan, The New Palgrave Dictionary of Economics (2008).

George (György, Georg) Katona (1901–1981) was born in Budapest. Katona studied psychology at the University of Göttingen, a dissertation on the psychology of perception. He worked at the University of Frankfurt, where he wrote an infamous paper on inflation's mass psychological aspects. Katona left for the USA, where he worked on developing the theory of psychological economics. He continued at the University of Michigan to form the Survey Research Center, which produced the University of Michigan Consumer Sentiment Index. Among his books are *The Psychological Approach to the Problems of a War Economy*, *The Powerful Consumer: Psychological Studies of the American Economy*, and *The Mass Consumption Society*. Katona (1942, 1960, 1964). Source: James N. Morgan, Katona, George, The New Palgrave Dictionary of Economics (2008).

Václav Mareš (1902–1998) was born in Prague, studied at Charles University, and at Ecole des Science Politiques in Paris, where he graduated in 1925. He received a doctorate at Charles University in 1926. After the War worked at Czechoslovak Embassy in Washington and after the communist takeover, joined the faculty of Penn State University, where he worked on international economics problems. Source: Rechcigl (2016) and various.

John (János) von Neumann (1903–1957) was born in Budapest. He published his first paper in mathematics at the age of eighteen. From 1921 he studied mathematics at the Universities in Budapest, Berlin, and later in Zurich. von Neumann completed his doctorate in Budapest in 1926.

Later worked as a privatdozent and the University of Berlin and then at the University of Hamburg. In 1931 received a professorship at Princeton, where he joined the Institute for Advanced Study. In 1944 together with Oscar Morgenstern, published the *Theory of Games and Economic Behavior*. Later became involved in developing electronic computers and was also involved in the Manhattan Project. His contribution to economic theory is enormous. His work substantially increased the mathematical sophistication of the economic theory and motivated a large number of theoreticians. von Neumann and Morgenstern (1944). Source: Thompson G.L., von Neumann, John in New Palgrave Dictionary of Economics (2008).

Oscar Lange (1904–1965) lived a large portion of his life in the Western countries and returned to Poland. We discuss his contributions in the main text of the book.

Lord Thomas Balogh (1905–1985) studied at the Faculty of Law of the University at Budapest, where he was a disciple of Ákos Navratil and István Varga. Later he studied at Berlin University. His first publication at the age of 23 was on History of German inflation (in Hungarian). With a scholarship from Rockefeller Foundation, he studied at Harvard University. From 1940 he became a fellow at Balliol College, Oxford, then at the Statistical Institute of Oxford University. He was close to Labor politicians and argued for the interventionist policy and exchange rate control. He worked for the Labor Cabinet Office after the 1964 victory and was appointed a life peer. He was close to the political left, but challenged socialist dogmas. His principal works include *Studies in Financial Organization*, *Unequal Partners*, *Facts and Fancy in International Economic Relations*, and *The Irrelevance of Conventional Economics*. Balogh (1947, 1963, 1973, 1983). Source: Streeten P., Balogh, Thomas, The New Palgrave Dictionary of Economics; Csikós-Nagy (1985).

William (Vilmos) Fellner (1905–1983) was born in Budapest, studied at the University of Budapest, and received a doctorate at Frederick William University in Berlin in 1929. Afterward, he was a partner in a family manufacturing enterprise in Hungary. He immigrated to the United States in 1938, staying first at Berkeley, and later became a professor at Yale from 1952. Fellner served at the Council of Economic Advisers in 1973–1975. Later he became a resident scholar at the American Enterprise Institute. His books include *Monetary Policies and Full Employment*, *Emergence and Content of Modern Economic Analysis*, and *Case for Moderation in the Economic Recovery of 1971*. Fellner (1946, 1960, 1971). Source: Tobin (1983).

Josef Soudek (1905–1993) was born in Bodenbach an der Elbe (Podmokly, Czech Republic). In 1924, he left for the University of Frankfurt am Main, where he studied economics and sociology. He graduated with a doctorate in 1928. From 1932 to 1935, Soudek was an editor of the economic section of the Frankfurter Zeitung. He immigrated to the United States in 1936, and from 1941 became a professor of economics at Queens College in New York. His work was mostly in the history of economic thought, especially on Aristotle Soudek (1952). Source: Leo Baeck Institute.

Karl Heinrich Niebyl (1906–1985) was born in Karlín, Prague. He studied at the Institute of Technology in Hannover, University of Paris, University of Berlin, and London School of Economics. He received a doctoral degree at the University of Wisconsin in 1936. In 1940 he began to work for the US government, but the administration terminated his position for concerns of his political activity. Later was teaching at Temple University. He has published *Studies in the Classical Theories of Money*. Niebyl (1948). Source: Hearing before the Subcommittee to Investigate the Administration of the Internal Security Act and Other Internal Security Laws of the Committee on the Judiciary, United States Senate, March 1957, available at books.google.com, accessed on 24 April 2020.

Eugen Löbl (Loebl) (1907–1987) was born in Holíč, today in the Slovak Republic. He studied in Bratislava and Vienna and had different business affiliated jobs before World War II. He was a member of left-oriented Slovak intellectuals around the journal DAV and joined the Communist Party in the early 1930s. In 1943 he participated at the conference in Atlantic City. After the war, Löbl worked as deputy minister of foreign trade and in 1949 was arrested, and in 1952, during the Slánsky trial, he was sentenced to life imprisonment. From 1963 he was involved in banking in Czechoslovakia and participated in the 1960s reform process. After the Soviet invasion, he left Czechoslovakia and lectured at different US universities and worked for the Slovak World Congress as the vice-chair. He published *Humanomics: How Can We Make the Economy Serve Us—Not Destroy Us*. Loebl (1976). Sources: Kačkovičová (2003), various.

Miloš Stádnik (1907–1977) born in Rakovnice, studied at Charles University and London School of Economics, and emigrated in 1968 to the United States, where he was on Bentley College faculty in Massachusetts. His works include *Národní důchod a jeho rozdělení se zvláštním zřetelem k Československu*, and *Sociální blahobyt a národní důchod*, both published in

Prague after World War II. Stádnik (1945, 1946). Stádnik had translated Keynes' General Theory into the Czech language, published in 1963. Source: Rechcigl (2016), various.

Lord Nicholas Kaldor (1908–1986) was born in Budapest. From 1927 to 1947, he studied and taught at the London School of Economics. Afterward, he moved to Cambridge University, where he became in 1966, a professor of economics. He was elevated to the peerage in 1974. Kaldor was an advisor to the British Chancellor of the Exchequer in 1964–1968 and 1974–1976. He believed that the market system with government intervention makes the economy more productive and equitable. Nine volumes of his Collected Economic Essays were published at Gerard Duckworth in London. His noted publications include *The Scourge of Monetarism*, and *Economics Without Equilibrium*. Kaldor (1982, 1985). Source: Wood A., Kaldor, Nicholas, The New Palgrave Dictionary of Economics (2008).

László Rostas (1909–1954) was born in Hungary. Kaldor initiated that he moves to England in 1939, where he collaborated with John Hicks on a book concerning taxation of war wealth. He had become one of the country's leading authorities on industrial productivity. His studies in this field led to his appointment at the Board of Trade. Hicks et al. (1941). Source: Kahn R.F., Rostas, Laslo, The New Palgrave Dictionary of Economics (2008).

Werner Stark (1909–1985) was born in Marienbad, today Mariánské Lázně. He studied economics and social science at the University of Hamburg, and continued at the London School of Economics. In the middle 1930s, he had taught at Prague. In 1939 he left for England, where he first published studies on Jeremy Bentham. From England in the early 1960s, he moved to Fordham University. After retirement, he stayed at the University of Salzburg. His work was multidisciplinary and translated to a number of languages. Source: Hagemann (2007), various.

Tibor Scitovsky (1910–2002) was born in Budapest. His father was the Hungarian Minister of Foreign Affairs, 1924–1925. He studied law at the University of Budapest and economics at the London School of Economics. He left for the United States in 1939, where he was a professor at Stanford University. He worked on problems of welfare economics, trade, development, and microeconomics. His books include *The Joyless Economy, Welfare and Competition: The Economics of a Fully Employed Society, and Human Desire and Economic Satisfaction*. Scitovsky (1952,

1976, 1986). Source: Adelman I., Scitovsky, Tibor. The New Palgrave Dictionary of Economics (2008).

Jan Viktor Mládek (1911–1989) was born in Bochnia in Poland. His family moved to Prague. He studied at Gymnasium in Prague, and law at Masaryk University in Brno, where he graduated in 1936. Before the war he studied at Sorbonne and Cambridge. During World War II, he worked in exile government, and participated at Atlantic City and Bretton Woods meetings, where Ladislav Feierabend, Antonín Basch, Ervin Hexner, and Mládek represented Czechoslovakia. From 1946 Mládek became one of the twelve executive directors of the IMF, later was in charge of different units. He was also a noted collector of arts. Among his publication *Mezinárodní finanční instituce Bretton-Woodské* published in Prague after World War II. Mládek (1946). Source: Šůla (1996).

John Hans Adler (1912–1980) was born in Tachov, today the Czech Republic. He fled Europe in 1937 and moved to New York. Adler graduated from Cornell University in 1941 and received a doctoral degree in economics from Harvard University in 1944. In 1951, Adler graduated from Harvard Law School and joined the Office of Management and Budget and, in 1961, the International Bank for Reconstruction and Development. He published, among others, *Economic Appraisal of Transport Projects*. Adler (1987). Source: various.

Evsey Domar (Domashevitsky) (1914–1997) was born in Lodz, at that time in Russia, today Poland. He moved to the United States in 1936, where he received a doctorate at Harvard. He worked at the Cowles Foundation and, from 1958, settled at the Massachusetts Institute of Technology till he retired. He was one of the founders of the growth theory, where he combined theoretical abstraction with historical knowledge. His noted book is *Essays in the Theory of Economic Growth*. Domar (1957). Source: Brown E.C., Domar, Evsey David, The New Palgrave Dictionary of Economics (2008).

Benedikt Korda (Benő Kornreich) (1914–2010) was born in Mukačevo, studied mathematics and physics at the Natural Science Faculty of Charles University. He escaped to Hungary in 1942, where he was called into forced labor. In 1944 Korda ran over to the Soviet side and worked as a translator. After the war, he joined the Communist Party and graduated from statistics and insurance sciences in Prague in 1951; in 1961 became a professor. He has written a variety of books on linear programming and mathematical methods in economics as *Matematické* *metódy v ekonomii*. Korda et al. (1967). In 1968 he left for Canada, where he became a professor at the University of Alberta. Source: various.

The second group of economists was born after the beginning of World War I, mostly during the interwar period, and professionally worked mostly after World War II.

George Jaszi (1915–1992). He was born in Budapest, attended Oberlin College, the London School of Economics, and received a Harvard doctorate. He worked at the Bureau of Economic Analysis, where he was a Director in the period 1963–1985. He helped to develop the national income and product accounts. Source: E. Denison Jasi, George, The New Palgrave Dictionary (2008).

Heinz Wolfgang Arndt (1915–2002) was born in Breslau in Germany (now Wroclaw in Poland), studied at Oxford University and the London School of Economics. Arndt became a professor at the Australian National University. His work includes *The Economic Lessons of the Nineteen-thirties*; *The Rise and Fall of Economic Growth: A Study of Contemporary Thought*. Arndt (1944, 1978). Source: Freeman R.D. Arndt, Heinz Wolfgang, The New Palgrave Dictionary of Economics (2008), and Hagemann (2007).

Lord Peter Bauer (1915–2002) was born in Budapest and studied economics at Cambridge and law at Budapest University. After World War II, he became a lecturer at London University, and in 1960 became a professor at the London School of Economics. He was elevated to the House of Lords in 1982. He influenced the development economics with his critical view of state interventionism as a non-efficient policy to tackle poverty. His work includes *West African Trade, Economic Analysis and Policy in Underdeveloped Countries, Dissent on Development, and The Development Frontier*. Bauer (1954, 1957, 1976, 1991). Source: Dorn J.A., Bauer, Peter Thomas, The New Palgrave Dictionary of Economics (2008).

Friedrich (Bedřich) Levčík (1915–1999) was born in Prague, where in the 1960s, he worked as the Head of the Department of the Economic Institute of Czechoslovak Academy of Sciences. From 1968 till 1972, he worked at the European Economic Commission in Geneva, and later till 1984, he was a director at Vienna Institute for International Economic Comparisons (Wiener Institut für Internationale Wirtschaftsvergleiche). His publications include, with different co-authors, *Industrial Cooperation between East and West*; *East-West Technology Transfer, Study of Czechoslovakia*; *Economic Crises in the East-European CMEA Countries*.

Levčík and Stankovský (1979), Levčík and Skolka (1984), Levčík and Kosta (1985). Source: Various.

Jaroslav Krejčí Jr. (1916–2014) was a son of Jaroslav Krejčí, the Czech Prime Minister during the German occupation between 1942 and 1945. He studied law at Charles University, but due to Czech universities' closure, he only graduated in 1945. His habilitation in 1947 was later not confirmed by the new communist government. He was arrested in 1954 and rehabilitated during the amnesty of 1960. After 1968 he emigrated, in 1976, became a professor at Lancaster University. His publications include *Social Change and Stratification in Postwar Czechoslovakia*, *Social Structure in Divided Germany, and Great Revolutions Compared: the Search for a Theory*. Krejčí (1972, 1978), Krejčí and Krejčová (1983). Source: Štrbáňová and Kostlán (2011, 316–320).

Alexandre Kafka (1917–2007) was born in Prague and studied in Geneva and Oxford. In 1940 family left for Brazil, where he taught at the School of Sociology and Politics in São Paulo. In 1949 Kafka joined the International Monetary Fund. He organized the Brazilian Institute of Economics at the Getúlio Vargas Foundation in Rio de Janeiro and worked as an adviser to Finance Minister. Kafka also worked for the United Nations and became a professor at the University of Virginia. Later again joined the IMF, where he was several times elected Executive Director. Source: various obituaries.

Anton Kotzig (1919–1991), after the 1939 closure of Czech universities, returned to Slovakia and received a degree from mathematical statistics. From 1940 he led a unit of mathematical statistics at an insurance company. From 1951 he was a professor at Vysoká škola ekonomická in Bratislava, and in period 1952–1958 was Rector of this university. From 1959 till 1964, he was the first director of the Mathematical Institute of Slovak Academy of Sciences. Later, Kotzig worked at Comenius University at the Faculty of Natural Sciences, also as a dean. He founded the Slovak school of theory of graphs. In 1969 he visited Canada and stayed in Montreal till the end of his life. On his sixtieth birthday, North Holland published a book, a collection of articles honoring Kotzig. Hammer et al. (1982). Source: http://www.mat.savba.sk/MATEMATICI/matematici.php?cislo=117, accessed 14 November 2018.

Ota Šik (1919–2004), we devoted a section to his contributions in the text.

Alice Teichová (Teichova, Schwarz) (1920–2014) was born in Vienna and became one of the leading economic historians of Central Europe. In 1944 she married Mikuláš Teich—who later became a noted scholar on the history of science. After the war, they moved to Czechoslovakia, where she received a doctorate in 1952 and taught at Charles University. Her husband got affected by purges in the 1950s. In 1968 after the Soviet invasion, they both left Czechoslovakia for West Germany. Later they settled in England, and she had received a professorship at the University of East Anglia. Among her works, we note *An Economic Background to Munich: International Business and Czechoslovakia 1918–1938*, *The Czechoslovak economy 1918–1980*, and *The Economic History of Central Europe*. Teichova edited together with the Herbert Matis, *Nation, State and the Economy in History*. Teichová (1974, 1988, 2000), Teichová and Matis (2003). Source: various.

Jan Adam (Glück) (1920–2006) was born in Malcov, Bardejov district in Czechoslovakia, and came to Canada in 1968. He became a professor at the University of Calgary. His works include *Wage Control and Inflation in the Soviet Bloc Countries*, Employment Policies in the Soviet Union and Eastern Europe, *Why did the Socialist System Collapse in Central and Eastern European Countries?: The Case of Poland, the Former Czechoslovakia and Hungary*, and *Planning and Market in Soviet and East European Thought, 1960s–1992*. Adam (1979), Adam (1987, 1993, 1995). Source: various.

Jan Maria Michal (1920–) was born in Nová Paka in Czechoslovakia. He studied at Charles University and the London School of Economics. He was a professor at the State University of New York in Binghamton. In 1960 he published *Central Planning in Czechoslovakia* by Stanford University Press. Michal (1960). Source: Rechcigl (2016).

John (János) Harsányi (1920–2000) was born in Budapest, where he received a doctorate from philosophy at the University of Budapest in 1947. In 1948 he left Hungary, began economic studies in Australia, later left for the United States with a Rockefeller fellowship. In 1959 he received a doctorate at Stanford. He held positions at Australian National University, Wayne State, and Berkeley. He received Nobel Prize jointly with Reinhart Selten and John Nash in 1994. His contribution is in game theory and welfare economics. His books include *Rational Behavior and Bargaining Equilibrium in Games and Social Situations*, and *A General Theory of Equilibrium Selection in Games*, with R. Selten. Harsányi (1977), Harsányi and Selten (1988). Source: Myerson R.B., Harsanyi, John C., The New Palgrave Dictionary of Economics (2008).

Karel Holbík (1920–2006) arrived in the United States in 1948 with a degree from Charles University in Prague; earned a doctorate in economics at the University of Wisconsin. His positions included Boston University, Harvard Extension School, and the US Naval War College in Newport. Source: Czechoslovak Society of Arts and Sciences, https://www.svu2000.org/remembering/karel-holbik/, accessed 12 May 2020.

Kazimierz Laski (Hendel Cygler) (1921–2015) was born in Poland. During WWII, he joined the underground resistance, wounded during the Warsaw Uprising. He studied political economy at the Academy of Political Sciences (Akademia Nauk Politycznych) and University for Planning and Statistics (Szkoła Główna Planowania i Statystyki) in Warsaw. In 1954 he received a doctorate at the Institute for Social Sciences at the Central Committee of the Polish United Workers' Party (Instytut Nauk Społecznych przy KC PZPR). He worked at the University for Planning and Statistics and other institutions in Poland. In 1968 emigrated and settled in Austria, where he worked at the institute WIFO, became a professor at the Johannes Kepler University of Linz, and had a career at Vienna Institute for International Economic Studies, where he was a director till 1996. Among his books, one finds *From Marx to the Market: Socialism in Search for an Economic System* written together with Wlodzimierz Brus, 1989. Source: various, https://wiiw.ac.at/kazimierz-laski-s-10.html, accessed 12 December 2019.

Włodzimierz Brus (Beniamin Zylberberg) (1921–2007) was born in Plock in Poland. He was an orthodox communist in the early years. However, in 1961, Brus published a reform-oriented book, *Ogólne problemy funkcjonowania gospodarki socjalistycznej*, which served as an inspiration for a generation of market-reform socialists. In the late 1960s, he was expelled from the Communist Party, and in 1972 he emigrated to the United Kingdom. He also published *Socialist Ownership and Political Systems* and *The Economics and Politics of Socialism: Collected Essays.* In 1989 he published *From Marx to the Market: Socialism in Search of an Economic System.* Brus (1961, 1973, 1975), Brus and Laski (1989). Source: various.

Jiří Jindřich (Heinrich Georg) Kosta (Kohn) (1921–2015) was born in Prague. Both totalitarian regimes persecuted him. He graduated from Vysoká škola obchodní in 1947, with Josef Macek influencing him during studies. He worked in the Economic Institute of Czechoslovak Academy of Sciences and was a member of the reform groups. Kosta left Czechoslovakia in 1968. He worked from 1970 till 1987 at the University of Frankfurt. His works include *Sozialistische Planwirtschaft: Theorie und Praxis, Abriss der sozialökonomischen Entwicklung der Tschechoslowakei*, and *Wirtschaftssysteme des realen Sozialismus*. Kosta (1974, 1978, 1984), Kosta et al. (1971). Source: Štrbáňová and Kostlán (2011, 308–313).

Jan Osers (1921–2012) worked in the Industry Research Institute in Prague, and in 1968 left for Germany. He was on faculty of universities of Mannheim, Heidelberg, and Karlsruhe. His work includes: *Forschung und Entwicklung in socialistischen Staaten Osteuropas*, and *Sozialistische Wirtschaftsmodelle*. Osers (1974, 1980). Source: https://www.morgenweb.de/mannheimer-morgen_artikel,-mannheim-zeuge-zweier-diktaturen-_arid,335787.html, accessed 14 October 2019.

Jacob Mincer (1922–2006) was born in Tomaszów Lubelski in Poland, spent World War II in prison and concentration camps. Later, on the Hillel Foundation scholarship left for Emory University, and received a doctorate from Columbia in 1957. He is one of the founders of the modern labor economics, and with Gary Becker, Theodore Schultz introduced the concept of human capital. Source: Welch F., Mincer, Jacob, in The New Palgrave Dictionary of Economics (2008).

Frank Meissner (1923–1990) was born in Třešť, in Czechoslovakia. In 1941 he earned a scholarship to attend an agricultural high school in Denmark, where he continued from 1943 at the Agricultural College of the University of Copenhagen. He moved later to Sweden. After the war, he returned to Prague, searching unsuccessfully for his family. Later he completed university studies in Copenhagen, and in 1949 settled in the United States. He was on the faculty of Cornell University. Source: various.

Marianne A. Ferber (1923–2013) was born in Mířkov, Domažlice, Czechoslovakia. She studied at McMaster University and received a doctorate from the University of Chicago. She became a professor at the University of Illinois. Ferber was a founding member of the International Association for Feminist Economics and served as a President of this Association. She published several books, as *Beyond Economic Man: Feminist Theory and Economics*, *Academic Couples: Problems and Promises* with Jane W. Loeb, and *Feminist Economics Today: Beyond Economic Man*, with Julie A. Nelson. Ferber (1993), Ferber and Loeb (1997), Ferber and Nelson (2003). Source: various.

Gregor Lazarcik (Lazarčík) (1923–2013) was born in Horná Streda in Slovakia. He studied in Slovakia and Brno. Lazarčík emigrated in 1948, worked in Switzerland, arrived in the United States in 1953, where he received a doctorate at Columbia in 1960. Lectured economics at Hunter College, and became a professor at the State University of New York. Source: https://prabook.com/web/gregor.lazarcik/198779, accessed 5 May 2019.

Václav Holešovský (1924–1981) was born in Prague, where he studied Russian and Czech language at the Charles University. He left Czechoslovakia in 1948 and studied at the University of Paris. Holešovský later received a doctorate from economics at Columbia. He was a professor at the University of Massachusetts at Amherst. His main works include co-authored *Czechoslovak National Income and Product, 1947–48 and 1955–56*, and *Economic Systems: Analysis and Comparison*. Holešovský (1977), Holešovský et al. (1962). Source: Ryavec (1982).

Alex Wynnyczuk (1924–2015) was born in Prague. After World War II, he studied law at Charles University and left the country after the 1948 communist coup. Initially lived in Munich, where worked as an economic correspondent of Radio Free Europe, and in 1955 emigrated to the United States. He studied at Berkeley and received a doctorate in economics at Columbia; became a professor of economics at Rensselaer Polytechnic Institute. He was involved in projects of measuring national income in former socialist countries. Source: https://www.legacy.com/obituaries/timesunion-albany/obituary.aspx?n=alexej-wynnyczuk&pid=175346970&fhid=4843, accessed 12 May 2019.

Herbert Kisch (1924–1978) was born in Prague. In 1938 was sent to France to stay with his uncle Egon Erwin Kisch. Afterward, he moved to Britain and joined the Czech Brigade of the British Army. After the war, Kisch studied economics and economic history at the London School of Economics. In 1950, Kisch emigrated to the United States, where he received a doctorate at the University of Washington in Seattle. He was teaching at Michigan State University. Posthumously his main work, *From Domestic Manufacture to Industrial Revolution, The Case of the Rhineland Textile Districts*, was published by Oxford University Press. It was initially published in German in 1981 as a volume in the series of the Gottingen Max-Planck-Institut für Geschichte. Source: Richard Tilly, Prologue: Herbert Kisch, the Man and His Work in Kisch (1989).

Boris Pešek (1926–2000) was born in Most in Czechoslovakia and arrived in the United States in 1950. Pešek studied at Iowa College and obtained a doctorate from John Hopkins University. He has held academic positions at Michigan State University and the University of Wisconsin-Milwaukee. He authored *Microeconomics of Money and Banking and Other Essays*, and co-authored *The Foundations of Money and Banking*, and especially *Money, Wealth, and Economic Theory*. Pešek (1988), Pešek and Saving (1967, 1968). Source: various.

Paul Medow (1926–2005) was born in Prague of Russian parents, studied economics at Columbia, where he received a doctorate in 1960. Later, professor of economic cybernetics at York University in Canada. He was a member of Karl Polanyi's seminar on non-market institutions in the late 1950s and the early 1960s. At York, he founded the Program on Political and Social Thought and Economic Research Systems Planning Group. Source: library of York University.

George John Staller (1927–2009) was born in Brno to a family of an eminent businessman and studied at the Law Faculty of Charles University, where he graduated in 1949. He left Czechoslovakia in 1949. He earned his bachelor's degree at Hastings College, doctorate at Cornell, where he was on faculty from 1960. Until today Cornell University keeps privately founded George Staller's lecture series. Source: https://news.cornell.edu/stories/2009/07/economist-george-staller-dies-82, accessed 30 September 2019.

Max Corden (1927–) was born in Breslau, Germany, today Wroclaw in Poland. He left at a young age to Australia, studied at the University of Melbourne, and received a doctorate from the London School of Economics. He became an eminent economist at the University of Melbourne, Australian National University, Nuffield College Oxford, and finally at John Hopkins. His famous book was *Inflation, Exchange Rates and the World Economy*. His ideas transferred into the Salter-Swan-Corden-Dornbusch model are still in use in economic policy studies. Corden (1971). Source: http://www.maxcorden.com, accessed 12 May 2020.

Janos Kornai (1928–) discussed in a more detailed way in the chapter on the socialist period.

Béla Balassa (1928–1991) studied law and economics in Budapest and left during the 1956 revolution. In 1959 he had received a doctorate in economics at Yale and worked at John Hopkins and the World Bank. Balassa-Samuelson theorem is a part of basic knowledge in economic policy matters. His book, published in 1962, *The Theory of Economic*

Integration, is a classic. Balassa (1962). Source: Jaime de Melo and Carl F. Christ, Balassa, Béla, The New Palgrave Dictionary of Economics (2008).

Jiří Skolka (1928–2000) was born in Plzeň, where he studied at Gymnasium. In 1951 he graduated at Czech Technical University, with a specialization in statistics. Skolka published together with F. Egermayer a book in Czech, *Časové řady v plánovaném hospodářství*. From 1956 he joined the Economic Institute of Czechoslovak Academy of Sciences, where he was active in a Mathematical-Economic Laboratory. He worked in the *European Economic Commission* in Geneva, from where—after 1968—he did not return to Czechoslovakia. He settled at Vienna at the *Österreichisches Institut für Wirtschaftsforschung*, where he became an expert in input-output analysis and published several books in this research field. Skolka and Egermayer (1951). Source: Štrbáňová and Kostlán (2011, pp. 446–450).

Jan Kmenta (1928–2016) was born in Prague. In 1949 Kmenta left his studies of statistics at the Czech Technical University and had arrived in Australia, where he received a degree in Economics in 1955, studying at evening courses at Sydney University. With Fulbright Scholarship, he studied at Stanford and received a doctorate in economics. He held academic positions at Wisconsin, Michigan State, and the University of Michigan. His famous, widely used textbook was *Elements of Econometrics*. Kmenta (1997). Source: Interview: Professor Jan Kmenta, interviewed by John Lodewijks, Econometric Theory, 21, 2005, pp. 621–645.

Baron Alexandre (Sándor) Lámfalussy (1929–2015) was born in Kapuvár in Hungary and left the country in 1949. He studied economics at Leuven and received a doctorate at Oxford University. Then he worked at commercial banks and later at the Bank for International Settlement. Lámfalussy served at the Delors Committee, which prepared the introduction of the European currency. He was founding President of the *European Monetary Institute*, the predecessor of the *European Central Bank*. The Belgian King made him a baron in 1993. Source: various.

Jiří Sláma (1929–2020) was born in Brno. He worked at Osteuropa Institut in Munich. His co-authored work includes *Der technologische Fortschritt in Österreich und in der Tschechoslowakei*. In addition, he has written *Kapital und Wachstum in den achtziger Jahren*. Kosta, Kramer, Sláma (1971), Sláma (1983). Source: various.

Vladimír J. Šimunek (1929–) was born in Brno, a professor at Kent State University, where he developed a specific econometric model. Source: Rechcigl (2016).

Radoslav Selucký (1930–1991) was born in Brno and studied economics at the university in Leningrad and Vysoká škola politických a hospodářskych věd in Prague. He emigrated in 1968 and worked in universities in South Carolina and Ottawa. His work includes *Czechoslovakia: The Plan That Failed*, *Economic Reforms in Eastern Europe: Political Background and Economic Significance*, and *Marxism, Socialism, Freedom: Towards a General Democratic Theory of Labour-Managed Systems*. Selucký (1970, 1972, 1979). Source: Various.

Jaroslav Vaněk (1930–2017) emigrated from Czechoslovakia in 1948, studied at Sorbonne, University of Geneva, and received a doctorate from the Massachusetts Institute of Technology. He was a professor at Cornell University. His research concentrated on the theory of trade and economics of labor participation and later on ecological economics. His books include *The Natural Resource Content of United States Foreign Trade, 1870–1955*, *General Equilibrium of International Discrimination: The Case of Customs Unions*, *General Theory of Labor-managed Market Economies*, and *The Participatory Economy: An Evolutionary Hypothesis and a Strategy for Development*. Vaněk (1963, 1965, 1971). Source: Horváth and Sedláček (2002).

Reinhard, Selten (1930–2016) was born in Breslau (today Wroclaw in Poland). He studied mathematics at the University of Frankfurt, where he received a doctorate in 1961. His habilitation thesis was a monography on multiproduct pricing. Selten later worked at the University of Bielefeld, and the University of Bonn. He had received Nobel Prize in 1994. His books include *General Equilibrium with Price-Making Firms* with Thomas Marschak, *A General Theory of Equilibrium Selection in Games* with John Harsányi, and *Models of Strategic Rationality, Theory and Decision* Library. Selten (1988), Selten and Marschak (1974). Source: Reinhard Selten's Nobel Prize Biography.

Iván T. Berend (1930–) a Hungarian economic historian who specialized in Hungary and Central Europe's economic history. Berend studied at Economic University and Eötvös Loránd University in Budapest. He received a university professorship in 1964 and became a member of the Hungarian Academy of Sciences in 1979. Berend worked as the Rector of the Karl Marx Economic University in Budapest from 1975 till 1982. Also, he was the President of the Hungarian Academy of Sciences from 1985 till 1990. He was also a member of the Central Committee of the Hungarian Socialist Workers Party. Since 1990 Berend worked at the University of California at Los Angeles. He has written a large number of books, translated into different languages. We mention two recent publication *History Derailed: Central and Eastern Europe in the Long Nineteenth Century*, and *An Economic History of Twentieth Century Europe*. Berend (2005, 2006). Source: various.

Luděk Rychetník (1933–2017) was born in České Budějovice, studied at Vysoká škola ekonomická in Prague, in 1968, emigrated to the United Kingdom, where he held different positions, most notably at the University of Reading. His work includes *The Production Function in Postwar Eastern Europe*. Rychetník (1971). Source: Various.

Jan Stankovský (1934–2013) was born in Brno and left Czechoslovakia in 1955. He studied at the Hochschule für Welthandel in Vienna. From 1966 he began to work at the Österreichischen Institut für Wirtschaftsforschung. He specialized in Austrian involvement in the international economic relations, East-West economic relations, and industrial co-operation. Among his books, see *Industrial Cooperation between East and West* with Friedrich Levčik. Source: Aiginger (2010).

Pavel Pelikán (1935–) was born in Prague, where he studied electrical engineering at the University of Technology. In 1965 he received a doctorate in economics at Charles University. Pelikán worked at the University of Toronto, University of Paris, and Ratio Institute in Stockholm. His books include *Kybernetika v ekonomii* with Oldřich Kýn, and an edited book on *The Evolutionary Analysis of Economic Policy*. Pelikán and Wegner (2003). Source: https://www.encyclopedia.com/arts/educational-magazines/pelikan-pavel-1935, accessed 12 May 2020.

Oldřich Kýn (1935–) left Czechoslovakia in 1968 and settled in Boston, where he had an academic position at Boston University. His books include *Kybernetika v ekonomii* published still in Prague, an edited book *On the Stability of Contemporary Economic Systems*. Kýn and Pelikán (1965), Kýn and Schrettl (1979). Source: http://oldrichkyn.com, accessed 12 May 2020.

Paul Marer (1936–) left Hungary in 1956 and received a doctorate at the University of Pennsylvania in 1968. He was a professor at the University of Indiana from 1975 and later worked as a professor at Central European University in Budapest. Among his numerous works, we mention *US Financing of East-West Trade*, and *Creditworthiness and Reform in Poland: Western and Polish Perspectives*. Marer (1975), Marer and Siwinski (1988). Source: various.

Michael Taussig (1938–2010) was born in Prague, arrived in the United States as an infant. He studied at the University of Colorado and received a doctoral degree at the Massachusetts Institute of Technology in 1966. He worked as a professor at Rutgers University in the area of income distribution and social security. His books include *Social Security: Perspectives for Reform, Alternative Measures of the Distribution of Economic Welfare*. Pechman et al. (1968), Taussig (1973). Source: Mila Rechcigl, In Memoriam: Michael K. Taussig, https://www.academia.edu/12646517/In_Memoriam_Michael_K._Taussig_1938-2010, accessed 10 May 2019.

Stanislaw Gomulka (1940–) was born in Krezoly in Poland. He was a professor at the London School of Economics. In Poland, Gomulka held positions after the break-up of socialism at the Ministry of Finance and the National Bank of Poland. His work is known in the field of economic growth, post-communist transition, and privatization. Source: various.

Milan Zelený (1942–) was born in Eastern Bohemia, studied at the University of Economics in Prague, and worked at the Czechoslovak Academy of Sciences. He left Czechoslovakia in the late 1960s, received a doctorate from operational research at Rochester. He was active as a professor at Fordham University in New York. Among his books, we mention *Multiple Criteria Decision Making*, and *Autopoiesis: A Theory of Living Organization*. Zelený (1981, 1982). Source: various.

Mikuláš Luptáčik (1944–) was one of the first graduates of the mathematical economics, which opened in the academic year 1961/1962 at Economic University in Bratislava where his teachers were leading Slovak economists as Unčovský, Fecanin, Laščiak, and Sojka. Later he worked at the University of Technology in Vienna and became Professor of University of Economics and Business in Vienna in 1999. His main research topics were input-output models, linear programming, and optimization. His books include *Nichtlineare Programmierung und Ökonomische Anwendungen*, and *Mathematical Optimization and Economic Analysis*. Luptáčik (1981, 2009). Source: various.

Zdeněk Drábek (1945–) was born in Uherské Hradište. In 1968 he received a university diploma at the Vysoká škola ekonomická in Prague, began to work at the Výskumní ústav zahraničního obchodu, then emigrated and studied at Cambridge. In 1979 he received a doctorate from Oxford University. After studies, he held positions at Buckingham University and the World Bank. After the fall of communism, Drábek returned to the Federal Ministry of Economy in Prague. He continued to lecture at different universities, the World Trade Organization, and the Joint Vienna Institute. Among his edited books, we mention *Managing Capital Flows in Turbulent Times: The Experience of Transition Economies* *in Global Perspective, Is the WTO Attractive Enough for Emerging Economies? Critical Essays in the Multilateral Trading System*, and *Can Regional Trading Arrangements Enforce Trade Discipline?* Drábek and Griffith-Jones (1999), Drábek (2005, 2010). Source: https://drabek.uk/curriculum-vitae/, accessed 04 August 2019.

Josef Brada (1945–) was born in Prague and received a doctorate at the University of Minnesota in 1971. His books include an edited volume on *Global Banking Crises and Emerging Markets*, and on *International Perspectives on Financing Higher Education*. Brada et al. (2015), Brada and Wachtel (2016). Source: https://wpcarey.asu.edu/people/profile/10411, accessed 12 May 2020.

Meir Gregory Kohn (1946–) was born in Kamenický Šenov in Czechoslovakia. From 1947, he became a resident of the United Kingdom and later of Israel and the United States. Kohn studied at the Hebrew University agricultural economics and received a doctorate in 1973 at Massachusetts Institute of Technology. From 1979 he works as a Professor of Economics at Dartmouth College. His books include *Financial Institutions and Markets* at Oxford University Press and an edited volume on *Finance Constraints, Expectations, and Macroeconomics*. Kohn (2003), Kohn and Tsiang (1988). Source: various.

Jan Vaňous (1946–) began to study at Vysoká škola ekonomická in Prague, but left Czechoslovakia after the Prague Spring. From 1970 lived in the United States, where he studied economics at Haverford College and received a doctorate from Yale University. Worked at different universities and from 1984 till 2002 was a President of PlanEcon, which provided economic analysis and forecasting concerning economies of Central Europe and the former Soviet Union. Source: https://www.nfneuron.cz/en/person/jan-vanous, last accessed 18 September 2020.

Jan Vincent Rostowski (1951–) was born to a Polish exile family in London and graduated from University College London and the London School of Economics. He worked as a Minister of Finance in Poland from 2007 till 2013. Among his books, we note *Macroeconomic Instability in Post-Communist Countries*. Rostowski (1998). Source: various.

Jan Švejnar (1952–) left Czechoslovakia in 1970, graduated from Cornell and received a doctorate at Princeton. He is one of the founders of the leading Central European educational institution CERGE-EI in Prague. His publications include an edited volume on *Participatory and Self-Managed Firms*, another edited volume on the *Czech Republic and Economic Transition in Eastern Europe*, and an edited volume on *Labor*

Markets and Economic Development. Švejnar and Jones (1982), Švejnar ed. (1995), Švejnar and Kanbur (2009). Source: svejnar.com, last accessed 18 September 2020.

After the break-up of socialism, a new group of talent flows from Central Europe to Western education institutions. We mention just some of them. Luboš Pástor is at the University of Chicago, Botond Kőszegi and Adam Szeidl at Berkeley, later at Central European University, Péter Kondor at London School of Economics, Jakub Steiner at Zurich and CERGE-EI, Miklós Koren at Princeton and Central European University, Attila Ambrus at Duke, Michal Horváth at York University, and a large number of others.

References

Adam, Jan. 1979. *Wage Control and Inflation in the Soviet Bloc Countries*. London and Basingstoke: Palgrave Macmillan.

———. 1987. *Employment Policies in the Soviet Union and Eastern Europe*. New York: Palgrave Macmillan.

———. 1993. *Planning and Market in Soviet and East European Thought, 1960s–1992*. Houndmills, Basingstoke, and London: Macmillan Press.

———. 1995. *Why Did the Socialist System Collapse in Central and Eastern European Countries?: The Case of Poland, the Former Czechoslovakia and Hungary*. Houndmills, Basingstoke, and London: Palgrave Macmillan.

Adler, John Hans. 1987. *Economic Appraisal of Transport Projects*, World Bank Series. Baltimore and London: The John Hopkins University Press.

Aiginger, Karl. 2010. *Jan Stankovsky Einem großen österreichischen Experten mit Visionen und internationalem Horizont zum 75.* Geburtstag, WIFO Monatsberichte, 2.

Arndt, Heinz Wolfgang. 1944. *The Economic Lessons of the Nineteen-Thirties*. Oxford: Oxford University Press.

———. 1978. *The Rise and Fall of Economic Growth: A Study of Contemporary Thought*. Melbourne: Longman Cheshire.

Balassa, Béla. 1962. *The Theory of Economic Integration*. Homewood: Richard D. Irwin, Inc.

Balogh, Thomas. 1947. *Studies in Financial Organization*. Cambridge: Cambridge University Press.

———. 1963. *Unequal Partners*. Oxford: Basil Blackwell.

———. 1973. *Facts and Fancy in International Economic Relations*. Oxford: Pergamon.

———. 1983. *The Irrelevance of Conventional Economics*. London: Weidenfeld & Nicolson.

Basch, Antonin. 1941. *The New Economic Warfare, Germany's Economic Conquest of Czechoslovakia*. New York: Columbia University Press.

———. 1944. *The Danube Basin and the German Economic Sphere*. London: Routledge and Trench, Trubner & Co.

———. 1945. *A Price for Peace: The New Europe and World Markets*. New York: Columbia University Press.

Bauer, Peter. 1954. *West African Trade. A Study of Competition, Oligopoly and Monopoly in a Changing Economy*. Cambridge: Cambridge University Press.

———. 1957. *Economic Analysis and Policy in Underdeveloped Countries*. Durham: Duke University Press.

———. 1976. *Dissent on Development*. Cambridge: Harvard University Press.

———. 1991. *The Development Frontier*. Cambridge: Harvard University Press.

Berend, T. Iván. 2005. *History Derailed: Central and Eastern Europe in the Long Nineteenth Century*. Berkeley, Los Angeles and London: University of California Press.

———. 2006. *An Economic History of Twentieth Century Europe*. Cambridge: Cambridge University Press.

Bíró, Gábor. 2019. *The Economic Thought of Michael Polanyi*. London: Routledge.

Bös, Dieter. 1974. In memoriam Richard Schüller (1870–1972). *Zeitschrift für Nationalökonomie* 34 (1–2): 238–240.

Brada, Jozef, and Paul Wachtel, eds. 2016. *Global Banking Crises and Emerging Markets*. Houndmills, Basingstoke, and London: Palgrave Macmillan.

Brada, Jozef, Wojciech Bienkowski, and Masaaki Kuboniwa, eds. 2015. *International Perspectives on Financing Higher Education*. Houndmills, Basingstoke, and London: Palgrave Macmillan.

Brus, Wlodzimierz. 1961. *Ogólne problemy funkcjonowania gospodarki socjalistycznej* (General Problems of Functioning of a Socialist Economy). Trans. The Market in a Socialist Economy. London: Routledge & Kegan Paul, 1972.

———. 1973. *The Economics and Politics of Socialism: Collected Essays*. Oxon and New York: Routledge and Kegan Paul.

———. 1975. *Socialist Ownership and Political Systems*. London and Boston: Routledge and Kegan Paul.

Brus, Wlodzimierz, and Kazimierz Laski. 1989. *From Marx to the Market: Socialism in Search for an Economic System*. Oxford: Oxford University Press.

Corden, Max. 1971. *Inflation, Exchange Rates and the World Economy*. Chicago: The University of Chicago Press.

Csikós-Nagy, Béla. 1985. Obituary Lord Thomas Balogh. *Acta Oeconomica* 35 (1–2): 213–215.

Dekker, Erwin, and Stefan Kolev. 2016. Introduction to The Social Theories of Classical Political Economy and Modern Economic Policy. *Econ Journal Watch* 13 (3): 467–489.

Dictionary of Political Economy. 1987. Originally published in 1894, edited by R. H. Inglis. Palgrave.

Domar, Evsey. 1957. *Essays in the Theory of Economic Growth*. New York: Oxford University Press.

Drábek, Zdeněk, ed. 2005. *Can Regional Trading Arrangements Enforce Trade Discipline?* London: Palgrave Macmillan.

———, ed. 2010. *Is the WTO Attractive Enough for Emerging Economies? Critical Essays in the Multilateral Trading System*. London: Palgrave Macmillan.

Drábek, Zdeněk, and S. Griffith-Jones, eds. 1999. *Managing Capital Flows in Turbulent Times: The Experience of Transition Economies in Global Perspective*. San Diego: E.M. Sharpe.

Fellner, William. 1946. *Monetary Policies and Full Employment*. Berkeley and Los Angeles: University of California Press.

———. 1960. *Emergence and Content of Modern Economic Analysis*. New York: McGraw-Hill.

———. 1971. *Case for Moderation in the Economic Recovery*. The American Enterprise Institute.

Ferber, Marianne. 1993. *Beyond Economic Man: Feminist Theory and Economics*. Chicago: University of Chicago Press.

Ferber, Marianne, and Jane W. Loeb. 1997. *Academic Couples: Problems and Promises*. Urbana: University of Illinois Press.

Ferber, Marianne, and Julie Nelson. 2003. *Feminist Economics Today: Beyond Economic Man*. Chicago: University of Chicago Press.

Figura, Ivan. 2018. Antonin Basch—učiteľ Imricha Karvaša, (Antonin Basch—Teacher of Imrich Karvaš). *Biatec* 26 (6): 29–31.

Grossmann, Henryk. 1929. *Das Akkumulations- und Zusammenbruchsgesetz des kapitalistischen Systems* (The Law of Accumulation and Breakdown of the Capitalist System). Leipzig: C.L. Hirschfeld.

Hagemann, Harald. 2007. German-speaking Economists in British Exile 1933–1945. *BNL Quarterly Review* LX (242): 323–363.

Hammer, Peter, Rosa Alexander, Gert Sabidussi, and Jean Turgeon. 1982. *Theory and Practice of Combinatorics, A Collection of Articles Honoring Anton Kotzig on the Occasion of his Sixtieth Birthday*. Amsterdam and New York: North Holland.

Harsányi, John. 1977. *Rational Behavior and Bargaining Equilibrium in Games and Social Situations*. New York: Cambridge University Press.

Harsányi, John, and Reinhard Selten. 1988. *A General Theory of Equilibrium Selection in Games*. Cambridge: MIT Press.

Hexner, Erwin, and Paul. 1943. *International Steel Cartel*. Chapel Hill: The University of North Carolina Press.

———. 1945. *International Cartels*. Chapel Hill: The University of North Carolina Press.

Hicks, John, Ursula Kathleen Hicks, and László Rostas. 1941. *The Taxation of War Wealth*. Oxford: Clarendon Press.

Holešovský, Václav. 1977. *Economic Systems: Analysis and Comparison*. New York: McGraw-Hill.

Holešovský, Václav, Thad Paul Alton, and Gregor Lazarcik. 1962. *Czechoslovak National Income and Product, 1947–48 and 1955–56*. New York: Columbia University Press.

Horn, Ede. 1853. *Statistisches Gemülde des Königreichs Belgien*. Dessau: Katz.

———. 1857. *Das Kreditwesen in Frankreich*. Leipzig: Verlag von Heinrich Hüber.

———. 1858. *Jean Law ein finanzgeschichtliche Versuch*. Leipzig: Verlag von Heinrich Hüber.

———. 1866. *La Liberte des Banques*. Paris: Guillaumin.

———. 1867. *L'economie politique avant les physiocrates*. Paris: Librairie de Guillaumin.

Horváth, Roman, and Tomáš Sedláček. 2002. Life and Work of Jaroslav Vanek. *Politická ekonomie* 50 (6): 859–869.

Kačkovičová, Mária. 2003. Eugen Löbl. *Biatec* 11 (1): 23–24.

Kaldor, Nicholas. 1982. *The Scourge of Monetarism*. Oxford: Oxford University Press.

———. 1985. *Economics Without Equilibrium*. New York: M.E. Sharpe.

Katona, George. 1942. *The Psychological Approach to the Problems of a War Economy*. New York: Columbia University Press.

———. 1960. *The Powerful Consumer: Psychological Studies of the American Economy*. New York: McGraw-Hill.

———. 1964. *The Mass Consumption Society*. New York: McGraw-Hill.

Kisch, Herbert. 1989. *From Domestic Manufacture to Industrial Revolution, The Case of the Rhineland Textile Districts*. Oxford: Oxford University Press.

Kmenta, Jan. 1997. *Elements of Econometrics*. Ann Arbor: University of Michigan Press.

Kohn, Meir Gregory. 2003. *Financial Institutions and Markets*. New York and Oxford: Oxford University Press.

Kohn, Meir Gregory, and S.C. Tsiang, eds. 1988. *Finance Constraints, Expectations, and Macroeconomics*. Oxford: Oxford University Press.

Korda, Benedikt et al. 1967. *Matematické metódy v ekonomii* (Mathematical Methods in Economics). Prague: Státní nakladatelství technické literatury.

Kosta, Jiří. 1974. *Sozialistische Planwirtschaft: Theorie und Praxis* (Socialist Planned Economy: Theory and Reality). Opladen: Westdeutscher Verlag.

———. 1978. *Abriss der sozialökonomischen Entwicklung der Tschechoslowakei* (Features of Social Economic Development of Czechoslovakia). Frankfurt: Suhrkamp Verlag.

———. 1984. *Wirtschaftssysteme des realen Sozialismus* (Economic System of Real Socialism). Köln: Bund-Verlag.

———. 1991. O pracích českých a slovenských ekonomů v exilu (Exile works of Czech and Slovak Economists). *Politická ekonomie* 9–10: 825–837.

Kosta, Jiří, Helmut Kramer, and Jiří Sláma. 1971. *Der technologische Fortschritt in Österreich und in der Tschechoslowakei*. Wien: Springer.

Krejčí, Jaroslav. 1972. *Social Change and Stratification in Postwar Czechoslovakia*. New York: Columbia University Press.

———. 1978. *Social Structure in Divided Germany*. London: Croom Helm.

Krejčí, Jaroslav, and Anna Krejčová. 1983. *Great Revolutions Compared: the Search for a Theory*. New York: St. Martin's Press.

Kýn, Oldřich and Pavel Pelikán. 1965. *Kybernetika v ekonomii* (Cybernetics in Economics). Prague: Svoboda.

Kýn, Oldřich, and Wolfram Schrettl, eds. 1979. *On the Stability of Contemporary Economic Systems*. Göttingen: Vandenhoeck und Ruprech.

Lederer, Emil. 1931. *Aufriss der ökonomischen Theorie*. Tübingen: J.C.B. Mohr.

———. 1937. *The New Middle Class*. Trans. S. Ellison. New York: State Department of Social Welfare and the Department of Social Science, Columbia University.

Levčík, Friedrich, and Jiří Kosta. 1985. *Economic Crises in the East-European CMEA Countries*. Köln: Index.

Levčík, Friedrich, and Jiří Skolka. 1984. *East-West Technology Transfer, Study of Czechoslovakia*. Paris: OECD.

Levčík, Friedrich, and Jan Stankovský. 1979. *Industrial Cooperation between East and West*. New York: Routledge.

Loebl, Eugen. 1976. *Humanomics: How Can We Make the Economy Serve Us—Not Destroy Us*. New York: Random House.

Luptáčik, Mikuláš. 1981. *Nichtlineare Programmierung und Ökonomische Anwendungen*. Königstein: Athenäum.

———. 2009. *Mathematical Optimization and Economic Analysis*. New York, Dordrecht, Heidelberg, and London: Springer.

Macek, Josef. 1955. *An Essay on The Impact of Marxism*. Pittsburgh: Pittsburgh University Press.

Marer, Paul. 1975. *US Financing of East-West Trade*. Bloomington: Indiana University Press.

Marer, Paul, and Wlodzimierz Siwinski, eds. 1988. *Creditworthiness and Reform in Poland: Western and Polish Perspectives*. Bloomington: Indiana University Press.

Michal, Jan Maria. 1960. *Central Planning in Czechoslovakia*. Stanford: Stanford University Press.

Mládek, Jan Viktor. 1946. *Mezinárodní finanční instituce Bretton-Woodské* (International Financial Institutions of Bretton-Woods). Prague: Ministerstvo Financí.

von Neumann, John, and Oscar Morgenstern. 1944. *Theory of Games and Economic Behavior*. Princeton, NJ: Princeton University Press.

Niebyl, Karl Heinrich. 1948. *Studies in the Classical Theories of Money*. New York: Columbia University Press.

Nikodym, Tomáš, Lukáš Nikodym, and Jana Brhelová. 2016. Antonin Basch and the Economic Nature of WWII: A Liberal Approach. *History of Economic Ideas* 24 (2): 141–164.

Osers, Jan. 1974. *Forschung und Entwicklung in socialistischen Staaten Osteuropas*. Berlin: Duncker and Humblot.

———. 1980. *Sozialistische Wirtschaftsmodelle*. Frankfurt: Campus Verlag.

Pechman, Joseph, Henry Aaron, and Michael Taussig. 1968. *Social Security: Perspectives for Reform*. Washington, DC: Brookings Institution.

Pelikán, Pavel, and Gerhard Wegner, eds. 2003. *The Evolutionary Analysis of Economic Policy*. Cheltenham: Edward Elgar.

Perlman, Selig. 1928. *A Theory of the Labor Movement*. New York: Macmillan.

Pešek, Boris. 1988. *Microeconomics of Money and Banking and Other Essays*. New York: New York University Press.

Pešek, Boris, and Thomas R. Saving. 1967. *Money, Wealth, and Economic Theory*. New York: Macmillan.

———. 1968. *The Foundations of Money and Banking*. New York: Macmillan.

Polanyi, Michael. 1940. *The Contempt of Freedom. The Russian Experiment and After*. London: Watts & Co.

Polanyi, Karl. 1944. *The Great Transformation*. New York: Farrar and Rinehart.

Polanyi, Michael. 1946. *Science, Faith, and Society*. London: Oxford University Press.

———. 1951. *The Logic of Liberty*. Chicago: University of Chicago Press.

———. 1966. *The Study of Man*. Chicago: University of Chicago Press.

Přibram, Karl Eman. 1907. *Geschichte der österreichischen Gewerbepolitik von 1740 bis 1860*. Leipzig: Duncker & Humblot.

———. 1927. *Die Probleme der internationalen Sozialpolitik*. Leipzig: C.L. Hirchfeld.

———. 1949. *Conflicting Patterns of Thought*. Washington: Public Affairs Press.

———. 1983. *A History of Economic Reasoning*. Baltimore: The Johns Hopkins University Press.

Rechcigl, Miloslav. 2016. *Encyclopedia of Bohemian and Czech-American Biography*. AuthorHouse.

Rosenstein-Rodan, Paul. 1943. Problems of Industrialisation of Eastern and South-Eastern Europe. *Economic Journal* 53 (210/211): 202–211.

Rostowski, Jan Vincent. 1998. *Macroeconomic Instability in Post-Communist Countries*. Oxford: Clarendon Press and Oxford University Press.

Ryavec, Karl W. 1982. Václav Holešovský, 1924–1981. *Slavic Review* 41 (2): 401–403.

Rychetník, Luděk. 1971. *The Production Function in Postwar Eastern Europe*. Oxford: Centre for Soviet and East European Studies, St. Antony's College.

Salz, Arthur. 1913. *Geschichte der böhmischen Industrie in der Neuzeit*. München: Duncker & Humblot.

———. 1930. *Macht und Wirtschaftsgesetz*. Leipzig: B. G. Teubner.

———. 1931. *Das Wesen des Imperialismus*. Leipzig: Teubner.

Schlesinger, Karl. 1914. *Theorie der Geld- und Kreditwirtschaft*. Munich: Duncker and Humblot.

Schulak, Eugen Maria, and Herbert Unterköfler. 2011. *The Austrian School of Economics: A History of Its Ideas, Ambassadors, and Institutions*. Ludwig von Mises Institute.

Schüller, Richard. 1895. *Die Klassische Nationalökonomie und ihre Gegner. Zur Geschichte der Nationalökonomie und Sozialpolitik seit A. Smith* (The Classical School of Economics and Its Opponents. On the History of Economics and Social Policy since Adam Smith). Berlin: Carl Heymans Verlag.

———. 1905. *Schutzzoll und Freihandel. Die Voraussetzungen und Grenzen ihrer Berechtigung* (Protectionism and Free Trade. The Conditions and Limits of Their Authority). Wien and Leipzig: F. Tempsky and G. Freytag.

Schumpeter, Joseph Alois. 1912. *The Theory of Economic Development*. Trans. Harvard University Press, 1934, reprinted by Oxford University Press in 1961.

———. 1932. Obituary: Ladislaus von Bortkiewicz. *Economic Journal* 42: 338–340.

———. 1942. *Capitalism, Socialism, and Democracy*. New York: Harper & Brothers.

———. 1954. *History of Economic Analysis*. Edited by E. Boody. New York: The Oxford University Press.

Scitovsky, Tibor. 1952. *Welfare and Competition: The Economics of a Fully Employed Society*. London: Allen & Unwin.

———. 1976. *The Joyless Economy*. Oxford: Oxford University Press.

———. 1986. *Human Desire and Economic Satisfaction*. Brighton and New York: Wheatsheaf and New York University Press.

Selten, Reinhard. 1988. *Models of Strategic Rationality, Theory and Decision Library*. Dordrecht, Boston, and London: Kluwer Academic Publishers.

Selten, Reinhard, and Thomas Marschak. 1974. *General Equilibrium with Price-Making Firms*. Berlin, Heidelberg, and New York: Springer-Verlag.

Selucký, Radovan. 1970. *Czechoslovakia: The Plan That Failed*. London: Thomas Nelson and Sons.

———. 1972. *Economic Reforms in Eastern Europe: Political Background and Economic Significance*. New York: Praeger Publishers.

———. 1979. *Marxism, Socialism, Freedom: Towards a General Democratic Theory of Labour-Managed Systems*. New York: St. Martin's Press.

Simon, Agnes. 2012. Intellectual Migration and Economic Thought: Central European Émigré Economists and the History of Modern Economics. *History of European Ideas* 38 (3): 467–482.

Skolka, Jiří, and František Egermayer. 1951. *Časové řady v plánovaném hospodářství* (Time Series in the Planned Economy). Prague: Prumyslové vydavatelství.

Sláma, Jiří. 1983. *Kapital und Wachstum in den achtziger Jahren*. Berlin: Duncker & Humblot.

Soudek, Josef. 1952. Aristotle's Theory of Exchange: An Inquiry into the Origin of Economic Analysis. *Proceedings of the American Philosophical Society* 96 (1): 45–75.

Stádnik, Miloš. 1945. *Sociální blahobyt a národní důchod* (Social Welfare and National Income). Prague: Knihovna sborníku věd právních a státních.

———. 1946. *Národní důchod a jeho rozdělení se zvláštním zřetelem k Československu* (National Income and Its Distribution with Special Attention to Czechoslovakia). Prague: Ministerstvo školství a osvěty.

Štrbáňová, Soňa, and Antonín Kostlán. 2011. *Sto českých vědců v exilu* (Hundred Czech Scientists in Exile), Prague: Academia.

Šůla, Jaroslav. 1996. Judr. Jan Viktor Mládek, významný český a mezinárodní finančník 20. Století (Dr. Jan Viktor Mládek, Important Czech and International Financier of the 20th Century). *Bankovnictví* 4 (24): 5–7.

Surányi-Unger, Theodor. 1931. *Geschichte der Wirtschaftsphilosophie*. Berlin: Junker und Dünnhaupt.

———. 1938. *Nationale und internationale preispolitik*. Jena: G. Fischer.

———. 1952. *Comparative Economic Systems*. New York: McGraw-Hill.

———. 1972. *Economic Philosophy of the Twentieth Century*. DeKalb: Northern Illinois University Press, published again in 2003 by Routledge, edited by E.R.A. Seligman.

Švejnar, Jan, ed. 1995. *The Czech Republic and Economic Transition in Eastern Europe*. San Diego: Academic Press.

Švejnar, Jan, and D. Jones, eds. 1982. *Participatory and Self-Managed Firms: Evaluating Economic Performance*. Heath and Lexington, MA: Lexington Press.

Švejnar, Jan, and Ravi Kanbur, eds. 2009. *Labor Markets and Economic Development*. London and New York: Routledge.

Swedberg, Richard. 1991. *Joseph A. Schumpeter, His Life and Work*. Princeton: Princeton University Press.

Taussig, Michael. 1973. *Alternative Measures of the Distribution of Economic Welfare*. Princeton: Princeton University Press.

Teichová, Alice. 1974. *An Economic Background to Munich: International Business and Czechoslovakia 1918–1938*. Republished in 2008, London: Cambridge University Press.

———. 1988. *The Czechoslovak Economy 1918–1980*. London: Routledge.

———. 2000. *Economic History of Central Europe*. New York: St. Martin's Press.

Teichová, Alice, and Herbert Matis. 2003. *Nation, State and the Economy in History*. Cambridge: Cambridge University Press.

The New Palgrave Dictionary of Economics. 2008. 2nd ed. Edited by S.N.Durlauf and L.E. Blume. Palgrave Macmillan.

Tobin, James. 1983. William John Fellner, 1905–1983. *Brookings Papers on Economic Activity* 14 (2): vi–vii.

Vaněk, Jaroslav. 1963. *The Natural Resource Content of United States Foreign Trade, 1870–1955*. Cambridge: MIT Press.

———. 1965. *General Equilibrium of International Discrimination: The Case of Customs Unions*. Cambridge, MA: Harvard University Press.

———. 1971. *The Participatory Economy: An Evolutionary Hypothesis and a Strategy for Development*. Ithaca: Cornell University Press.

Varga, Evgeny. 1935. *The Great Crisis and Its Political Consequences. Economics and Politics, 1928–1934*. London: Modern Books.

———. 1946. *Izmeneniia v ekonomike kapitalizma v itoge vtoroi mirovoi voiny* (Changes in the Capitalist Economy as Result of the Second World War). Moscow: Gospolitizdat.

———. 1953. *Osnovnye voprosy ekonomiki i politiki imperializma—posle vtoroi mirovoi voiny* (Basic Problems of Imperialist Economics and Politics—After the Second World War). Moscow: Gospolitizdat.

———. 1964. *Politico-economic Problems of Capitalism*. Moscow: Progress Publishers.

Wolowski, Louis Francois Michel Raymond. 1848. *Etudes d'economie politique et de statistique*. Paris: Chez Guillaumin et Cie, libraires. Republished in 2016 by Wentworth Press.

———. 1864. *Les finances de la Russie*. Paris: Guillaumin.

Zelený, Milan, ed. 1981. *Autopoiesis: A Theory of Living Organization*. New York: North-Holland.

———. 1982. *Multiple Criteria Decision Making*. New York: McGraw-Hill.

Index[1]

[1] Note: Page numbers followed by 'n' refer to notes.

J. Horvath, *An Introduction to the History of Economic Thought in Central Europe*, Palgrave Studies in the History of Economic Thought, https://doi.org/10.1007/978-3-030-58926-4

T

CPI Antony Rowe
Chippenham, UK
2020-12-15 11:32